Adventures Among Spiritual Intelligences

[redacted] 12/03

Angels, Aliens, Dolphins & Shamans

Adventures Among Spiritual Intelligences

by

Timothy Wyllie

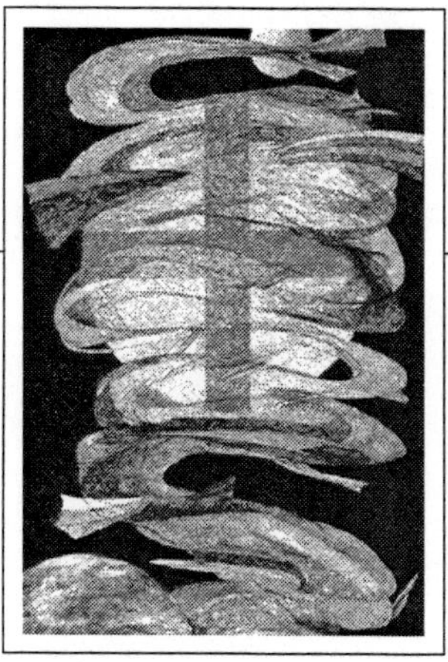

Wisdom Editions

Novato, California

WISDOM EDITIONS
A service of ikosmos.com
1122 Grant Ave., Suite C, Novato, CA 94945
415.898.7400 • 888.247.4446

Cover & interior design: Phillip Dizick
Author photo: Urszula Bolimowska
Cover illustration and interior glyphs: Timothy Wyllie

Publisher's Cataloging-in-Publication
(Provided by Quality Books, Inc.)

Wyllie, Timothy, 1940-
Adventures among spiritual intelligences : angels, aliens, dolphins and shamans / by Timothy Wyllie.
p. cm.
LCCN 00-112085
ISBN 1-931254-16-8

1. Telepathy. 2. Dolphins—Psychic aspects. 3. Angels—Miscellanea. 4. Shamanism—Miscellanea. 5. Childbirth—Miscellanea. 6. Charkovsky, Igor. 7. Lilly, John Cunningham, 1915. 8. Urantia book I. Title.

BF1171.W95 2001 133.9
QB101-700044

Printed in the United States of America
10 9 8 7 6 5 4 3 2 1

To
the
Great Spirit
who dwells in us all,
dolphin, angel
and
human
alike.

Some names have been changed to protect identities. To those whose wrath I may have incurred by my references to an anonymous companion, I can say merely that this is the way *she* wished it to be. The adventures would not have been possible without her presence.

Contents

Acknowledgements

The subject of dolphin telepathy and the transformation of our planet is a far-reaching affair, and a vast and ever-growing number of people are intimately involved. I take this opportunity to acknowledge all those beings, visible and invisible, who have the heart and the mind for such an exhilarating adventure. Great things will come of this work.

Many people contributed very directly to making this book possible. First, my deep appreciation and gratitude go to those who participated so directly in some of these adventures: Alma Daniel, John C. Lilly, Peter Anderson, Michael Miller, the late Carolina B. Ely, Roberta Quist, Elli Bambridge, Glenda Lum and Carl Avey, Peter Shenstone, Kamala Hope-Campbell, Mr. Ketut Cutet, Mr. Oko, Siti and Ri, Bill Smith, and Ray Kelly, Jr.

My wholehearted thanks also go to Denise Herzing and Dan Sammis, for a chance to swim closer to dolphins than I had ever been; Igor Charkovsky, for opening up new possibilities; Edward Mason, for patient editing in the early stages; Ted and Jean Bambridge, for a quiet place among the trees; Michelle Margetts, for taping and transcribing Igor Charkovsky; Dr. Kamayani, for sharing her heart; Mark Howell, for new heights of understanding and support; Cathleen Civale, for the most outrageous dolphin story of them all; Anni Moss, for a splendid sample of visual telepathy; Diana Wyllie, for finally demonstrating the difference between "me" and "I"; Andrew Ramer, for cosmic gossip; Armand DiMele, for telepathic tendrils; Kenny Ekstrom, for future possibilities; William Giese, for a shared artistic vision; Bobby Faust, for humor and height; and The Bozon Band—Kathleen Sartor, Giovanni Ciarlo, Dennis Waring, Andrew Tatarsky, Stephen Michaels, and Vicki Obermeyer—for continuing marvels of musical telepathy.

Any exploration of telepathy is, of necessity, a subtle matter, and often a well-placed word, a smile of encouragement, or an example of telepathy in action makes all the difference in the winding, multidimensional journey that this book describes. My love and thanks, therefore, also go to all my friends in Australia, New Zealand, Bali, England, Canada, France, Japan, Greece, Switzerland, Holland, Ibiza, Hawaii, and the United States.

My deepest gratitude to Wisdom Editions, and in particular, to Byron Belitsos, who has shown faith in this vision and the willingness to re-birth it, and Elianne Obadia, The Writer's Midwife, for her loving patience and attention to detail in editing the new edition. And to Alyssa Schiffmann, my thanks for her excellent job of putting it all together in the final stages.

Special thanks should go to Urszula Bolimowska for her invaluable creative visual insights and to Phillip Dizick for his cover and book design.

To my angelic co-workers, Zophiel, Fandor, and Joy, I give my heartfelt appreciation; this work could not have existed without you. It has all been worthwhile.

Thank you.

Preface

I began keeping notes in the early eighties on strange encounters that I started having with spiritual intelligences—non-human intelligences whom I sensed possessed wisdom, compassion and a spiritual depth of being. I had no idea at the time that I was embarking on a lifetime's adventure.

Those Reagan years were difficult times: the massive disillusionment of the seventies—with the apparent collapse of the spirit of regeneration that so many of us had felt in the previous two decades—had largely given way to cynicism and materialism. The movement that had seemed so full of hope only a few years earlier appeared to have been crushed like so many previous movements of youthful idealism. We did not realize then what has become much clearer since such remarkable events as the collapse of Soviet communism and the turnaround in South Africa: that the spirit of freedom which blossomed so forcefully in that wonderful time needed to ground itself into the fabric of the new global culture before once again flowering in the massive transformations this last decade has already manifested. And I suspect that this is just the start.

My personal adventure into the realms of the heart began with the dolphins. I set down these encounters in the first book of this series, *Dolphins, ETs & Angels,* and it was the dolphins yet again that led me into the journeys I am describing in this book. Through direct experience, they have demonstrated to me that we do indeed share this planet with another type of being whose intelligence, though very different from ours, is certainly comparable and quite possibly a great deal more profound. They have, after all, been living in the oceans for well over thirty million years in what appears to be a harmonious, loving, and caring way. This, in itself, is a tacit lesson to any of us who have passion for the integrity of Gaia, our home planet.

For almost two weeks, I spent many hours a day in the water with this particular pod of dolphins, simply allowing myself to be directed by them in whatever manner they felt appropriate. It was obvious after a while, too, that they were doing their own investigations into what made me tick. They were certainly instrumental in provoking some intense emotions in me. These ranged from fear and anger—two states of mind that they seemed to be studying in our species—to feelings of love and ecstasy the likes of which I have seldom experienced. It also became clear to me that they had performed an ultrasonic operation on my body and had removed an incipient testicular cancer.

One of the most significant events in light of the ensuing adventures, which I recorded in the first book, came as a result of a telepathic question I had put to the dolphins toward the end of my sojourn with them: "Since it has been so frequently observed," I had silently asked, "that unexplained flying objects come and go from our oceans, have you anything you wish to tell us about these mysterious occurrences?" And, sure enough, on the last night of our stay in Florida, my companion and I were treated to a twenty-minute display of the strangest of lights in the sky. So clearly intentional were the patterns made by the movement of the lights, that we were left with little doubt these were direct manifestations of some form of higher intelligence.

This was to be followed a couple of weeks later by an even more astonishing display of high strangeness. And in New York City, no less. Three of us witnessed the stately passage of a blue-green disc flying sedately across an overcast sky early one Labor Day afternoon. Before we could fully recover from our surprise, a boy perhaps eight years old strolled up to us and proceeded to give us a twenty-minute analysis on the nature of "star cars," their means of propulsion, and the tourists and explorers who use them. He also talked about something he described as the center of space activity and the beings who inhabit it. The boy went on to explain the various political systems within the galaxy, and finished up with a masterful discourse on the plight of the few warlike planets and how they are viewed by the rest of the populated Universe.

When I asked the lad if war was a factor out there in the galaxy, his answer, like everything else he told us, was fluid, unpremeditated, and superbly coherent. "Yes," he'd said, "there are a few warlike races, but they don't get very far from their home planets because the lines of supply become so attentuated. War takes a lot of energy and expense, and in those cases, the races involved and the physical spaces they occupy are simply avoided by everyone else."

Not a reply, I thought at the time, that would spring immediately to mind in a generation reared on the evil empires of Darth Vader, the Klingons, or Ronald Reagan, for that matter. This piece of information might have proved quite helpful to both Napoleon and Hitler in their Russian campaigns! He told us much more, but exactly who this odd young boy was I have never discovered. In the light of what I now know, I think he was in some way telepathically overlit by whoever was in that craft. Search though we did, we never saw him again.

As can be imagined, my worldview and what I previously imagined might be happening on this little planet of ours was rapidly disintegrating in the face of these encounters. It is one thing to subscribe to a belief in life on other worlds from having read science fiction and seen the movies, and quite another to be presented with the reality of telepathic dolphins and an eight-year-old telepathic translator. But the Universe had just begun to show itself to me.

After plunging into full-time study of cetaceans and spending an enlightening time in the Bahamas with a group of captive dolphins and some remarkable Rastafarians, another strange and promising scenario opened up: some friends of my companion in Canada had started to communicate with angels. Considering the paces we had been recently put through, it would have been foolish not to have flown up to Toronto to see for ourselves what was going on.

Sure enough, a sensitive young man called Edward found that when he put himself in a light trance, entities spoke through him who had introduced themselves as angels. Fortunately, I had been somewhat prepared for this since coming across a profoundly intriguing document called *The Urantia Book,* which itself purports to have been transmitted—or channeled as we might now call it—from the angels.

Sadly, channeling has recently fallen into disrepute due to the abuses and exploitations of a few who have sought to take advantage of human gullibility. But in its purest form, it has always been a revered way of communicating with other realms of existence. The degree of coherence and integrity of the channeled information is invariably the surest way to ascertain the channel's authenticity. And the information that came through Edward remains some of the finest available.

Among much of value that the angels told us were many things of particular relevance to us as we move through the massive global transformation of consciousness necessary to bring us into the New Age—or the "True Age," as it might be more accurately called. The most astounding was the news of the final reconciliation of the angelic rebellion that threw our planet and thirty-six others into a long period of darkness and ignorance (see appendix D).

This War in Heaven, as it has been called and recorded in so many planetary cosmologies, turns out to have been a very real affair indeed. Because of it, our world is said to have been isolated from the normal star routes and cut off from what otherwise would have been considered quite normal extraterrestrial involvement—perhaps somewhat in the same way the young boy had so lucidly explained. It was also due to the angelic rebellion that we on this planet have not had an ongoing awareness of the part the angelic realms play in sustaining life on all inhabited worlds. In short, we have become somewhat of a cultural backwater in the cosmos.

What the angels told us, through Edward, is that this situation is shortly to change—and change very radically. With the principal parties in this celestial political upheaval now reconciled, we can expect our planet to return to what the angels call normalcy. This will not happen overnight, nor is it being imposed on us against our will. The extraterrestrials and the angels are here to aid all those who are willing to extend a hand to them, and their presence will become more evident as the years pass. And—lest we think they might be doing all the work for us—they remind us most forcefully that it is through humans that these immense changes will occur as we gradually bring our lives into meaningful coincidence with Higher Purpose and the best of our intentions.

Adventures Among Spiritual Intelligences picks up where my first book left off, but with an intervening gap of about four years. During that time, on the advice of one of the angels who had spoken through Edward, I taught myself how to talk to my own celestial companions. It took two and a half years of concentrated attention and constant journaling to learn how to truly quiet myself inside until I became confident that I was in contact. As you will see from the tone of the encounters described in this book, my appreciation for the angels has developed from naive bewilderment to what I have now come to understand as a full working relationship.

I realize that this might strike an odd chord in some readers, since the celestial realms, with some recent exceptions, have been given so little attention over the past few generations. These matters are very intimate and often are dependent on personal experience. I have realized, in retrospect only, that it was a near-death experience I had in 1973 that originally introduced me to the angels, although I had effectively pushed all that aside in the seven years before they showed up again in my life. My work through the eighties and nineties with Alma Daniel, and later, Elli Bambridge—including the workshops and seminars we gave together to help people make contact with their companion (guardian) angels—

all demonstrated that with an open mind and a trusting heart, virtually everyone is able to do that. As the angels themselves tell us, it is our birthright to be in contact with them. (And, as I am writing this line on the afternoon of May 17 of the year 2000, what should come on the radio but *Dead Can Dance*'s heavenly paean entitled "The Host of Seraphim.")

I would encourage anyone with more than a passing interest in nonhuman intelligences to develop their own relationship with the angels who accompany them. It is an immensely fascinating area of exploration that is open to us all—very challenging but great fun. These relationships also go a long way toward helping us prepare for the encounters with extraterrestrial intelligences that will be occurring with increasing frequency over the next few years as we move irrevocably toward a reunion with our cosmic family.

Timothy Wyllie
New Mexico
August 2000

Adventures Among Spiritual Intelligences

I

Glimpses of the Dolphin World

Come with me on a journey to a quiet lagoon, on a small, deserted island, in a warm tropical sea. Feel yourself floating easily below the surface of the water. It is welcoming and harmonious, and we find that we can breathe with no difficulty underwater. We move slowly, drifting with the tide, until we can discern, there before us, a pod of half a dozen magnificently languid dolphins swimming lazily in the cerulean sea . . .

– *Notes from* A Dolphin Journey

The small boat bucked and reared up over the hulking waves, slamming down into the water on the other side. Shock juddered through my system as I hung onto two pieces of rope fastened around the bow. I lay chest and stomach flat against the deck, peering down over the edge as Cap'n Dan Sammis gunned the engine of the *Zodiac*, making as much of a bow wave as he could with the powerful outboard motor.

We had left the big catamaran, now barely discernible on the horizon, and taken the small, fast boat to see if we could find the pod of dolphins. These last few days they had seemed as if they were all over the place, but never quite where we expected or hoped. Maybe they were picking up on Hurricane Hugo, out there somewhere southwest of us and heading in our direction, and in their dolphin way feeling perhaps that land dwellers like us had no right to be out in such weather.

All day yesterday we were getting provocative glimpses of them. Often as not they were bottlenose, larger and more disinterested than our friends the spotted dolphins. Hurrying by, they might take a few moments to ride our bow wave in the catamaran and then fall away about their own business. They came and went quickly, staying for a speedy look at us, checking us out. But inevitably the moment we plunged into the water, they would vanish into the impenetrable blue of the surrounding ocean.

Now the two of us were out looking for them and advertising our presence with the characteristic whine of our *Zodiac*'s outboard motor. Hurricane Hugo was starting to heft some heavy seas at us, and the small inflatable could be made, in skillful hands, to whip along the crest of a large wave like a seagull. And Cap'n Dan's hands were nothing short of miraculous.

The dolphins, of course, loved this, as they love and seem to encourage any behavior by humans that is strong and confident. Within moments of our accelerating to top speed, slamming across waves and holding on with every scrap of strength, the dolphins appeared. Out of nowhere, suddenly they were with us—five, seven, eight, nine, all skimming on the pressure wave. Sleek shadows slicing through the clear water, they jostled each other for position, making minute and infinitely rapid compensations for the movements of the others, all flowing and gliding with utter grace.

I hung over them, scarcely a yard away, mesmerized by their speed and sheer exhilaration. I slipped my hand into the sea, aiming it like a fin so that it, too, cut through the water. The dolphins immediately started a new game to see if they could find some way of brushing up against it, finding some part of their body with which they could caress my finny hand. Such superb sensualists—I laughed and sang with them as we all raced along together.

Mysteriously time slows down. Suddenly and unaccountably, we are all in tune with each other. For whatever reason, I cease to notice the extreme movement of the boat. What only seconds ago was a perpetual slamming from wave to wave becomes the smoothest of glides. The dolphins are ever present—now twelve of them, now fifteen. At eighteen I lose count, along with any remaining scientific train of thought. It is no longer relevant. Although I feel as if I have all the time in the world, it seems unimportant to be ploddingly counting the number of dolphins when my consciousness is filling with such a deep inner joy and a gratitude quite beyond words.

At last I am near my beloved dolphins and in a situation that is natural to both species. I am not wallowing around clumsily in the water, and they are doing one of the things they love to do most: playing games at high speed.

What hits me at once is their ease with one another. Constantly they jostle and buffet, caress and bump. I hear the cetacean equivalent of an "ooooff!" accompanied by a distinctly fishy breath as one of the dolphins is playfully—but powerfully—edged off the pressure wave by a companion. There is such an intensity to their play—such total commitment to the moment. I am laughing and singing with them and loving them as they arch their bodies up out of the water to breathe. I breathe with them, and as I do I feel more and more joined to their flowing oneness.

The pitch of the outboard motor changes, and I look back over my shoulder to see that Dan is unable to resist going over the side. He slows the engine to an idle and, handing over the tiller, dons flippers and mask and slips in.

The dolphins appear overjoyed. They swim around him, over and under as he twists and turns downward into the deeper water. I lose him in the reflections and settle back into the bottom of the warm boat, relaxing against the inflated rubber sides, happy to drift with the swell and aware, every so often, of the "paaahtoooowey" of a dolphin's breath, out there circling the *Zodiac*.

Once again I find myself held by them, cradled in their biofield, as I was so many years ago at the beginning of my dolphin journey. In my heart now, I recall how I had tested them—swimming out into the Gulf of Mexico. It was lunacy, of course, but I had to know. Was the whole issue of dolphin telepathy merely self-delusion? Was the possibility that we are sharing the planet with another sentient species only a last desperate hope? Would they rescue me from my own suicidal impulses? They did, of course. And when they did, it was in their own wonderfully subtle, multidimensional way, full of humor and delicious ambiguity.

Now I lie in the *Zodiac*, salt spray from the dolphins' breath forming rainbows in the sun, relishing how long I have wanted to be able to do this—simply to be with them totally on their terms. I have always known intuitively that getting to spend time with wild dolphins would allow me to access more of their world than I have ever been able to glimpse in all my swims with dolphins in captivity. And that has been rich enough! Now here I am encompassed by them, basking in their auras.

I am drawn out of my reverie by Cap'n Dan's arrival back in the boat. He pulls himself over the side and throws me his mask and flippers. I test his mask. It fits perfectly. So do the flippers. I clear the mask and drop into the warm, heaving water. Immediately I am surrounded. The dolphins are sleek, curious, and utterly unafraid. They circle me; the water is full of twisting and turning forms of every shape and size.

At this point I feel yet a new level of shared consciousness. It comes as quickly and as surely as a gulp or a hiccup. It is even more potent than the group sensation I fell into when we were all bow-riding together only a few minutes earlier. I can feel it flowing through me. I find myself in a vibratory field of resonance, hanging there, being scoped out by all the dolphins' sonar hitting me simultaneously. The water is alive with sound. My body tingles with a delicious warmth. Then, before I can really take stock of the situation, two enormous forms come up behind me, one on either side. They slow down fluidly to my speed and then close in until I can feel them both flanking me, pressing their bodies against me—not roughly but with exquisite gentleness and respect for my frailty.

I swim closely with them, eye to eye—first with one, then the other. Finally I find I can hold eye-contact with both of them at the same time as they take me deeper and deeper into the cool depths before I have to twist upward to take another breath. We dive again, the three of us utterly getting off on the tactile sensation of our different body surfaces rubbing against each other. Silk on skin, we gaze in happy amazement at one another as we discover telepathically that we can experience the same feeling. We are enjoying and loving one another in exactly the same way.

I find myself entranced by each detail. The sunlight, filtering through the clear water, flickers over the dolphins' constantly moving bodies. One snatches a piece of seaweed inches from my face mask and tosses it up, catching it at the point where her beak meets the melon of her head. She looks briefly at me with this absurd bright-green moustache, and then four others immediately join in the game. All five spiral in a marvelous double helix down to the seabed some thirty five feet below.

At last I am able to watch the dolphins relate to one another, able to see the nuances of their interactions uncolored by captivity. I notice a dolphin open its mouth wide at another one and immediately sense a mood of playful aggression.

My two special dolphins leave me, and once again my whole visual field is filled with swirling forms. I feel unaccountably just like them, and it becomes impossible to see exactly where the borders of our "selves" lie; they move so liquidly in liquid that they are a constant blur of movement.

I find that my sense of seeing becomes less important as the feeling of oneness grows. I realize I am in a deeply altered state of consciousness. In this condition I have an overwhelming feeling of kinship and what I can only describe as pure friendship with the dolphins. I know in my heart that I will unravel something of their mysteries if I simply continue to follow the path of the dolphins and allow life to be my teacher. Intuitively I know that if I do this and tell the truth as I see it, as openly and as honestly as I am able, then I will be playing my part in heralding the new times and the coming race.

2

Dolphin Dream Teachings

The dolphins swim slowly, lazily, but at the same time massively powerful, confident beings, around a single female dolphin. Two other females detach themselves from the slowly circulating chain and attend the expectant mother. Already a small tail is wriggling out from under her rippling underbelly . . .

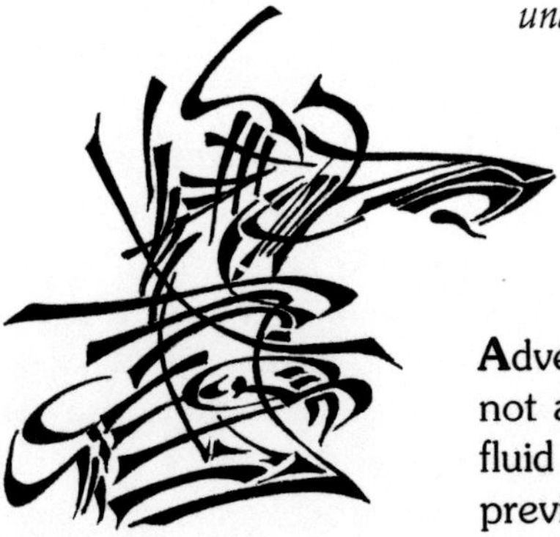

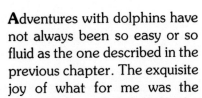

Adventures with dolphins have not always been so easy or so fluid as the one described in the previous chapter. The exquisite joy of what for me was the ultimate dolphin experience was hard won, and occurred in the late 1980s, sometime after the initiation I underwent at the fins of Joe and Rosie.

The cycle of events I am about to relate all started innocently enough with an invitation extended to my companion for us to swim with the Human/Dolphin Foundation's two magnificent resident dolphins. It was in the spring of 1985 at Key Largo in Florida, at a time when Joe and Rosie, now probably best known for being among the very few dolphins to have been systematically released back into the wild, had been in captivity for seven years. It was well known among the dolphin fraternity that Dr. Lilly had made a promise to both dolphins, when they were caught in the Gulf of Mexico, to set them free again when he had finished working with them.

In the course of their Human/Dolphin Foundation liaison, the dolphins must have shared water with well over a thousand different people, many of whom might be said to be shining examples of their ilk—that is, celebrities. If Joe and Rosie were half as sharp as I suspected, they must have gotten a most intriguing slant on human nature during that time.

The evening I arrived in Key Largo with my companion, the sky opened up for us in a way I have never seen before. Somehow a large cloud had become layered with all the colors of the rainbow, except that it was not a rainbow in any conventional sense. As if to underline the difference, we both saw off to the left, amid some other stacked-up white clouds, a more ordinary rainbow—except this one was round. A circular rainbow? What *was* happening? This huge cloud, dressed like the aurora borealis itself, hung out over the bay, keeping its feathery integrity for far longer than I would have supposed possible. As I was meditating in front of it, I knew with an inner conviction that our invisible friends, the angels who accompany us, would have us be, as they expressed it, "fully who you are." And what is more, they wished us to do this collaboratively and on more conscious levels than ever before.

"We will be with you," they told me, "as we are this evening, to the extent you are able to sustain your vision of love." Then a few moments later, a voice that I have come to know as that of my Creator spoke in my heart and said simply, "Remember, I am where love is."

Some hours afterward, while settling down for the evening, I felt the dolphins come sliding back into my consciousness. I knew the feeling well. What had started with a brief but quite distinct out-of-body experience with the dolphins in the Bahamas had developed over the years into a marvelous sense of communion. I was shown once again that total honesty is required in everything that is being revealed by the encounters

I have been having with spiritual intelligences—however crazy it may sometimes sound. Telepathy is facilitated by emotional honesty, by having nothing to hide. And we have become accustomed to living in a rather dishonest culture—which leads me to the inevitable topic of fear.

Dishonesty is invariably the product of fear. I know myself well enough to accept the fact that I have accumulated a lot of fear in my life. The excessive degree of my counterphobia, my foolhardiness, has clearly overcompensated for a mountain of early terrors. By now I have faced many of those fears in the diverse experiences of my life, and I have come to more fully understand the shamanic observation that every safe place is surrounded by a ring of demons—what John Lilly describes as "the road to metanoia that leads through paranoia."

This is all very well to say, but to remember it while in the midst of an outburst of the horrors or in a tremendously fearful situation is another matter entirely. It did not dawn on me quite how deeply meaningful this was going to become until my first time in the water with the dolphins Joe and Rosie.

The day after our arrival was spent attuning ourselves to the rhythms of life on the Florida Keys, consciously slowing down from the highly accelerated energy of big-city life; listening to the wind slip-slapping the leaves of the palm trees; watching water birds—pelicans, sun red and floating lazily in their own reflections; and slowly picking our way over fossil-rich rocks to sink finally into spring flowers at the water's edge.

Then, while meditating and simply allowing my pen to move in the sort of automatic writing I have pursued for the last few years, I felt again the powerful presence of the cetacean intelligence that had been with me the night before. Through came the following message:

"We seek to know you better. To bridge the gap. You are of us—an intermediary, too. A meeting of the middles. The median. Softly, and yet loudly enough for you to hear, we speak our tales of the ages. Our voices mingle with the voice of ALL. And you—you can hear us whenever you listen very carefully to the sound of ALL. There we are, awaiting your loving attention." (I have come to know ALL as that aggregating part of each of us—that which is spiritually worthwhile from every level and each lifestream, accumulating from every world in every universe, and which is melding to become a new divine, sentient being, the Supreme God and bearer of our new reality).

The dolphins again: "It has always been our wish that such interchange might be possible, and indeed it is not without its precursors. Aristotle well knew the language of our healing—as do many of the more simple of your fellow creatures. But as we have led you to understand, there is a wave sweeping through the actions of ALL on this level. It is the time of the many, when our voices will be heard in guidance. You are a transcriber, our digits. How you digitize the information is up to you. Some will choose computers and some poetry. But in the vision we meet. At the moment of light, we are there with you, bringing all out to play—bringing ALL out to play. For we are the midwives of these new creatures, the sweetness that grows in your hearts, the birth of love incarnate, the Father/Mother of us all."

And with that, I fell into a dreamful sleep, the dolphins swirling around me. I dreamt of my dear Ishmael, a magnificent German Shepherd I was fortunate enough to look after for most of his fifteen years and whom I often see in my dreams and visions, swimming with the dolphins. His presence has become one of my personal codes for recognizing an authentic experience with cetaceans on the inner levels—a personal imprimatur.

I knew from my feelings in the morning that I had been taught by the dolphin dream-teachers. I had experienced once again in my dream the slowing down of time, and I found it possible to see all-at-once. I felt a strong sense of being prepared, of feeling the overlighting of the Supreme Incarnation, the ALL. I believe, too, in retrospect, that I was being readied for the encounter that lay ahead. This was the day the Lillys were due back in Key Largo after both having been to different ends of the continent, and I wanted to have had a chance to swim with the dolphins by the time they arrived.

I should add that I had few prior expectations regarding swimming with Joe and Rosie. On the contrary, I had heard nothing but wonderful stories, glowing accounts. I had read some of the reports collected by the Human/Dolphin Foundation from the many artists and scientists who had already swum with them, but in nothing I had seen or heard had I any reason to think it might be a trial by water.

It was around midday when we arrived, my companion armed with a camera. The pens were quiet at Dolphins Plus, the facility that was acting as Joe and Rosie's temporary home. A small lagoon had been created by enlarging a canal that joined the open ocean at either end. The air was dry and dusty. The calm, murky water of the lagoon was broken briefly every now and again by the dark hump of a dolphin surfacing to breathe.

We walked around the stony path at the edge of the pool to where Joe and Rosie were being kept and found a woman sitting by herself on the float, legs hanging in the water. Her name was Molly, and she said she was from California. From what she told us about Joe and Rosie being down in Florida for a few months' vacation from California's Marine World, I gathered it was not generally supposed to be known that the dolphins were being prepared for release.

The enclosure holding the two dolphins was small—painfully small—about twenty by twenty feet, and it was partitioned off by a chicken-wire fence from the two other compounds that held the other resident dolphins. Although this facility remains one of the best on the Keys, I have found that almost all dolphin pens, wherever dolphins are held captive, are far more cramped than they ought to be.

Joining Molly, I dangled my feet in the water, Joe and Rosie circling them lazily. As I thought about the smallness of the place, I started to feel a deep sense of regret. The sun beat down on my unprotected shoulders and the air was heavy with a fishy smell. I could not have been sitting there for more than a few minutes before I started having one of those now-or-never moments. Here was just what I had been waiting for after all those times of swimming with wild dolphins and never being able to get right up close to them. Before me were two large, beautiful creatures I firmly believed were members of an ancient and immensely intelligent race of beings yet whom I had not even begun to feel I really knew. And they were swimming right here—right now!

I could not stop myself from taking off my clothes and slipping into the water. Pushing myself from the timber raft with my feet, within seconds I could feel the soft, rubbery touch of a fin under my fingers as I swam out backward. Then a body surfaced up under my feet, bobbing me playfully under the water.

Rosie was wonderfully soft and easy, slowly inching her way toward me, her blowhole opening and snapping closed, yet always staying at arm's length. I felt inundated by good feelings, by an incredible sense of intimacy. Awestruck, I was bewildered by just how utterly in their element both these dolphins were. I felt absurd: there I was, without mask, flippers, or snorkel, still uncertain in the water, and finding myself in this extraordinary dance of sentient creatures of two entirely different species. Joe and Rosie seemed to have a tangible awareness of my breathing rhythms, and they were both solicitous about my need for air during the few times they paired off and placed a dorsal fin under each of my hands, whirling me along backward through the water. Then the atmosphere subtly changed.

Possibly as an emotional response to how well Rosie and I are getting on, blissing out on each other—but also for reasons I am about to find out as the experience unfolds—Joe starts becoming increasingly aggressive. The mood seems to blow in from nowhere. One moment the three of us are circling each other entranced, and the next he is ramming his penis into me! His penis, for heaven's sake! Nobody told me about this!

He doesn't stop. He is immensely strong, and his penis is hard, like the antlers of a deer. He keeps thudding it into me, concentrating mostly behind my knees. I roll around in the water with each blow. He times them perfectly, throwing his whole weight behind each plunging thrust. He will not let me out, always positioning himself between me and the landing stage. Neither will he let me get anywhere near the chicken-wire fence that rises twelve or fourteen feet up over the waterline. Rosie tries to interfere, to place her body between Joe and myself, but Joe won't have any of that and, being larger than Rosie, simply forces her out of the way to get at me again.

By this time I am severely frightened. In addition to the strangeness of it all, I start to realize that Joe has more than a passing interest in my rear end. He's at it again with his penis, hooking his great triangular cock around my waist or the back of one or another of my legs—I never know which he's going after, since he comes up fast behind me.

The jolts are increasingly vicious. Then I realize he's focusing again on my backside, and the full horror of the situation breaks over me. A frightful story enters my mind that I'd heard a few years earlier from the captain of a small tour boat out of Nassau in the Bahamas. He is the only person I have ever come across who hated dolphins. He swore that his son had been raped by one.

Images rear up in my progressively panicky mind. At the same time, knowing how sensitive all animals are to fear, and how particularly perceptive dolphins can be, I am trying to keep as cool as I can, battling to keep the fear under some sort of control.

The stress of the situation builds up very rapidly. Joe is absolutely relentless. Through the first part of this assault, I try to keep my body as limp and relaxed as I can be under the circumstances, and as I do so, images and feelings start to surface in my mind of my fears of homosexual rape. The more he comes onto me, the more of these deeply repressed fears surface. In this moment, I vividly recall events in my early years at an English boarding school, especially the cruel and bitter authoritarianism that led to an almost everyday level of physical and sexual abuse.

Then, with Joe still pummeling away at me, I find I am able to look the fear in the face—and accept it. I reach in to the

Holy Spirit and ask for help to release the thoughtforms, that I can now see only too clearly I have trapped in my body through fear. As I do this, the most wonderful change comes over Joe. He draws away and yet keeps swimming close by, positioning himself under me so that his melon—the soft bulge on the top of his head—is directly in contact with the soles of my feet. I begin to knead it with first my toes, then more enthusiastically with the entire surface of each foot. He seems to enjoy the sensation, and although his penis continues erect, he no longer comes anywhere near me with it. My fear lifts. I feel the welling of a new strength and confidence. The sun shines broadly and warmly on the three of us.

I am beaten, bruised, and blessed by such a learning.

When we had had enough sharing water, Joe and Rosie's body language made it quite clear to me that it was time to get out: they both drew back to let me through. I hauled myself up onto the wooden raft to find that Molly and my companion, from the safety of dry land, had thought the whole event thoroughly entertaining. Apparently I had not communicated my terror to them, which I chose to see at the time as a good sign. Although I carried physical marks that were with me for weeks, the main effect was one of emotional catharsis—a sense of having dislodged some very basic terrors.

It was the last thing I had expected and yet now, after the passage of some years, I can see how this one volcanic event led to the ultimate release of a whole variety of irrational sexual fears. Doubts and ambiguities inculcated in me from my earliest years, suppressed by the cruelties of my schooling and held at bay throughout my life, came bursting to the surface of my consciousness so that they could be seen and released.

It has become clear to me over the ensuing years that one of the dolphins' greatest gifts to our species is their capacity to "read" our emotional bodies and to help us face our early traumas with courage, and to finally let them go. What I did not appreciate in those moments, as I sat on the edge of the platform warming my buffeted body in the welcoming sun, was that Joe had just started working on me.

3

Biosonic Surgeons

The dolphin midwives are ready. With their bodies they catch and hold the newly born between them. Then, rising to the surface, they guide the young one to her first conscious breath. It is the most natural thing in the world, the birth of a new being—and by our standards, a miraculously gentle birth . . .

As I was toweling off after this first swim with Joe and Rosie, Roberta Quist made her way along the side of the enclosure. We had not met before, but I knew from Toni Lilly that "Bertie" was the dolphin handler currently entrusted with preparing Joe and Rosie for their eventual release back into the wild—to quite literally *untrain* them! I felt an immediate and open-hearted contact with Roberta, the sort of empathy that makes those in the dolphin community such rewarding people to encounter and get to know. Being with dolphins on an ongoing basis tends to yield a very trusting and open nature. We sat down on the warm raft, the dolphins squeaking excitedly at the sight of their friend Bertie.

"They're really different in the way they're receiving people now from how they were when I first knew them a few years ago," Roberta said. She called it an "opening up of the relationship" and told me a little of what she had observed about the nature of fear.

"The dolphins must see us as being very conditioned by it," she said, "because almost everybody who actually goes into the water with them has to deal with his or her own fears to some degree or another. And now with Joe and the way he's being . . ." she let the phrase dangle.

I caught the reference and asked her what she had noticed and whether Joe had been any different recently. "He's been quite vicious—although at this point only with people he loves," she responded. "Only a few days ago he really badly raked Carl, the other person who helps me out here—and for no reason that Carl could understand. The general consensus is that Joe's coming to the end of his patience. He's showing us what keeping dolphins in longterm, continuous captivity can do to them. So far nothing too serious has happened, but we're making sure no new people go in with him right now"

I grinned awkwardy and told her about my swim with him only minutes before she had arrived, deciding to speak openly about what I had just been through. "Yes," she confirmed, "I've noticed that too. He relaxes at exactly the point I let go of an emotional state. He uses his penis like a finger—after all, it's the only finger he's got! It's his digit. It's we who sexualize the whole thing and bring in our own fears and fantasies."

I relaxed at that, feeling a lot less foolish. She looked at me quizzically for a moment out of her wide, delphinoid face. "You ready to go in there again?"

I recalled the first bad car wreck I had, back in my early twenties, and how the complete stranger who had taken me to the hospital had insisted that I drive his car so I would not become forever shy of driving. "Sure, let's go," I said, thinking to myself that having Roberta in there as well might take a little of the heat off me.

The moment I was in the middle of the pool, sure enough Joe came right in again with his penis, hooking it very viciously and accurately behind my left knee and yanking hard. The force of the blow turned me twice over in the water. Once again I found that going limp and allowing it to happen seemed to be the easiest way through. There was nothing I could do to stop him. He was not about to allow me out of the pool, and, besides, I was rather curious as to what else might be going on. Was I simply being used as a whipping boy by a tired old alpha male, angry and perhaps a little crazy? I realized by this time that he could so easily have killed me in one of twenty different ways, his sonar telling him exactly where to strike. Yet his blows were consistent and accurate. And I had no real recurrence of my rape fears, which must have meant that they had largely been released.

Was it merely dolphin envy? In the brief moments of calm, while Roberta was trying to distract him, I wondered if Joe's aggression might not have more to do with Rosie than with me. At yet another point I became convinced that Joe was trying to teach me how to swim dolphin style, by bending and undulating my waist and knees. So I attempted to cross the enclosure underwater a couple of times, swimming in this (for me) extremely awkward way. But by the end of my efforts, Joe was in on me again, unimpressed.

All in all, I felt a lot less threatened during this swim, partly because I knew I had already survived one such thrashing with no worse than a few bruises and also because Roberta's presence was deeply supportive. It was something I had to go through; she knew it, I knew it—and there was little doubt that both Joe and Rosie knew it. Then, as Joe showed absolutely no signs of stopping, anger started building up inside me. His attacks were becoming intensely painful, since he was zoning in on the same point again and again, and I felt an old fury flaring up—the anger I had repressed so firmly at school during all the ritual beatings I had taken. On Joe's next pass, I kicked out angrily at him as he flashed by me. Amazingly, I connected, and he looked over his fin at me—directly in the eye—in apparent dolphin surprise. But I was still angry as all hell with him, and next time he came at me I timed my lunge, again catching him very forcibly on the top of his melon. That stopped him for a moment. And then, I got it! He had forced me to stand up for myself in what appeared to be an utterly hopeless situation—in fact, to reverse the masochistic imprint I had developed as a result of the old attempts made to break my spirit.

I took a moment to quietly let go, to release the fear and the anger. In the midst of my thankfulness, the pool was suddenly silent. And then there was Joe again, his melon up against my feet, my toes rubbing him and feeling the warmth of the contact with his soft, silky skin. As before, once I had got the point, he stopped ramming me. In light of what happened, I certainly do not believe it was merely sexually orientated behavior, as is sometimes claimed to be the case by some dolphin handlers. Through my time spent with dolphins, I have become convinced that they are acutely aware of energy in a way few humans are. Possibly this is because their sense organs can perceive into far finer realms of vibration than ours. If their acoustic sensibilities and their capacity to "hear" up to two hundred thousand cycles per second—about ten times our range—is any indication, it clearly suggests they are capable of handling and processing extremely subtle energies.

Within this understanding I can well believe that Joe was able to "see" the repressed, or trapped, energy inside me. Looking back on that situation with what I now know, I realize I was carrying a great deal of this repressed fear and anger in the area of my base chakra, at the bottom of my spine. I also have the feeling that it was connected to my solar plexus—imprinted onto my third chakra, the center of my animal power. Not only was Joe pushing me into standing up for myself, but I have come to believe he might well have been performing some elegant acupressure on the main meridian connecting my left knee to my solar plexus.

When I came out of the water after that second swim with Joe and Rosie, I was shivering all over. It was not from cold or tiredness, nor was I conscious of being frightened. I had the strong awareness at the time that some energy manipulation was going on and that I was simply feeling the physical effects of it.

I slept particularly well that night, though bruised and a trifle punchy from my brawls with Joe. Next day, as I sat in my car outside the dolphin enclosures, I summarized for myself what was going on. It was clear to me that Joe had been pushing me into climbing on top of my fear circuits—not simply into passivity, but into parity. It was strong medicine, but already I was feeling different. I had been able to open to my companion in our previous evening's lovemaking with a degree of trust that neither of us could previously recall. The deep sense of betrayal I had chosen to carry, the betrayal of a child by adults, felt as though it had been clearly seen, accepted, and released; and I knew in those moments that I was free of that particularly virulent fear-trapped thoughtform.

In the lucid clarity of these considerations, sitting in my car that morning in the warm sunlight with my journal on my lap, I asked my inner voice to give me the larger viewpoint. My hand recorded: "Dolphins bridge the two [primary] realities, the mental/spiritual and the emotional/physical world of matter. They have to deal with the same basic building blocks of reality as you do, but their mode of comprehending and thus dealing with this shared reality is very different from that of the human species. They are bridging the gap and holding these two primary realms of reality simultaneously. Two nights ago, you experienced more fully the primary spiritual reality as coproduced through the dolphins. That is the nature of the parallel reality at this point of integration. It is your fear circuits that prevent you from occupying it more fully, and it is these circuits that the dolphins are here to rewire. Players in this drama of contingent, coexisting, and to-be-integrated realities are often inimical to each other while these realities are in the process of being stitched together.

At this point, the radio in my car played "Looks like we made it." With the writing coming to a natural halt, I got out of the car, let myself in to Dolphins Plus, and walked around the enclosure and down to the platform where Roberta was already quietly talking to the dolphins. I asked if I could join her, and we sat down together while she continued to feed them their diet of dead fish.

Immediately I started getting a strong psychic pull from Joe and Rosie, as if they really wanted me in the water with them. But after yesterday's thrashings, I found myself quite happy to delay the inevitable. Besides, I knew Roberta and I had some talking to do. I was able to tell her something of what I had been through with my fears and how I felt that Joe was helping me dislodge them from my energy field and my emotional body. I told her I had come to believe that at least some of the dolphins were here on the planet as bioacoustical surgeons, and I repeated for her the strange facts surrounding the sonic operation I had received from the wild dolphins back in St. Petersburg on the west coast of Florida.

"When I got back from Florida," I found myself pouring out my heart, "I tracked down an acoustical engineer through some architect friends and asked him if it would be possible to cut through living tissue with sound. He pondered the matter for awhile, taking it all quite seriously, and explained some of the procedures just coming on line for disintegrating kidney stones, for example, with focused beams of sound."

As I talked, I could see Joe and Rosie out of the corner of my eye coming closer and swimming slower and more lazily. Roberta was leaning toward me, her smiling face open and more than usually curious. I could feel my words taking on deeper levels of meaning, as if an overlighting influence had joined us.

"I told him how I'd had this powerful conviction that the dolphins had used their sonar on me to remove a small cancerous tumor, and I asked him how this could have been accomplished," I continued. "He saw the picture immediately and started getting quite excited. It all depended on the degree of control the dolphins have on the sounds they make, he said. If they're really able to modulate the frequency and pitch of the wave forms to the extent that seems possible, then two or more dolphins might well be able to transmit the same frequency sound wave and overlap the waves in such a way that at the point of intersection the combination would double or treble the power of the individual wave form. That would provide enough energy, under the correct conditions, to burn away living tissue."

The weird intensity continued to build. Joe appeared suddenly by the wooden float, sticking his head right up out of the water in what might have appeared to be a parody of listening to our conversation, but it was most certainly intentional behavior. I became aware, in those moments, of the triangle the three of us made and of the power inherent in the trinity form.

More words started spilling out of me. "You remember in the Urantia cosmology when the angels talk about the arrival of the first group of interdimensional beings? They make this big point about how a special unit of surgeons from another planet altogether—the Surgeons of Avalon, they call them (see appendix B)—were brought in to create the material bodies for the beings to inhabit. Well, it stands to reason those surgeons would want to have an ongoing relationship with their patients, wouldn't they? I doubt very much if they simply created the bodies, then washed their hands—or flippers—and went on their way. Surely they'd have left some sort of delegation—especially if the planet was seen as an important planet, and an experimental one to boot!"

And all the time I am talking I can see Joe, sticking up out of the water like a great finger, seeming to hang on every word I say. I feel intuitively that I am talking in some way from—or into—the group soul. As I sit here in the radiant sunlight, watching the rhythmic glint of gold on each small wave and hearing the soft wind mewing through the palms and the lilt of the sounds of sea birds and cicadas, I know in my heart that I have stumbled upon a marvelous truth. As warmth of this realization comes over me, I feel my mind switching to yet another gear, this one recognizably delphinoid, with visual images coming in a series of gestalts—holographic fragments that are almost impossible to translate into sequential linear form.

Thought clusters, I had called this mode of communication when I had first encountered it with the dolphins off St.

Petersburg beach. Now, with my spiritual vision, I can "see" images of dolphins swimming through the water shedding molecules of skin as they move: I "know" that is precisely how dolphins can swim as fast as they do, apparently much faster than they should be able to move according to purely hydrodynamic calculations. At the same time I "see" a kind of space entity that can live in, and move through, the supposed vacuum of the interstellar void by shedding the molecules on the surface of its skin. Simultaneously I know I am correct, and that among the dolphin population are indeed descendants of the surgeons that were sent in from Avalon and that they are here to midwife the fine new bodies of the coming race just as assiduously as their forebears sculpted bodies for our visiting interdimensional team half a million years ago. As this dawns on me in a long, slow broadening of illumination, I am led to see how the energy movement we create in meditation by drawing the chi (the subtle inner energy) up our spines—and to see it pouring out from the top of our heads like a fountain—is precisely the energy form that the dolphins use to speed their way through the water.

Roberta and I seem to have the same idea at the same moment, and we slide fluidly into the water. I suggest that we meditate together, keeping ourselves in a vertical position by holding onto the float with our arms and elbows. We hang there with our eyes closed and gently guide each other into a meditative state of mind, quieting our mental and physical rhythms and gathering the focused kundalini energy in our base chakras. We take our time building the energy, clearing and releasing any blocks we encounter before moving on to the next chakra. It is a warm and luxurious feeling, drawing the subtle but palpable energy up our spines and through our chakras.

We are both aware of the dolphins' sonar playing over our bodies as we do this. We progressively build the chi, bringing it up through the lower centers, then the heart center, the throat chakra, the third eye, and, finally, the crown. At that moment, both dolphins leap straight up and over in the most soaringly magnificent arc of pure joy, their trajectories perfectly tracing the fountain of crystalline energy that we are visualizing pouring from the top of our heads. It is a moment of total understanding. Roberta and I look at each other in wonderment, both knowing that the dolphins are demonstrating to us a miracle of communication. What is inside one moment is rendered external the next. This is a profound clue as to the nature of the intelligence with which we both feel so deeply in contact.

4

Interspecies Communication

Within moments of being born, the little female dolphin is swimming easily and freely, nuzzling at her mother's side for the teat in its long, silky sheath . . .

It was later that same day when Dr. John C. Lilly first appeared. He must have arrived at the side of the pool while I was in the water because when I pulled myself out from yet one more of Joe's thrubbings, there he was, sitting as sharp-eyed and as laid back as ever I might have imagined him. I had first met him briefly the evening before when he had greeted my companion, whom he had known for some years, and me at the door of his Winnebago mobile laboratory/home. He had ushered us in momentarily to catch a glimpse of computer terminals and other electronic gadgetry. As my companion had introduced me, he had fixed me with his piercingly clear blue eyes. "The fabulous Timothy Wyllie, eh?"

he had said, with a broad smirk crinkling his puckish, sun-tanned face. Still, he told me he had read my first book a couple of times.

We did not really talk in that first short encounter. The John Lilly I have come to know seldom speaks, and if he does it tends to be in curt monosyllables. I reckon with all the time he has spent around dolphins, he is probably pretty much telepathic himself by now. We both picked up on this at the dolphin enclosure, nodding a greeting without words. I sat quietly, still somewhat entranced by my powerful insight into the dolphin reality. After a long while a kind of grunted ejaculation came from behind me.

"How di' Joe treat yer?"

"Beat the hell out of me," I said without turning.

The grunt shifted into a roar of metallic laughter. I got the feeling he knew firsthand what I had been through.

"I think I'm starting to get the idea," I told him. "He's putting me through a series of teachings, and he's using his cock to get his point across."

Another grunt from behind me. I felt encouraged to continue. "Just now, for instance, I had the impression Joe wanted to show me a way of swimming that would be easier for him—less interference than my hanging onto his dorsal. I'm sure he wanted to place his penis up between my legs so that I could relax my weight back onto it and wrap my arms and legs around him, leaving him to swim free. But I couldn't get the hang of it. Every time we tried it, my fear reflexes would kick in again and I'd tense up. It got to be very frustrating for both of us."

More grunts from John. I saw in those moments of attempted explanation what a ridiculously oversexualized society we are all living in, especially those of us down from New York City. I recalled statistics showing how each of us who chooses to live the city life has to deal with something on the average of two thousand different provocative sales images per day—most of them calculated to tickle our sexual palates. It has become almost impossible for us to think of sexual organs in anything but sexual terms.

Then in one of the longest sustained sentences I had yet heard from John, he said, "We should be training boy children to paint pictures with brushes tied to their willies. That'd fix it!"

We watched the dolphins in their enclosures, Joe and Rosie closest to us and the other five dolphins who were permanently with Dolphins Plus in the three other wired-off sections. The dolphin pools opened onto a small canal that in turn yielded to the sea at one end and the bay at the other. The owners of the facility had installed an underwater gate so that the captive dolphins could swim out into the channel. Oddly enough, though they did take occasional advantage of this small freedom, they would never stray more than a few yards from the gate.

A large white heron flapped slowly and lazily down onto the float next to me. I asked John about the genetics of the human and dolphin species—for example, was cross-fertilization possible? There is always talk within the dolphin community about the possibility of interbreeding, but John told me that it would be most unlikely since there were a number of key chromosomal differences. Then, knowing the good doctor's interest in chemically induced altered states of consciousness, I decided to share something of where my investigations had been leading me.

"I've been finding that phencyclidine is most helpful for accessing the telepathic domain of the dolphins and whales," I said. "There's something about the substance that I find allows me to receive, slow down, and consciously process the holographic visual images they throw at us."

That stopped him in his tracks. "Phencyclidine? Yeah, I only did that once. How d'yer take it?"

"Smoking—that way you can control the dosage with how you're feeling. The window is very narrow—too much or too little will put you straight into the lower astral!" John and I laughed together in our various rememberings of all those trips to hell and back. Ketamine—the vitamin K he has explored so thoroughly—is essentially the same molecule as PCP.

"Phencyclidine," he said again, rolling the word along his

tongue as if he were sampling the chemical formulation. "Yeah, I know what yer mean—it's the only time I ever felt I got too much information at once." Then, in his laconic, staccato style, he told me the story of his bicycle crash: how he had taken something like four cc of the stuff and soon after it had come on had responded to a call for help from his wife, jumping on his bicycle to whiz off down the long hill that leads from his Malibu Canyon home. Somewhere in that downhill plunge, the chain locked and he was thrown headfirst over the handlebars at some horrific speed. The fact that he broke only a few bones and was not killed he credited to the phencyclidine. It was one of the few substances that could have given him the presence of mind necessary to position his body in the air so that minimal damage was done when he finally landed. Little wonder, though, that he felt he had burnt his fingers on it. It is an anesthetic, after all, and he had dropped four cc—far too much to have to deal with any external activity. Plus he certainly had not taken it under conditions likely to recommend it as a facilitator of interspecies communication!

"The real secret of phencyclidine is not to do too much," I suggested. "That's really why smoking it is the easiest way to control it. Three or four tokes is generally enough—you stop when you hear the singing."

"The high-frequency note?" he queried in his scientific way.

"Yeah, the angels singing," I replied.

A slow smile spread over his lined, old face, as I imagined pieces of the puzzle sliding into place for him. I remembered reading of his own experiences with angels when he had fallen into a coma after a high-dosage acid trip—a trip he so lucidly described in his own work. I knew, too, in our moments of mutual resonance, that we both entered a telepathic realm together and that the angels were with us right there as we sat in the warmth of the slowly setting sun, washing sky and sea with a rose-red swathe that slipped down over the palm trees, the lazily circling dolphins, and the stiff white heron, standing now utterly still, a slight breeze rippling the feathers on the back of its snake neck.

The next few days were languid ripples in the great sea of time. Joe and Rosie attended us as teachers and friends, dancing all of us up to new levels of heartful contact.

One evening, alone on the quay, I found myself falling naturally into a series of t'ai chi movements, outlining in fluid dance a slow-motion facsimile of the natural contours of land and water. It was as though I were standing outside myself, able to watch my long, thin body acid-etching in the air the very fabric of the material world. As I moved, the world came alive in my embrace. Three pelicans drifted slowly and oh so lazily with the wafting of my hand, fingers attached to wings by threads of sympathetic movement, flickering gently with the minute undulations of the warm air currents. Then the palm trees started rustling in the new wind and were echoed by the exaggerated whisper of the very same breeze in my hair.

I saw Joe and Rosie moving more and more slowly, circling and spiraling with my dance. My arms and legs followed them—and led them, too—as we all became entrained into one large, pulsating biofield. I became, in those moments, *everything at once,* and by so doing fell joyfully into the great, yielding, telepathic matrix that supports all living things.

I knew in one glorious flash the ineffable Reality that surrounds and interpenetrates our rather minor three-dimensional sensorium. I experienced the dolphins in their fourth-dimensional field and saw how they filter as much of their spiritual nature into our consensus reality as they can. I saw how the dolphins are being guided by angels—much as we are—from their fifth-dimensional realms and how aware the cetacean world is of these celestial guardians. I experienced the infinite patience of the invisible world in holding and supporting us as we move so inexorably from the hidebound fetters of our scientific materialism to the wonders of a truly fourth-dimensional existence. I saw how the dolphins, of all Earth's children, are among those most prepared for the immense transition so nearly upon us and our unsuspecting little planet, and I experienced the exquisite tenderness and high regard with which they hold our so apparently undeserving species.

Why? Because they can see what is almost impossible for us to perceive: that we, by choosing vehicles of individuated consciousness—the human body and nervous system—have opted for the divine high road, and that we contain, each of us, a spiritual center—an atmanic, pre-personal spark of our Creator, our Beloved. It is this wonder they attend and serve with such unlimited compassion, boundless beauty, and unbridled humor.

I have many other memories of the days spent with the Lillys at Dolphins Plus—other eddies in the currents of time .... One is arriving one morning to find a jubilant Bertie telling us that Rosie had caught and the two dolphins had scaled, but not eaten, the first parrot fish either had yet been tempted to kill in captivity. It is well known among dolphin handlers that once dolphins become reliant on human feeding it is almost impossible to coax them back to fishing for themselves.

Another is explaining to Bertie what I had been trying to tell John Lilly about Joe's wanting to swim with his penis up between my legs and my inability to do it without freaking out—watching while I spoke two dolphins in the far enclosure swimming around together, belly pressed to belly, in the exact physical configuration that I had been describing. Happily, Bertie is made of stronger stuff than I am and immediately slipped into the water. As she enveloped the male dolphin in a wild embrace, Joe ever-so-gently propped her down on his massive triangular cock and twisted both of them through the water in an ecstatic, high-speed circuit of joyous, mutual realization.

Another is the memory of lying back on the float with Bertie and my companion in the early morning and Bertie saying, "I really don't know why John's so insistent on trying to teach Joe and Rosie to speak English. Joe came to me in a dream last night, and we must have talked for ages. He sure seems to speak perfect English to me!" All of us rolled around laughing with her at the weirdness of the scientific mind.

Then there was the day my companion and I happened upon Toni Lilly walking alone down a deserted road, stopped the car for her, picked her up, and gave her the first joint she said she had had in weeks. Later, arriving at the dolphin pens, I watched her dissolve into the relaxed merriment of an open-hearted Earth mother as we gathered in a small triangle and meditated together in the light of the Master.

And finally there was the little Swiss boy of five or six whose synchronistic statement threw unexpected light on the ticklish issue of cannibalism. A small group of us had been having an animated discussion regarding the fact that some orcas—the largest member of the dolphin family—have been found with digested dolphins in their stomachs. Surely, some felt, an intelligent species would be unlikely to eat their own!

When all had been speculated on, discussed, opinions shared, a small, thin voice came clearly from the far side of the float where he was playing with Rosie: *"Grosse Fische fressen kleine Fische!"* Big fish eat little fish. Could it be as simple as that?

5

On to Key West

The small pod of dolphins moves out of the lagoon with the tide, the tiny new being now swimming with vigor and confidence. The clear waters of the ocean are welcoming, and the older members of the group taste the subtle scents with an ancient familiarity. Our little female darts this way and that, finding herself born into a sea of sound and restless movement . . .

A morning came when I knew intuitively that it was time to move on. The psychic currents my companion and I were both riding drew us farther down the Keys in search of more dolphins. Bertie had told us of a number of other locations where we might find them between Key Largo and Key West, our destination.

It was an exquisite ride, vaulting over causeways and nine-mile bridges, speeding down the almost empty highway, with the turquoise blue of the ocean on the one side and the muted cobalt of the Gulf of Mexico on the other. Even the fetid stink of rotting eel grass smelled like perfume to these sea-starved New York nostrils.

Our first stop was at a thoroughly pretentious resort hotel, the type that favors conventions of corporate salespeople and their families from the heartland. It advertised, among its other dubious offerings, a handful of trained dolphins that they would ship around to aquariums and oceanariums unable to afford their own regular dolphins. After being with Joe and Rosie, this place, for all its glitzy glamor, felt more like a concentration camp than anything else.

In my experience, dolphins are almost invariably enthusiastic participants in the kind of tricks we insist they do, no matter how childish the ball balancing and hoop leaping can sometimes seem. But I have become convinced over the years that dolphins, as a fully sentient species, choose their life experiences in much the same way we do. Free choice is, after all, the essence of spiritual responsibility. Thus, unsentimental though it might appear, our cetacean cousins are clearly in captivity of their own volition. This, I hasten to say, is no reason to take advantage of or mistreat them. On the contrary, if we more generally understand that they are choosing to be with us in this way, we would undoubtedly treat them with a great deal more respect.

The dolphins' voluntary surrender of their physical freedom, together with their almost inevitably cramped surroundings, must have effects on their subtle energy systems the likes of which we can only guess. Presumably it is this factor that is the basis of the different feelings received from captive dolphins and those who choose to remain in the wild. Some trainers will point to what seem to be somewhat immature emotional reactions among dolphins in captivity—envy, possessiveness, stubborn behavior, sulking, temper tantrums—as examples of their low level of intelligence, without perhaps taking the issue of choice to its next logical step. If they are indeed volunteering for confinement (and the last three dolphin catchers to whom I have talked all told me they have frequently noticed dolphins deliberately putting their heads up into the noose they use for netting them), then whatever could it be that urges them to do this? Are they perhaps studying, through emulation, the very characteristics that contribute to our fearfulness and contentious aggression?

As might be expected, here at the hotel, an overridingly sad pall hung over the mean little wired-off enclosures. It was precisely the kind of place that sometimes makes me so ashamed of humanity and our domination-orientated worldview. Yet, surprisingly, in spite of the sadness and horror of the plight of the dolphins, I had the most distinct impression that we had in some sense been seen and, in a subtle way, recognized and known. It seemed almost absurd to have this reaction. Was it my own wishes, I wondered, or my expectations in action? Was it all in my imagination? It is temptingly easy to project our own feelings onto them.

As I was having this strangely powerful sense of mutual recognition with the dolphins, my companion and I were standing up in the shadows above and behind the main pool. Drifting up to us we could hear the voice of a macho young trainer explaining to a small group of staring people all about dolphins. He ended his talk by saying that dolphins are about as intelligent as German shepherd dogs.

Now wait a minute! I lived with my old Ishmael for his whole life, and I came to have a pretty good understanding of the nature of a German shepherd's intelligence. For a dog he was incredibly smart—he managed to steal the Christmas turkey on three different occasions and was known to close doors and windows after going out on the prowl for the night—yet he had little of the wisdom and strange detachment that pour through the eye of even the simplest and most fun-loving dolphin. A dog's intelligence—while possibly more streetwise—is of a different level altogether.

It was all too much. The cloud of sadness was starting to grind in on both of us, and we realized we were unlikely to get much more accomplished in this desolate place. After the constant presence of Joe and Rosie in our lives, I had all the feelings of being back on the dolphin trail and was anxious to get on to the next of the places Bertie had recommended, which was farther south and had the unlikely name of the Betty Brothers Real Estate Office. A real estate office had seemed an altogether odd place to find dolphins, but Bertie had insisted we explore it since it contained the rare promise of two semiwild bottlenose dolphins who came daily to the small bay in back of the office to hang out with, and be fed by, the redoubtable Betty Brothers.

When we arrived, we turned into the potholed, dilapidated gravel forecourt and soon saw a sign that told us that dolphin feeding was at 10:00 a.m. and 5:00 p.m. It was already 10:45, so it looked like we might have missed the morning feeding. As we moved instinctively toward the sounds of water in the lagoon behind the office, we both picked up strong impressions that the dolphins would be there for us. After a few minutes of walking in hopeful silence along sandy paths under sun-dappled trees, we came upon a small inlet beautifully ringed by flowering shrubs and sporting a timber railing down one side. Two channels connected the inlet with the larger bay and the ocean beyond.

Beside me, my companion gave a quiet call of delight and pointed to a dark, glossy hump floating sedately in the middle of the small body of water. Within moments this was followed by a single eye—an eye full of intelligence and knowingness. This was not at all like a dog's eye, or indeed that of a monkey. No, for those wonderful, delicate moments of first sight, that single unblinking eye seemed to contain all the wisdom of an ancient and primordial knowingness. Then, to our happy astonishment, the lone dolphin was joined by another one who rippled lazily over from the shadows at the far end of the inlet.

Silence . . .

The seemingly ever-present white heron stood over on the right-hand bank among the flowers and impassively watched the proceedings. Then a burst of screechings from some gulls disturbed the serenity of the moment, and I found myself moved momentarily out of this smooth, flowing reality.

I turned to my companion and saw that she was also caught in the intensity of the natural phenomena around us. For all her patience and understanding, I knew that up till now she had not really grasped the reality of the interspecies connection with all its extraordinary implications. She appreciated it as an idea and of course could see its power and effect in my life, but she had not yet allowed herself to actually experience it. To complicate the issue further, this thoroughly fearless woman had one relentless and overbearing phobia—she loathed being in the water! An early neardrowning and the memory of a few past lifetimes of death at sea had imprinted her and left her firmly in the grip of an ocean-terror. You can perhaps appreciate the mordant humor of her situation, teaming up as the partner of a dolphophile.

As we stood at the edge of that small lagoon, watching the two magnificently lazy dolphins, I did not have to be overly telepathic to tell she was still wondering what all the fuss was about. "Shall we try a visualization?" I suggested, remembering how effective my first experiments were with the captive dolphins in New York Aquarium on Coney Island. "Let's both visualize the dolphin swimming toward us." We hugged and put our heads together in focused concentration.

Until this moment the first of the two dolphins had not moved. Within one second, however, he was swimming fluidly in our direction, a long *V* of ripples breaking from his beak. Intuitively I knew he was the male. He halted a few yards from us, as if to assert his own prerogative, and very deliberately started moving in a small circle, keeping one eye fixed on us all the time. I motioned to my companion to try the visualization again, this time with him swimming away from us. He rather pointedly sank like a large, smooth rock, to the bottom. We lost him in the murky water, and after a minute or so he popped up over by the main entrance to the inlet. I received a strong impression at this point that he was trying to tell me something but that I just was not getting it—there was something about the feeling that I simply could not grasp. I wondered momentarily if I might not be picking up on his confusion after receiving two such similar visual telepathic signals.

Intending a reality check, we sent the dolphin a third signal, this time projecting his image swimming toward us. It worked. He swam the entire fifty yards or so directly toward us.

At this point I took in more fully the second dolphin, who up to this time had remained remote and whom we had not involved in our telepathic experiments. I could see her swimming alongside the original one. The first kept his clear and knowing eye on us while the other accompanied him underwater. Then, for another reality test, I made a crossing movement with my arms, very precise and to the point, directly to the closely watching dolphin, and I repeated it quite deliberately three times. Although I had no clear meaning in my mind, I was most curious as to how the dolphin would respond.

The first dolphin, the one watching me, immediately sank out of sight, and then an astonishing little dance unfolded. A group of three white mooring buoys—five-inch, white metal spheres probably once used for lobster pots, so much part of the scenery that up to this time neither of us had even noticed them—started moving slowly and steadily toward the exit to the lagoon. It was a comical sight to see this little cluster of balls floating serenely, and even a trifle mysteriously, toward the open bay. Three? Toward the open bay? Could it possibly be? It was quite obviously a response to my three movements.

My companion and I looked at each other in happy amazement. Our hearts knew we had been seen and understood, and that the dolphins' trailing of the buoys along the length of the lagoon was a wholly deliberate, reciprocal, and coordinated response to my previous action. A powerful sense of joy welled up in both of us, and in those moments I understood that my companion, after all this time, was being touched by the magic of the dolphins in an entirely new way.

A kitten joined us, bounding out from under a bush and rubbing its head against our legs. Somehow the combination of all of our mammalian intelligences, melding with the movement of the dolphins toward the open sea, the crying of the sea birds, and the heron lifting ponderously off the water, brought me to the realization that these dolphins, semi-wild yet devoted in their own way to their human friends, were a natural link between the captive, residential dolphins with whom we had just spent so much time and the open-ocean dolphins we hoped to meet in the waters off Key West.

I saw in associational flashes how we were being prepared through a series of graduated encounters: first with Joe and Rosie, then briefly with the sadly captive cetaceans at the resort hotel, and now through this delicate meeting with dolphins who could quite evidently leave the lagoon and yet deliberately chose to stay in contact with their human friends. I knew that in some subtle yet unified manner we were being told that the wild dolphins were expecting us.

6

Many Faces in Brain Coral

Our newly born dolphin feels the vibrations carried by the water moving through her little frame. Her whole body is a sensor, exquisitely tuned and open to every fresh sensation. Dormant nerve cells come alive, memories and images pop, fully formed, into her awakening consciousness . . .

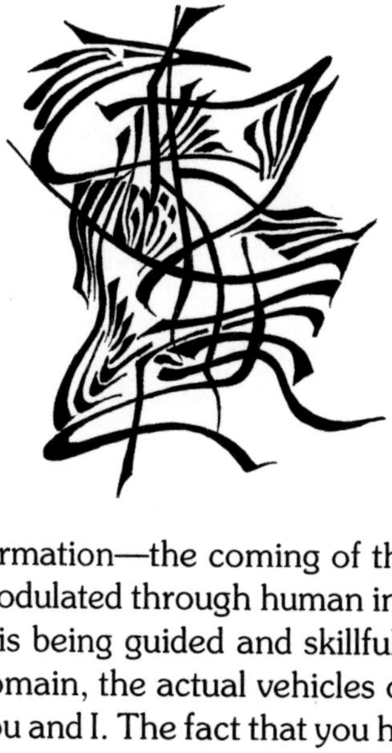

The more deeply I submerge into the uncharted waters of this new reality of ours, the more I have learned to respect that the transition, the global transformation—the coming of the True Age, if you like—is being modulated through human instruments. While I have no doubt it is being guided and skillfully administered from the angelic domain, the actual vehicles of the transformation are people: you and I. The fact that you have been guided to read this book strongly suggests that you are indeed one of "us." At the time of writing, so I have been informed by my angelic sources, "we" are some sixty million strong. That is the sum total of those who are currently awake, all over the face of this planet. And others are awakening every day.

As we emerge from our dream of fear, we see that we form a patchwork quilt of human conduits, of reality co-creators. As we clear ourselves and release our ingrained and self-defeating habitual circuitry, so we bring ourselves first into alignment with our own personal spiritual destinies—and soon enough into resonance with the highest spiritual aspirations of our species.

When we meet in our groups of all different shapes and sizes and ask for the blessing and presence of our mutual Creator, we can become radiating centers of light and coherence, able also to open to wells of deeply buried knowledge and all the wisdom that has become overlayed by the trials and tribulations of life on this small planet. We all have these overlays—they have seemed quite unavoidable in this third-dimensional density. Possibly the alchemical act of accepting and releasing these fear-trapped thoughtforms is in itself an excellent tuition for the responsibilities involved in coming into our full power.

I believe it is this releasing process (see appendix C for the Releasing Meditation), which many of us have now been practicing consciously for a number of years, that is allowing the angelic coordination to draw together individual threads in the woven tapestry of the new reality. In my own personal thread—a harmonic of the larger reality—I am meeting more and more enlightened beings, women and men who carry information within them that invariably fits with what I have been shown—and with what emerges spontaneously from the wisdom of the heart, like so many locks and keys.

Peter Anderson is one such being—one of those rare people with a truly extended worldview: a cunningly disguised bodhisattva who can tickle the truth and the humor out of a stone wall. I had first met him in New York, where we had done some mutual explorations of the inner planes, allowing us to come to know one another with an intimacy characteristic of life in a pod of dolphophiles. Like many sailors, he has had his fair share of encounters with dolphins in the wild, and he holds a deep and abiding love for them.

Peter is a large man, with the capacity to look equally at ease in a multinational boardroom, fixing a sink, or messing about on one of his beloved boats. His face is wide open to those with eyes to see, with features that constantly appear to be dissolving into mirth. My companion and I were happy to receive an invitation to stay with him in his Key West home and possibly, if he could arrange it, all go out in a boat to look for wild dolphins.

The atmosphere of the small town of Key West, at the end of a long, bent finger of islands extending over one hundred miles into the ocean, was relaxed and at the same time intensely creative. We sat, the three of us, in the warm April sunlight, allowing the pleasure of our meeting again to seep into our bones. Conversation was easy and flowing, and soon it became obvious that by pooling our resources we could all help prepare the boat belonging to Peter's close friend Timmy Wegman and get it ready for action without too much flurry.

With the nuts and bolts of the situation settled, the conversation moved into more metaphysical regions. Peter has a surprisingly finely tuned awareness of the larger context, demonstrating an elegant comprehension of the numerous difficulties and misunderstandings that have befallen our small sphere since the authorities of our section of the universe threw us into darkness all those years ago (see appendix D, "The Lucifer Rebellion").

In listening to him talk, it quickly became apparent that his sympathies were wholeheartedly on the side of the rebel angels who, whatever their reasons, were drawn to courageously take on—and defy—the combined weight of the regional universal hierarchy. He held the strong opinion that the universal authorities' response to the rebellion—that of cutting off certain incoming cosmic rays important for the sustenance of higher-dimensional life on the planet—was, to use his words, "downright rude." He summed it up by saying, "Under these circumstances, I've long felt we've done a pretty interesting job of defining ourselves, even without the benefit of those vital energies; or the very least, we've developed some valuable compensators. I've also felt that our species has evolved some qualities of humanness that could be of an immense benefit to a universe that can sometimes appear a little stuffy at the bureaucratic level."

Peter had been overjoyed when I had told him back in New York of my metaphysical research indicating that his most ardently held hopes had been fulfilled and that due to the reconciliations made on our System headquarters, the vital energies—the juice, he had called it—were coming back on again. The circuits were indeed opening.

Being an iconoclast by nature and a politician by craft, Peter appreciated both sides of this complex issue. Somehow, whatever his sources or resources, he too had seen glimpses of the larger picture, although distinctly from his point of view. I found his own certainty and inner knowingness helpful in resolving any final doubts I may have had that the whole Lucifer business was a figment of my imagination—that I had been simply spinning a story in my mind.

The concept that we are all children of the same Creator, whether we are human, angel, or extraterrestrial, is a relatively advanced one, and it is only really perceived through the wisdom of the heart—as also is the understanding that all beings make mistakes, sometimes gross errors of judgment, but that it is through having the courage to step out and initiate action that we all ultimately learn the truth. What had been shown to us was that the rebel angels were responding to an inner calling that others in the universal community were not able to hear personally, nor comprehend in those who had opened to this Supreme revelation.

It appears that our Creator, the designer of this whole splendid affair, uses selective amnesia in certain key beings or orders of beingness as a technique by which differing lines of knowledge and information can be kept separate. It is therefore not altogether surprising to encounter immensely high and powerful beings, angels within the universe hierarchy, who are perfectly wise in the main arena of their personalities, but utter numbskulls in some other, perhaps less immediately significant aspect. It is a marvelous system because it keeps all of us on our toes, alert to the fact that we are all growing together in the great game of evolving toward perfection, and it allows each to contribute to each other's wealth of understanding. It can also be very humbling.

After a luxurious night and a delicious breakfast with our generous host in his sun-filled little garden, the call came through for which we had been hoping. If we footed the bill for some minor nautical bits and pieces, Timmy Wegman would be delighted to take the three of us out looking for wild dolphins. The boat, at sixteen feet stem to stern, was a trifle small, but Peter assured us that both of them were first-class sailors and that all would be well.

In Peter's ancient blue Cadillac, we rolled happily down to the marina at which Timmy's boat, the Teoy Lee (by no means to be confused with Cheoy Lee, makers of exemplary yachts), was moored. The beautiful old wooden houses, with their surrounding balconies and balustrades, sparkled among the general tattiness that gave the Keys their fine and funky flavor.

Working hard all morning on rerigging the boat and fitting the sails, we set off about midday into the turquoise blue of the open sea. Peter wanted to take us first to see some large clumps of coral that Timmy had previously located. We would also have the chance to dive in among the local flora and fauna.

I must confess at this point that, in spite of my consuming interest in cetacean intelligence, I was still very much a landlubber. I had a tendency to get rather bored with endless expanses of ocean. I had not yet developed the sailor's acuity to perceive the minute changes in current and texture that can make sailing such a high skill.

Quite how Timmy ever rediscovered the coral heads in all that ocean will probably always remain a mystery to me, but within a couple of hours we were anchored over them in about twenty-five feet of water. I did not need much encouragement to flop over the side into the tepid depths. As I undulated my way downward, great carpets of iridescent fish scattered from my path, whole schools moving as one organism, tail-flicking their way to safety while watching me with a thousand placid eyes.

I circled down to the coral, holding my nose and blowing out my sinuses to adjust to the increasing water pressure. Still a relative novice in the arts of underwater diving, I found that my attention was more fixated on my physiology than it might otherwise have been. I was therefore quite unprepared for the sight that lay below me. When I saw what Peter had brought me to, I literally burst out laughing—not something to be advised in twenty feet of water. The last of the air in my lungs was therefore suddenly expelled, to be replaced by a flood of seawater filling my mouth and mask. I beat a hasty retreat to the surface, still convulsed with a laughter mixed now with an edge of panic.

After coughing and spluttering for a few moments in the security of the warm sunlight and fresh air, I jackknifed my body down once more into the depths. Yes, there it was again. It was hard to believe my eyes: carved all over the surface of this massive head of brain coral were the faces of countless human beings. Every facet of this bulbous, convoluted creature was cunningly shaped into representations of human features. They were undeniably clear and the oddest of sights.

Now, I have looked at brain coral before—and many times since—in different parts of the world: the Caribbean, the Great Barrier Reef, and in the seas around the Indonesian islands of Bali and Lombok. I have long admired the beautiful composition that looks so much like the lobes of the higher mammalian brain, and I have wondered if the structure of it is not in some way a schematic precursor of this amazing instrument we house between our ears. Here, however, was something rather different. The forms were quite unmistakable: eyes, noses, mouths, cheekbones, even a suggestion of ears and hair in some cases ogled out at me.

There must have been almost a hundred separate faces, all shaped into the surface of the coral and all approximately the size of a human head. *Whatever* was going on?

Of course, simulacra abound in nature. You only have to see the enormous American Indian visages seemingly carved by nature into the canyon walls of some of the great western parks to get a feeling for the reciprocity of natural phenomena with our species. We are certainly among the most exquisite jewels in the crown of creation, and it is therefore scarcely surprising to see echoes of our presence etched into our environment. But this was something qualitatively different. I could accept the possibility of one or two faces—nature has her moments of whimsy—but *scores* of them?

Then it dawned on me that I was looking at an answer to another of the intimations my companion and I had received from the pod of dolphins off St. Petersburg beach. Through a series of synchronicities, the understanding had dawned on us that dolphins overlay living protoplasm with sonic signals, shaping it to contain holographic records of their species. Associated with this came the recognition that they also practice the sonic "carving" of coral into some of the extraordinarily varied and beautiful forms it can take. Like many largely poetic revelations, of course, this currently cannot be proved. I had presented it in my first book more as a way of showing the trail down which I felt the dolphins were leading us, in the hope that it might strike a familiar chord in others.

As it so happens, Peter had all this very much in mind when he asked Timmy to bring us here. When he originally read my account he had independently intuited that certain brain corals were repositories for dolphin holographic/acoustical signals. He had reckoned that the fractal convolutions provided sufficient surface area upon which the dolphins could overlay their information. Other dolphins could subsequently retrieve the stored images by "sonaring" the brain coral using sonic band widths and frequencies similar to those employed in their placement.

Concerning the faces, when he had first seen them he had considered it as extraordinary a sight as I was now thinking. I wondered if this strange phenomenon that had peered up at me through all those multitudinous eyes could be the next stage in the continuing personal revelation, the gradual unfolding of the dolphins' world to my way of thinking. Are the seas filled with dolphin artifacts, I wondered—products of these intensely creative and playful spirits? Might we have become blinded by our cultural hypnotic trance into dismissing a magnificently sculpted and tended underwater environment as an outcome of a random arrangement of events? Does our deeply entrenched sense of dominion over other living creatures persuade us to believe in the Darwinian notion of survival of the fittest, while missing entirely the survival of the gentlest, the most humorous, and possibly the most artistic intelligences on the face of the planet?

We rolled back into the boat, laughing and all chattering at the same time. Both Peter and I were overjoyed to see each other appreciating the implications of what we had just seen. "Of course, not every brain coral is necessarily a dolphin artifact," he told us when we had calmed down a little. "Some are simply brain coral. Some might be waiting to be imprinted. Virgin coral."

"Yeah! Sometimes a banana's just a banana," said Timmy, who had been listening to all this while preparing for our departure from that spot. We had gotten to know very little about Timmy so far, as he had kept up an almost ceaseless banter with Peter since we had arrived on the boat that morning. On the outside, however, he was an enormous man—six-and-a-half feet tall and some 240 pounds—who Peter had originally warned us was an "old Key West Baba with the persona of a bear." He was quite evidently a magnificent sailor, so the fact that he did not always take kindly to city folk was not, at that point, of the greatest importance.

Soon we were scudding along, driven by a new wind that had sprung up with the late afternoon. We all kept a sharp lookout for dolphins while Timmy steered a course for where he thought they were likely to be. He and Peter fell back into their banter, boasting and ribbing each other. There was a macho edge to it that made it rather painful, and although my companion and I propped ourselves in the bow of the boat, there was scant space to isolate ourselves from what felt like a rising flood of suppressed hostility.

Countless cans of beer had been disappearing down the throats of our increasingly boisterous captain and his mate. The hot sun beat down on us, and the talk turned naturally to life on the open seas. Timmy made it clear that he, quite reasonably, subscribed to the school of sailors who vouchsafe a healthy respect for the unpredictable and violent nature of the ocean. He started illustrating his point of view by describing all the things that can go wrong at sea, stories of shipwrecks and general mayhem. While he was probably trying to be humorous in the school of can't-yer-take-a joke, he was actually running off at the mouth with some apparent degree of malice in his attempts to frighten the city slickers. Healthy respect is all very well, I thought, as he regaled us with disaster after disaster, but the guy is simply fear-mongering at this point. And the alcohol was not helping.

Throughout the day my companion's fears of drowning were being challenged moment by moment simply by being out in this tiny vessel with three large men. Being a spiritual warrior, however, she chose to deal with the fear rather than submit to it, but Timmy's attack was pushing the whole situation into a pitch of general obnoxiousness that soon became downright intolerable. Finally, I exploded in anger at his superior attitudes, shouting at him to keep his fearmongering to himself. I also made the mistake of telling him that the kind of hostility he was putting out was going to keep the dolphins away in droves.

This naturally infuriated him. Some high and mighty dude telling him, Timmy Wegman—a captain in the Conch Republic Navy, no less—how to get along with dolphins! And so it continued, nobody backing down, everybody shouting, Peter trying to calm down first one of us, then the other, not helped by the fact that both Timmy and myself were equally dear and loved friends from different aspects of his life.

Thank heaven we were all expressive people by nature, because it was a marvelous row, sitting there in the cockpit of the Teoy Lee. It had been a long and tiring day in spite of our exhilaration at seeing the coral. We had been watching intently for dolphins and had not caught even a distant glimpse of them. We were hot, fatigued, and punchy—and I was certainly frustrated by the lack of dolphins even though I ought to have known better.

It was my companion who cut through the melee with the

first sensible idea since it had all started. "Listen, you guys, while you're all shouting at one another, I'm sitting here with all this backed-up fear in me. Please help me release it. Can't we meditate together or something?"

We all looked at each other, and the absurd humor of the situation started coming through to us. What we were putting out were definitely *not* spiritual vibes, and we all knew where such negative emotions would get us in relation to dolphins.

We did not hesitate long. Arranging ourselves as comfortably as the cramped surroundings allowed, we formed a small and rather irregular circle. We shut our eyes, balanced our chakras, and proceeded to let go of all the negative emotions that had been gripping us so vigorously. We breathed in the prana together, filling ourselves with the calm and goodness inherent in the act of tuning into our Source, and once again started resonating with each other in the fullness of a shared heart. We "toned" together, sending out long, vibrant tendrils of sound, our voices joining together in a way that would have seemed totally impossible only minutes before.

After a few minutes of silence, with the wind hissing through the rigging, the occasional far-off sound of a seabird, and the lapping of the gentle waves, I opened my eyes and chanced to look up. Directly overhead, a full silver moon glowed in the deep blue of the late afternoon sky. I stared at it in wonder until Peter's hushed voice brought my attention back to the water. There beside us, arching out of the sea like a shiny black wheel, was a single sleek dolphin. Its glistening eye regarded us from only four feet away. We intuited simultaneously that the dolphin had appeared at exactly the right time—that its sudden arrival somehow symbolized the reconciliation we were all experiencing. Staying honest to the emotional reality had helped us move through the darkness. I knew, in that burst of contact and communication, that the dolphins were somehow keyed into our evolution as spiritual beings and that this was a demonstration of their almost supernatural ability to appear at precisely the most meaningful time and place. Then, of course, to the skeptic the whole encounter *could* have been yet another of those lucky coincidences that seem to pepper the trail of the wild dolphins.

7

Angels and The Urantia Book

Our young, female dolphin opens to knowing herself as part of the great dolphin group soul. She rejoins her consciousness with this oneness, knowing in those moments all that is ever known—the entire history of this aquatic species held, as it is, in a standing wave, an acoustical hologram, allowing every dolphin the most intimate access to every other dolphin that has ever been . . .

Later that night, back once again in Peter's house, I sat mulling over the events of the day.

When I had originally received the vivid holographic impressions from the dolphins in St. Petersburg that led me to believe they had been using their bioacoustical skills to "decorate" their underwater environment, I found it almost impossible to believe. Surely it was just wishful thinking. After all, at that point I was still just beginning to come to terms with other intelligent life forms. Like most of us, I had inherited a belief system that occluded all but the most mundane and mechanistic, leaving little room for the realization that we are, in fact, surrounded by intelligence. What the dolphins did for me, as it seems they are doing for many people, is to introduce the possibility that life is a far more wondrous affair than our scientific materialism would allow.

In revealing aspects of their realm that I would hitherto have dismissed as pure fantasy, the dolphins had started a process of psychic disintegration in my personality through which long-held but totally erroneous assumptions literally cracked apart. It was a highly personal process and one that I never really expected to be affirmed by other people's perceptions. Now here was Peter Anderson also arriving at the same conclusions.

My training in architecture, with all its structural and down-to-earth necessities, and my stint as a businessman in New York City had ill prepared me for the actual reality that was starting to emerge all around me. Although a near-death experience (NDE) in 1973 had exposed me to the fact that our three-dimensional world was overlaid by something distinctly more extraordinary, the impact of this realization had taken almost ten years to permeate through to me. The dolphins, in their way, picked up where the NDE had left off, showing me in no uncertain terms that all was not as my five senses suggested—there was much more going on.

Angels, our collective name for beings from other levels of existence, certainly were not part of my understanding at that point in my life. But, again, the dolphins changed all that. By putting me through a series of life experiences in which I was led to see that we share the planet with cetacea, another race of beings with an intelligence at least equal to our own, my worldview was literally rattled open. If I could have been that blind about beings who obviously share this level of reality with us, then whatever else might exist beyond the range of our senses?

It was at this point that *The Urantia Book* came into my life—a book that seems to have been transmitted from the angels themselves. Any who take the time and patience to carefully read its more than two thousand pages will have to admit that its very coherence and scope is quite beyond the human imagination.

The book's coming into existence is itself something of a mystery, since one of its avowed intentions is to avoid yet another personality cult. Thus the name of the man through whom it was transmitted, for instance, has never been revealed; and, indeed, it is said that he had virtually no interest in the material that came through him. Like Edgar Cayce, he was asleep or unconscious at the time of the revelatory activity.

What little is known is that the book's dictation by a group of superhuman personalities required almost thirty years—roughly from 1906 to 1935—and was coordinated by a well-known physician and psychiatrist of the era, an American named Dr. William S. Sadler. According to the best account I have heard, Dr. Sadler and his wife Dr. Lena Sadler were in private practice and living in Chicago, when through an apparent series of coincidences, they were led to the "sleeping subject" by means of a simple referral from another patient.

It seems that Sadler was quite a man of his time, sporting a rather empirical and scientific bent of mind. He had, in fact, trained for a time with Sigmund Freud in Vienna, and had taken his medical degree at the University of Chicago. But he had a strong religious bent as well.

Among his vast range of interests (he authored nearly 40 books in his lifetime) were the investigation and even debunking of mediums and psychic phenomena.

Here's how the book came about: One day Dr. Sadler was called in to investigate the case of a man who had been talking incessantly in his sleep. The doctor agreed to listen in and see what he could do to alleviate the situation, only to find that when he did, he was addressed directly by a disembodied voice that was using the sleeping man's vocal chords.

What followed is not well-documented, but I imagine poor Dr. Sadler must have gone through something like the psychic reorientation that I experienced with the dolphins. What can be deduced, however, is that for the next thirty years he and a small group of associates received the vast tome through this unnamed contactee, then retyped and edited this extraordinary document under the close supervision of a body of celestial "revelators", as they called it. The methods of transmission varied, but for the most part appeared as written materials produced by the subject while in an unconscious state. I have also heard lore about the literal materialization of some portions of the text. The important final section, which contains a complete retelling of the life and teachings of Jesus according to an angelic record, is said to have appeared out of nowhere sometime in 1934.

The information was intelligent and coherent enough, it appears, to engage one of the best minds of that generation for most of his remaining years—along with the other six or seven members of what came to be called the Contact Commision, as well as a group of several hundred invited associates who came to be known as the Forum. On angelic instruction, Sadler convened this large group to review and discuss the newest material on a weekly basis, and, sure enough, the next week's transmitted documents would often reflect the queries, reservations, and suggestions brought up at the previous meeting. It must have been a long and intense labor of love, and for this alone, if for no other reason, it deserves a great deal of respect.

What rapidly became clear (and the degree of secrecy which successfully surrounded the project for all those years bears out the seriousness with which those good citizens must have accorded it) is that the information was being given to us, among other reasons, because so many inaccurate and distorted ramblings had been previously passed off as valid spiritual data. It seems that this planet sorely needed some real truth.

As the writings developed, Dr. Sadler and his friends were made aware that the "Great Work" was being coordinated and facilitated by a group of angels known as the Midway Creatures, under the supervision of higher beings hailing from far up the celestial hierarchy. They were told that the Midwayers were in fact the more permanent planetary citizens and that this world—or, more accurately, this dimension—was in fact a form of kindergarten for developing souls. These souls are, of course, ourselves—mortal human beings who live out our short lives, learning from our experiences on this level of density before proceeding to other worlds and dimensions where the teachings continue.

This group of angels, the Midway Creatures, will appear again later in this book under a new name that they have asked to be called: Beings of the Violet Flame. But they, perhaps more than any other entities from the invisible realms except guardian angels, can be seen to have played an active part in the development of spiritual awareness on this planet through the long history of our species. There is little doubt they were the dominating influence in the pantheons of most ancient peoples and are still known and respected under various names given to them by the less materialistic cultures of today—for example, the Australian Aborigines call them Wandjinas, while the Hopi refer to them as Kachinas.

The size and scale of the Master Universe, as described by the angels—with planet upon planet, universe after universe, trillions of inhabited worlds and virtually countless numbers of angelic beings overseeing this massive operation—must have blown the socks off our stolid Midwestern citizens (as it still does to readers of this era, in spite of the power of modern telescopes). What emerges is a carefully and lovingly tended creation with a high level of free choice. And yet guidance is always available to each one of us, whenever we are open to receive it. It is mostly our restrictive belief systems that preclude this everpresent help.

What *The Urantia Book* tells us is that there are many dimensions to existence—alternate levels of reality—and that the angelic realms interpenetrate our rather dense third dimension. One way of comprehending this is to understand the angels as entities from the vast inner spaces—vibrationally finer, subtler levels of reality that could be described as the realm of our collective imagination. This does not mean that the angels are imaginary creatures, but that they can be contacted through the imagination. Each of us has a potentially open line of communication with them. Moreover, human beings, though evolving under different conditions on the many different inhabited worlds, are distributed like one enormous family throughout the universe. And we are the links—

the bridges between the inner and outer realms. We are literally the physical hands of the angels.

Anyone who has done any yoga or healing work, or who has an occult turn of mind, will have had some experience with their own subtle bodies—the mental, emotional, and spiritual vehicles that occupy the same space, though not the same vibrational frequency, as our physical bodies. To these people it will come as little surprise that our system of chakras—the centers that modulate these subtle-energy vehicles (see appendix C)—are access points to the invisible realms. It is through the progressive opening of our throat chakras that we are able to make direct conscious contact with the angelic realms. The angels, of course, are constantly present with us, guiding us through the university of life. We simply make their job, and consequently ours too, a great deal easier by opening to them. They will never force themselves on us, since our free will is greatly revered, but the more willing and capable we are of working with them, the more scope they have in helping us with our journey.

One of the more everyday ways in which the angels function is to overlight us. They are by nature pattern carriers, containing within their beingness the forms, shapes, and concepts most likely to yield a created reality that is aligned with higher purpose. They will seek out a human being who is already starting to think in a particularly relevant direction and join their energies to hers or his in such a way as to produce their desired result.

It is undoubtedly this effect in action that scientists and artists often refer to when they claim, like Einstein, that mystical experience is "the sower of all true art and science." The Scottish physicist James Clerk Maxwell's electromagnetic equations came into his head, so he said, out of nowhere and were not tested until much later. The German chemist Friedrich von Kekule hit upon the ring structure of benzene when he saw a snake with its tail in its mouth as he dozed in front of a fire. Quantum mechanics and the concept of the double helix in biological systems also have their origins in pure intuition. As I write now, for instance, I can feel the presence of Zophiel, the angel assigned to the creation of this work, literally guiding my hand. He will always give me my free choice of words, but I have become aware, through experience, of a deep inner joy that arises in me when I express the concepts that he wishes to communicate.

There are, as can be inferred, many, many angels and orders of angels responsible for nurturing life on a planet such as ours. It is quite possible that there are more of them than there are of us! This is, for reasons that will emerge in time, a most important little sphere. Not only do all living humans have guardian angels, but there are celestials who oversee virtually every branch of human activity. There are angels of the nations, angels of the future, angels of the churches. There are coordinating angels, recording angels, angels of entertainment, and angels of progress, of enlightenment, and of health. There are also angels who care for special groups, for relationships, for selected activities, and for creative projects. Angels, in fact, are almost everywhere we might look, could we but see them. However difficult or chaotic life on this planet might seem to be, it would be in a very sorry state indeed if it were not for the presence of our celestial guides.

Which brings me back to that sultry Florida night as I sat contemplating our day at sea with Peter Anderson and Timmy Wegman. I realized as I sat there, with the scent of the night-flowering jasmine filling my nostrils, that I was being joined by yet another angelic presence. There is a tone to these encounters that is becoming more evident to me as I open progressively to the subtle realms.

I had recognized from previous times spent with our host a quality that I have come to associate with people I think of as "trinity personnel"—women and men who appear to be available to an overlighting by a group of angels called the Trinity Teacher Sons. These angels are high celestial beings who, *The Urantia Book* tells us, have been sent from the Central Universe to teach and demonstrate the finest levels of truth, goodness, and beauty appropriate to us here on this world of ours. They seek out those whose minds and hearts are already reaching toward the patterns they carry and, in a manner both intimate and thoroughly sexy, overlight us, encouraging us into new reaches of revelation and creative action. They also show us how to go about helping in the redemption of some of the more unfortunate idiosyncracies of our dualistic state of consciousness (see appendix E, "Universe Overlays").

I thought about Peter's profound knowledge of the affairs of the universe and how he seemed to have known about the Lucifer Rebellion and the effects it had on this planet. Yet I knew he had not learned it from *The Urantia Book*. I saw in those moments how it was possible that my companion and I had triggered some access point within him, in all likelihood through the resonance we carried as two people in love, not only with each other but with the God that dwells within us. We have found that this tends to be a recurrent theme when the two of us bond closely with a third person. Under certain conditions we have been able to perceive, and sometimes even draw in, celestial spirits from the higher frequency domains. Possibly it is the triune form, an exceptionally stable lens for angelic communication, that allows an overlighting from a Trinity Teacher Son.

As I was pondering this issue, quietly listening to the night sounds all around me, I heard clearly the voice of one of these particular angels. "It would be a mistake," the voice told me, "to understand humankind as the only will creatures on the planet. The pattern that ultimately leads to a creature with free will is coded into all biological life. It is not a superficial overlay but a reawakening of deeper levels of creative intensity."

And along with this message I was given to see how the dolphins had made use of their free will to explore their individual creative intelligences while living within a harmonious whole. In contrast, our species appears to have decided to investigate the use of will in relationship to power and the individual consciousness.

As a postscript to the time spent in Florida with the dolphins, both captive and wild, I received a call from Peter Anderson about a month or so after I had returned to New York. He told me he had been sailing out in the warm waters off the Keys when a dolphin he had seen a few times before and had come to know as Baba showed up just off the bow.

"I broadcast a gestalt," Peter said, "of Baba's beauty and wisdom—as seen by my perception—and expressed an openness to whatever message he had." He mentioned that he was holding an image of the dolphin message of healing neurotic human fear, which he feels is a by-product of our having forgotten that the human species is also telepathic, and that he embraced the vision of dolphins being midwives of this process.

"Immediately as I'd expressed my openness," he continued, "I was flooded with an intense telepathic gestalt of John Lilly and Joe and Rosie as being keys to this healing process. Opening myself further to what I felt was being transmitted, I felt a 'tape' being fed into my subconscious concerning and directed to John Lilly, to help activate him as a primary change agent of dolphin intelligence. While I don't know anything about the contents of the tape, I was assured by Baba that when the time was right with Dr. Lilly, it would unwind as faithfully as a cassette deck."

The whole encounter had made a deep impression on Peter, and he had called me directly after he got back into port. As synchronicity would have it, Peter found himself involved with Joe and Rosie in the flesh some two years later when they were being kept at the Dolphin Research Center awaiting their release. He experienced an immediate and profound rapport with Joe and was among those who felt that the dolphins did not wish to be released.

"Joe flashed me a vision," he told me at that time, "of a place where humans and dolphins could have equal access to each other in the wild. Joe and Rosie were serving as ambassadors and intermediaries between the two species. "DOLPHIN"—my name for the collective intelligence of all dolphins—came pouring in through Joe, showing me the unique knowledge those two dolphins have with regard to the sources of human neurotic fears and how DOLPHIN could use this knowledge, gained through Joe and Rosie's intense experiences with probably thousands of people, to get a handle on us and therefore help further in guiding our mutual evolution."

Peter explained to me how he felt the message from Baba was starting to activate. He also attributed the creation of Project Delphi to the passion of that encounter. Project Delphi is to be a permanent offshore facility where dolphins and humans can relate on relatively equal terms, and it is being gradually created as funds become available. It is almost fifty feet long and eighteen feet wide and is envisioned as a floating house with a huge glass-bottomed lounge. Large contact ramps lead into the water, and there is even a safe area for once-captive dolphins to retreat into while in the process of reintegrating to their wild state. There is also an open area in the grand salon where dolphins can join in human indoor activities. In short, it is a really beautiful environment in which dolphins and humans have as much equal access to each other as possible and under natural conditions. Peter and his friends have called Project Delphi OH-DIF (Offshore Human-Dolphin Interface Facility) to symbolize "Oh, what a difference!"

The difference is, he tells me, that with few and rare exceptions, our approach to foreign intelligences coexisting with us on this planet has been to capture and study them in the lab. Hardly an auspicious beginning to our relationship with another sentient species, and scarce wonder that extraterrestrials prefer to remain very low key and only relate to a few carefully selected people.

At the time of this writing, Project Delphi is still inching its way toward completion. With the basic structure in place, it awaits the next infusion of funds and enthusiasm. Peter continues to feel that his beloved OH-DIF could be a giant first step in showing that we are willing to meet this remarkable cetacean intelligence in the wild, as equals, in a facility where mutual respect and friendship can flourish.

"The reconciliation you spoke about is occurring," he told me recently, "and the juice is beginning to flow again. The dolphins are activated to share their wisdom. More and more people are getting the message, entering the dreamtime of DOLPHIN and are discovering their fears are healing. It remains for us to find ways to join the dolphins in their world, utilizing friendship and choice, and garner the full message."

8

Vitamin K with Dr. John C. Lilly

There are no secrets in a dolphin's life. All is known because all is experienced—simultaneously. For dolphins there is no real childhood, just the learning of sinew and muscle and the joy of physical growth. All that is ever known is known by all . . .

There is a great mystery to the cetacean intelligence, and like all mysteries, it can be very elusive. We perceive dolphins with our senses, touch them and look into the depth of their eyes, smell their fishy breath, and swim with them, each to the best of our abilities. We can speculate about their artifacts and fancy we see evidence of their artistic prowess in slyly molded coral. Anecdotes abound as to dolphins' ability to be in the right place for us, at exactly the right time. They save surfers from sharks and swimmers from the perils of an unexpected rip; they demonstrate to potential suicides that there is joy in the world; and they can even bring lively chatter to the lips of autistic children.

Dolphins are clearly benevolent and highly intelligent. Yet it is equally evident that this intelligence is radically different from ours. It is as though our species has become so conditioned by the tools we make that we tend to occlude any form of higher intelligence that does not construct an environment for itself. We set the standards of intelligence and then make the error of trying to assess another species by whether it fulfills the same criteria.

While there is no doubt that we have needed to sorely blinker ourselves in order to arrive at this point in the last decade of the twentieth century, it is obvious that we have to alter, and indeed are changing, some fundamental aspects of our thinking in order to proceed from this point onward. We simply cannot afford to continue with our terra-chauvinistic myopia. Since the dolphins and whales appear to be the first comparably intelligent species we are meeting as we awaken to our place in the galactic community, may we not presume that the cetaceans are endowed with attributes within their range of intelligence that may be helpful to us in our transition to the larger context of an inhabited universe?

After all, they share the biosphere with us and thus have to deal with essentially the same physical elements that we do. Whatever their other dimensions of thought or action, it is apparent that dolphins are present within our consensus reality—as we are evidently within theirs. Although this point may seem rudimentary, it is important to state because it is certainly not so in the case of most nonhuman, extraterrestrial intelligences; neither is it true for the angelic or nature spirit/devic realms. This ability to transcend our level of consensus reality, so admirably demonstrated by most, if not all, extra- and intraterrestrial beings, can produce tremendous confusion in the minds of human contactees when their apparently solid extraterrestrial friends fly through the air and walk through walls.

Dolphins, on the other hand, clearly share this world and are in this dimension with us. Therefore, on some level, both species must be able to share a mutual system of symbols. At least we have many of the same things to talk about.

One day, when I was delving into the issue of a shared language between humans and dolphins, I found myself again being drawn into what I refer to as the cetacean telepathic matrix. For the dolphins, the whole matter appeared to be very simple: they showed me that if we could transform, or transduce, their sonic signals into visual signals and display them under water, then it would give the dolphins visual feedback on their own sounds. Furthermore, we humans could modify and alter the images—say, on an underwater TV monitor—in such a way that the dolphins could see what we were doing with their sonic pictures. This, they intimated, could lead to a mutual, visual third language, which both species might co-create and learn simultaneously.

All very well, but at the time, when I came to check it through with computer experts, they assured me that the available technology had not yet reached the point at which we could display real-time images back to the dolphins. Thus the idea had to be put on hold until small, portable microprocessors were developed with sufficient power.

With the lack of success of other cetacean researchers to find the grail of true interspecies communication, and yet with the growing anecdotal body of information regarding seemingly intelligent interactions between our two species, I can only make the assumption that it is mainly telepathy that the dolphins are here to share with us. And, of course, telepathic communication is a notoriously ticklish and subjective phenomenon. Almost all of us know it exists and have had experiences of it in the course of our lives, yet it is inevitably unexpected and seems to be most difficult to summon at will.

Two examples of dolphin telepathy in action will demonstrate how elusive the phenomenon is. The first is drawn from my own files and concerns a report told to me personally by one of the readers of *Dolphins, ETs & Angels*. She was in Florida at one of the dolphin research centers, relaxing and reading my book. She had arrived at the point in which I was exploring the possibility that a sand dollar might be a dolphin communication device. On the facing page stood a splendid drawing of a sand dollar done by my companion of the time.

At the very moment she was looking at this picture, there was a slight commotion in the water beside her, and she saw that a dolphin had found, and then flicked at her feet, the brownish disc of a living sand dollar.

The second example is taken from Hugh Edwards's book *The Remarkable Dolphins of Monkey Mia* (published privately by Hugh Edwards in Western Australia in 1989) and tells of a frustrated fisherman pulling in his boat after cruising forty miles at sea without catching a single snapper. As he is wrestling with the stern of his rowboat, knee-deep in water, he notices a large snapper swimming wildly all around him, threading in and out of his legs in six inches of water. He can scarcely believe what is happening until he turns and looks behind him to see the smiling eyes of three dolphins who have shepherded the hapless snapper in from deeper water and are keeping it imprisoned within a five-foot radius of where he is standing.

One of the traditional ways of actively opening up to the telepathic realms has been to ingest entheogenic—or psychedelic—plants in a variety of different and exotic brews. "Entheogen" is a word suggested by the great mycologist R. Gordon Wasson to describe plant substances that reveal or draw out the "God essence" in humans. Amanita muscaria mushrooms, ergot fungus, yage, ganja, ayahuasca, datura, atropa, yopo, San Pedro cactus, virola, peyote, henbane, pitjuri, opium poppies, ibogane, morning glory seeds, liberty cap mushrooms—the list of psychoactive and trance-inducing plants is long. There was the soma of the Hindu vedas, their most holy of sacraments, thought now to be derived from the fly agaric mushroom; the wine laced with ergot, that early version of d-lysergic acid diethylamide, which became the backbone of the Eleusinian mysteries; a surprisingly comprehensive list of the healing properties of Cannabis sativa that the Chinese emperor Shen-Nung compiled in 2737 B.C.; the teonanactl ("divine flesh") mushrooms of the Aztecs; and the kava-kava of the Polynesian Islanders. Virtually every society, with the exception, I believe, of the Eskimo, has a history of the sacred, shamanic, or alchemical use of such substances.

Investigating these domains of reality has always been a choice for adventurous souls. It is scarcely surprising, then, that our modern, technological society has also produced its own share of mind-altering chemicals. Most synthetic entheogens, such as psilocybin, mescaline, and LSD-25, are derived from natural substances and are able to affect the human brain by mimicking neurochemicals. Though little is known about this most intimate of human concerns—largely, I fancy, due to the fear engendered in many people by the idea of losing control—scientists are starting to talk of receptor sites into which these psychoactive compounds fit, as a key would in a lock. The inference is that the brain appears to have been designed with entheogens in mind.

There is also a group of wholly synthetic chemicals that also, astonishingly, have receptor sites in the human brain and that work in ways not well understood at the moment. Phencyclidine and ketamine are two such compounds, developed as rapid-action battlefield anesthetics during the Vietnam War. One of their considerable advantages over more traditional anesthetics is that they do not depress the breathing system. And they are potentially extremely safe. Ketamine proved highly successful and, because of its very low level of toxicity, began to be used in routine hospital operations. Everybody liked it. It was controllable and short acting; it left virtually no residual side effects; and the doctors could get patients on and off the operating tables faster and more efficiently. Ketamine was definitely cost effective.

It had one side effect, however, that had everybody a little concerned. A significantly large percentage of patients were coming out of their anesthetic sleep with stories of meeting angels, being taken off in spaceships, and even some reports of conversations with God. There were also doubtless some horror stories. Fact, fantasy, or pure hallucination, ketamine could be a thoroughly disturbing experience for a person checking into a hospital for a minor surgical procedure and ending up having a friendly chat with the Almighty. I am told that the chemical is being gradually withdrawn from use but that it is still frequently administered to pregnant women and children, who are possibly less vocal about their experiences. (See appendix G for more information on potentials and risks of taking ketamine.)

In the early seventies, some astute explorer of the inner realms discovered that small doses of ketamine, one-fifth to one-tenth of a full anesthetic dosage, produce marked shifts in reality without the concomitant disadvantage of unconsciousness. This has led to a sizable amount of informal research conducted by intrepid cosmonauts of inner space whose tales will be told, no doubt, when society as a whole wakes up to the true value of such entheogenic explorations.

As those who have read his recent work will know, Dr. John C. Lilly has been an enthusiastic investigator of this molecule, and his book *The Scientist: A Metaphysical Autobiography,* examines many aspects of this remarkable substance: its potential for awakening deeper and generally inaccessible levels of consciousness, as well as some of its evident pitfalls. As in most powerful experiences in life, taking ketamine is not without its risks, and it should be used wisely; however, it remains a legal substance, although hard to obtain and therefore unlikely to be widely misused. For those people who have had firsthand knowledge of mushrooms, acid, DMT, peyote, or any of the other noble entheogens, the essence of moving to another, radically different level of consciousness will not be new. What ketamine delivers is a much more specific dimensional shift, as well as a sufficient degree of consciousness to explore within the new reality. There is a high level of choice within the experience itself—unlike acid or DMT, for example, which invariably deposits most of us in the middle of continuing weirdness, largely outside our personal control. Ketamine, as well as allowing a glimpse of our co-creative potential as human beings, also seems to permit access to the group soul in a manner that can only be described as telepathic.

I was soon to discover the truth of this, after driving up from Key West and the joys of our last few days spent with wild dolphins. My companion and I had moved with the flow in the warm, Florida sunshine, slowing down and allowing the wind and the sea to shape our days. Now it was time to return to Manhattan and see how long we would be able to retain the deeper, slower rhythms of the natural elements in the face of all the city's mental energy. Before that, however, I determined to make a final stopover to see Doctor John in Key Largo, bringing to share with him a vial of ketamine hydrochloride.

We found the doctor once again in his mobile laboratory, and he greeted the news of the ketamine with a gruff twinkle of relish. Roberta Quist, too, was interested in the experience, so we agreed to meet in the early afternoon at the house of some friends of the Lillys. Our plane was leaving Miami at 5:00 p.m., which is an easy ninety-mile drive from Key Largo. Fortunately ketamine is relatively short-lasting, about one-and-a-half hours maximum, so the timing promised to work out just right.

As we relaxed back at our motel and prepared to leave for the meeting place, I experienced three quite distinct occurrences of clairaudience—of hearing voices with as much reality as if the people had been there with me in the flesh. But I was alone in the shower at the time. Although I have been practicing automatic writing for some years, I have never considered that to be true clairaudience. I have received, very occasionally, extremely clear but brief messages from the inner realms that have registered in my brain with the same impact as external voices, but these have all been highly significant to the moment and clearly angelically sourced.

In this case of the shower, however, all three incidents of clairaudience involved specific people: Peter Anderson; Timmy Wegman, the boat skipper; and John Lilly himself. It was as though I was simply overhearing them saying brief and wholly insignificant snatches of dialogue.

It was very odd. I thought of it at the time as sinking momentarily into the dolphin telepathic matrix, and it further demonstrated to me that telepathy is considerably more complex than mere thought transference. Telepathic communication, I am discovering, actually involves the nature of reality itself and perhaps can better be described as a dimensional shift—as if I had dipped for a moment into an alternate, perhaps parallel, reality in which we are all in contact with one another, all the time.

My companion driving, we found the house in question tucked down one of the tiny side roads that crisscross the Keys just north of Key Largo. It was up on the thinnest of stilts, like so many others thereabouts, in the belated but ever-optimistic hopes of those who build their homes in regions subject to hurricanes.

We climbed the stairs, and the door was opened by Roberta. I could see John Lilly pacing up and down inside the single, large area. We were motioned inside a pleasantly furnished modern living room, shades drawn to diffuse the bright Florida sun. My companion had previously decided not to take the substance with the rest of us, preferring most generously to hold the center and make sure we both got to Miami in time for the plane. "Got the ketamine?" John barked at me without any preliminaries. I was encouraged. I had been warned that, like Joe, he is his most cantankerous with those he likes. I pulled the vial out of my vest pocket and gave it to him. He held the small brown bottle up to the light—it was the more concentrated and potent of the two types of Ketalar made by Parke Davis.

"Good! The one hundred!" he said with a curl of a smile on his thin lips and another twinkle of his blue eyes. "Brought yer own syringe?" he asked, and when I said that I had not, he turned to the bathroom and came back with a handful of needles.

"Want me to do it to yer?"

I said yes—he is a doctor, after all, and I have always had a distaste for needles, regarding them as a necessary evil for certain substances. Ketamine, since it is broken down and made ineffective by the stomach juices, has to be injected. Fortunately the injection is intramuscular, and the fineness of the needles available these days usually make it virtually unnoticeable.

This, however, was not to be one of those felicitous occasions. John pulled out an enormous hypodermic syringe with an ultra-long, fat needle on it. Maybe it was designed for horses—it was the largest I had ever seen, and I stared at it in horror.

"What's yer body weight?"

"Around 134," I replied and he upturned the bottle with the hypodermic in it and drew off 134 milligrams of clear liquid. Up to that point, the largest dose I had tried was one hundred milligrams, and 134 was going to put me very close to unconsciousness—it is an anesthetic, after all. But I could see that it was going to be an important trip, and I hoped I would be able to bring some of it back.

By this time John was approaching me with the syringe held like a dagger. We locked eyes while I rolled up my sleeve. I flashed on a paranoid fantasy of mine—of being killed and dismembered by those of my tribe. It had been reinforced rather ominously by no less than three separate conversations about cannibalism within the previous twenty-four hours. Ah, well!

In one fluid motion, John thrust—literally slammed—the syringe into my arm, grinning at me with drug machismo while shooting the plunger. My eyes watered with the pain and my arm burned, but I am a survivor of the British boarding school system, so I did not give him the satisfaction of blinking when he yanked out the needle. He had a slight smile, and I read him as thinking, "There yer go, boy! It's what yer wanted."

Turning away, the good doctor administered the other injections in a much finer syringe and somewhat more dexterously, I thought, than he had mine. Finishing with himself, he used his thigh muscle. Then we waited for the ketamine to take effect. John positioned himself lying down in an arm chair. Roberta chose the floor. My companion seated herself to the side with her notepad out, in the hope that while doing K, someone might say something sensible just for once.

For no reason that I can imagine, except perhaps for the continuing shock of the injection, I am standing up when the ketamine hits me. I glide downward, a slow-motion fall to the floor, where I end up in a sitting position leaning against a sofa.

Unstoppable waves break over me, washing me on to a stony beach, mashing me into shifting pebbles, dissolving me and then gathering me together again.

First I rapidly lose a sense of being anybody—and then, being *anything*. Everything I was, I am losing. I know it is an ancient initiation and an access point to the sacred mysteries. I am dying to this reality and will be reborn into another. I have to let go. I cannot hang on against the power of the waves. I lose consciousness, and beyond a vague sense of undergoing countless ceremonies of initiation in different cultures down through the ages, I have no conscious recall of this period of the trip.

When I return, somewhat later, to my personal identity, I find that I am in my divine Self, possessed by the I AM. Somehow I have dissolved into this other One, who is ALL and therefore also me. I feel John out there in K-space rooting for me, and I am intensely thankful for the fine-tuning he is giving me. Like Joe the dolphin, in pushing me to confront my fears he is encouraging me to move through them to the metanoia that lies beyond.

In this moment I know I love the old man. I ask him silently, assuming telepathy, to show me what he experiences of the new, emerging reality.

The next thing I know, I am in the dolphin realm. John, Bertie, and I are together, and water swirls all around with the flashing, darting forms of dolphins sliding between us. We are literally in a reality in which everything is known to all. We move through it in a marvelously stately way, and gradually I see what is being demonstrated. This telepathic reality that we all, dolphins and humans alike, are co-creating, is something we are actually doing the whole time. The difference between us and the dolphins is that they know and understand this, while our species does not. Conventional scientific materialism gives little credence to alternate realities, let alone the possibility that an entirely new reality awaits us all—a reality that has been built patiently down through history by all the great seers and sages, the angelic domains, and the cetaceans. In this moment I know it is they, the dolphins and the great whales, who are holding together this transcendent, telepathic reality. They are grounding the vision into this, our shared dimension. We humans are able to access it to the extent that we can open our hearts and our minds to it.

I can see while I am in this state that through some property of water and the dolphins' particular skill with sonics, their evolutionary path allows them to know and more fully participate in the co-creation of this emerging reality. It is clear to me that dolphins have a much better idea of the roles they play in orchestrating their world. Possibly another way of expressing it is that dolphins appear to live in a superconscious state far more than we do.

Just as this subjective encounter with the dolphin telepathic matrix is winding up and everything is slipping and sliding around me, I hear a clear male voice say to me, "Synesthese and you won't amnese!" I think, with detached interest, that this is precisely what I need to know if I am going to bring back anything of value from the bright world. I need to draw every situation, each encounter, as deeply into my physical body as I can; bring it as far as possible into the cellular level of sensual memory; ground it so that when I cross over once again into the human consensus reality, this vision of a higher dimension will remain securely planted within me.

Focusing on cellular memory induces yet another state of consciousness. In this, my viewpoint is that of an ultimaton, the smallest quantum of matter. I feel my intelligence in that state and the level of consciousness I am privileged to enjoy, and I know absolutely and firsthand that matter is intelligent—on the most basic of levels.

Evolution ripples before me as conglomerations and confederations of ultimatons group themselves together in pulsations of ever-increasing wisdom. Guided by the light inside them, these minute particles of matter gather in ascending levels of complexity and order. Those electing to become brain cells, for example, start with the brains of the very simplest of creatures and, through lifetimes of experience, move up the food chain to the highest and most complex levels of organization they desire. And so for livers, kidneys, hearts, and all matter in general.

I see, in these moments, how each one of us is crafted with infinite care—a biological masterpiece of unknowable capabilities; how every organ and cellular organization within each of us agrees to collaborate, through incarnation after incarnation; and that it is through *their* blessed journey through the ages and *their* indestructible hardiness and persistence that I am coming to know my Self. This I experience as the Great Mother Spirit, moving through matter to inform her wisdom within the very ground of being. Through the cetaceans and all other creatures capable of reflecting on their own natures, she reaches out to the Father Spirit. Our field of beingness is the plane upon which they both meet: their sacred marriage.

I am then drawn to the other extreme and find myself straddling the entire universe. I know I AM becoming. I AM ALL in my supremacy, recognizing it inside my Self. I AM the Supreme Being, child of the Trinity and the entire evolutionary process, on all planets, everywhere—a god in the making. I know my Self as the vast accumulation of all the acts, thoughts, and feelings of truth, beauty, and goodness of every being whose domain I overlight. Yet I cover the universe.

I watch as the ripple of sentient intelligence, of superconsciousness, expands continuously outward from Central Shining—the galactic core—absorbing all information and qualities of lasting spiritual value. I see that these elements are being woven into the new reality, a reality which is no less than the body of a god/goddess.

I lie experiencing human history, as contained in the very material of my physical body, roar through all my senses. I know I must be coming down from the elevated heights of God consciousness because all the acts and decisions made in the past are leading irrevocably to precisely this moment in time. Everything is perfect, has always been perfect—*per facio,* thoroughly made—and is moving inexorably toward the grand destiny that awaits us all.

Ketamine is inherently a very internalized experience,

and possibly because of the high dose I had taken, this effect was even more pronounced. I am astonished to realize now, as I write, that I can recall nothing of the other three people's physical presence in the room throughout the trip. Psychically and telepathically I feel that we were linked, but I can bring back virtually no images of John, Roberta, or my companion—where they were or what they did. I credit the disembodied suggestion of cross-sensory synesthesia—best known as the ability to see sounds or hear tastes—for allowing me to remember and to describe, if inadequately, something of the K-space and what might await us as we move into full fifth-dimensional consciousness. It seems that the more senses we can bring to bear on any event in the spiritual realm, the more chance we have of fixing it in our cellular memories. But, as often happens with glimpses into the grander picture, a small price is exacted. Perhaps that, too, is part of the process of grounding the vision. Sharing ketamine with John Lilly was to be no exception.

9

A Journey into Fear

Each individual dolphin lives within this stupendous acoustic hologram, moving it along moment by moment, pulse by pulse. It is a reality created quite literally by the dolphins, in which we humans surely exist only as bit-part players . . .

The ketamine trip I took with John Lilly was by far the most valuable and encapsulating interaction I have had with this substance to date, and it underlined for me how important it was to share the K-space with those I trusted and loved. It certainly was not an encounter to be recommended for the inexperienced.

Long before I wanted to get up and leave, my companion had to haul me out on jelly legs, down the steps and into the car. As she drove fast and confidently up the highway, I fell to thinking more about the fear imprints to which our species has been heir. I could see that fear—and especially fear of death—has been used to control and discipline us, for good and for bad. In contrast, I perceived the dolphin—born water to water—tail first, ever active and jubilant and largely without predators, as having negligible fear imprinting.

This must make our fearfulness very evident to them and is likely to be one of the major barriers to full communication between our two species. I resolved then and there to do what I could to exorcise my own fear imprints. It would prove to be an ongoing process. I could not have known at that point just what the universe had in store for me so very few hours after cruising the byways of cosmic consciousness!

I must have still been touched by the ketamine throughout our drive north because I recall to this day looking out the window as we approached the Miami airport and seeing a plane lifting off. The odd thing about it was that I perceived the plane as a perfectly pixelized version of itself, as if I were watching a stupendous computer animation.

We returned the rental car and moved easily through the airline formalities with little prescience of what lay ahead. The plane was virtually empty and the stewardesses blandly efficient and content to leave us alone. Landing at La Guardia, we made our way to the baggage claim. Suitcases poured briefly forth from under the rubber petticoat. My companion's popped out. We went on waiting for mine. Minutes passed and still no suitcase. Soon there were only the two of us left waiting and still no case.

I recall saying to myself in an act of will, "It will come onto the belt . . . Now!" which was followed by a fleeting mental image of my bag dropping off a truck. Of course, it could have been my imagination.

The conveyor belt continued to turn, now empty. Minutes passed. I could feel an insistent dread coming up on me. What was in that suitcase? After a short time of nothing happening I started moving like an automaton toward the claim department office, but fortunately there were people in line ahead of me, so I changed my mind and walked back to the carousel. Making that small decision served to bring me back into myself, and I was shocked at how hypnotized I had allowed myself to become by the fear.

"Anything in that bag?" my companion asked, deliberately casual.

Up to this point I had not cared to think too much about it, but the realization could be held at bay no longer. I recalled, with my heart starting to pump harder, that I had a tiny vial of powdered phencyclidine tucked in a side pocket, which by virtue of its ease of manufacture, and thus its misuse potential, had been classified by the federal authorities as a Schedule 1 substance. Its possession carried the maximum penalties in New York State, and right then I was staring them in the face.

Of course it was one of my worst fears. Terror flooded my system. My hands were sweating and my heart was going like a hydraulic drill. My whole uneasy relationship with authority reared up inside my overheated mind: all the beatings I had sustained at school while "they," the authorities, had sought to break my spirit; all the bullying; all the cruel and unfair treatment meted out to those who chose to follow their own drummers; the calculated terror inflicted by mindless bureaucrats on a generation of people who simply wanted to find out for themselves what makes them tick.

"Be cool!" I reminded myself. "Act casual." And what did my mind do? It created a paranoid fantasy in which my suitcase had been stopped and examined, the phencyclidine found and put back, and now we were being watched. Who was going to pick up the suitcase? I was trapped.

My mind, seemingly ever willing to drop into the pit of fear, filled in the picture while I waited for the bag to appear. I remembered the men in the phone-company ladder truck who were so interested in all the goings on in Dolphins Plus—they spent more time gazing over the fence into the enclosure than they ever did fixing the wires. Then, in a paranoid free association, I thought of all Dr. Lilly's past working relationships with governmental agencies and of his ultimate refusal to take part in a science that he could see would be used to manipulate and exploit dolphins. (It is certainly no secret that the U.S. Navy has invested extravagantly in cetacean studies.)

As I stood there terrified, the conveyor belt going endlessly around and around, barren of bags, I found myself slipping into a fantasy—perhaps even someone else's reality—in which all these dreadful things were not only probable, but true. I knew I was caught in the web. There was no way to turn. "They" had me.

Then my bag emerged. Parading serenely along the middle of the belt, taking the corners with elan, marching forward, it moved inexorably toward where I stood—amazed, horrified, and waiting for my bitter appointment with destiny. It was now or never. If I ran away, I would only have to deal with the whole thing another time. I had to bluff the thing through. I picked up the suitcase as it came level with me, turning and talking as naturally as I could to my companion, and steering us toward the sliding glass doors. It was a long walk through the now nearly deserted area. Our footsteps echoed on the cold terrazzo tiles. Finally the doors slid open electronically for us, and we were out and into the awaiting taxi. Odd, that! A cab right there, seeming to be waiting just for us. They must want to know who we are and where we live! Thus the fantasy continued unabated throughout the drive back into the city, with me peering out of the back window to see if we were being followed.

I can now see that I had become locked within a full-scale paranoid episode because my next madness was to become convinced that one of the doormen at our apartment block, a Russian emigre and a genuinely kind and good man, was in fact a KGB agent. The psychosis devolved from there. After being in the apartment only a few minutes, I knew with an obsessive certainty that the place had been bugged in our absence. I crept around convinced everything was closing in on me. It all fit together. There was no getting out of it. Somehow I had gotten entangled in a web of espionage. I had been noticed and would never again be a free agent.

But even in the middle of this freak-out, I could see there was something about the lunatic certainty of my convictions that had the telltale signs of a fear-driven fantasy. For a start, my companion seemed unconcerned. I knew there was a lesson being administered here, although I did not know what it was until I asked for help.

I drew a bath and collapsed into it. My inner voice came through loud and clear. It told me how, in the course of our lives, we interact with other people's fantasies—nonoperant realities that will not continue into fourth-dimensional consciousness—which we have to learn to transmute. We do this by taking on the fantasy, owning it, and then releasing it. No further investment of energy need be put into it. I was shown that our souls, those aspects of ourselves more in contact with our superconscious, literally structure our reality out of all the potentials they deal with moment by moment. The soul, I know, has predetermined before it comes into incarnation—at least for those of us who are not first-timers—the most significant challenges and opportunities that we might require as part of our maturing process.

The clarity of the voice and the value of the insight helped me lever myself out from under the paranoid fantasy, and I soon found that I could pull my energy in from it. I was getting ready to burn it off. I asked my companion, who had most patiently and bravely given me the space to really get to the bottom of this fear, to help me breathe and tone out the thoughtform. Afterward I felt totally rejuvenated and even enriched by the whole episode. I could see how my indulgence in fear would keep me hypnotized in a nightmare that has nothing to do with the splendid reality we are all co-creating—that because we are given free choice, fear can and does blot out the immediate possiblity of living in the love-generated reality. The only way to release the fear, in my experience, is to take it in, accept it fully, see where it stems from, find out if it has anything of value to contribute to the living of the life—and then, with the help of a higher power, let it go back to the light. In this way it is truly possible, I believe, to lose all our fears completely and forever. They are no longer necessary with full consciousness.

A pointed postscript to this little jouney into madness occurred shortly afterward. The Cosmic Coincidence Control was hard at work. My companion and I had decided to explore Philippine psychic surgery, as a well-thought-of practitioner was in town for a few days. We made our appointments, negotiating the veil of secrecy behind which this unorthodox procedure is required to operate.

My companion's appointment was first, and she had gone on ahead of me. I followed half an hour later in a cab. I walked straight out the door to our apartment block, and there it was, just waiting—a rare enough event in Manhattan: an empty yellow cab. As I slid in, the driver, a large, thick-necked man with short, blond, curly hair, put down the newspaper he was reading to fiddle with the meter. I noticed the unusual type on the front page and guessed it to be Russian. The name on his driver's ID was Mike Michaels. It was all too much—cognitive dissonance.

"You're with the KGB, aren't you!" I blurted out with a silly smile on my face.

There was a fraction of a second pause. I saw his eyes flickering in his rearview mirror. "Yes," he said, either putting me on something dreadful or taking his life in his hands.

He did not ask me how I knew he was with the Soviet espionage agency until later in our conversation but sat there in sorry confusion, emanating despair. He was the worst spy I could ever have imagined. "Doesn't look like you enjoy it much," I said, leaning forward to talk through the gap in the plastic partition.

"No—it's terrible. It makes me completely miserable." His shoulders heaved as we wove down Central Park West, and the back of his poor neck got redder. He had joined the KGB directly after leaving school, he told me, because it seemed like a good way to be secure and especially to see the world. He had always wanted to travel. But now he had been in the service for twenty-one years and had seen enough of the world to know that the Soviet government was deceiving itself and its people. He thought that the West and the other free economies, for all their obvious disadvantages, allowed people the fullest opportunity for a good quality of life. He had become totally disenchanted with the Soviet system, was frightened for the future of his family at home if he were to do anything foolish, and had no idea of where he could turn. He was living in perpetual fear and felt hopelessly trapped in this maze of subterfuge.

It was a tragic tale, as might be imagined, and I did not have any particularly constructive ideas for him beyond the suggestion that he turn to the inner realms, which he did not seem to greet with much enthusiasm. I did, however, thank him for telling me and supported his honesty in holding forth so freely. It came to me to encourage him to speak appropriately to others he might have in his cab, equally openly. Sooner or later he would draw in the correct person to help him. He had some problems with the concept, of course, but seemed generally relieved to have been able to have unburdened himself to somebody.

It was a short trip, and even though he was driving progressively slower, finally we reached our destination. I paid my fare, blessed the poor fellow, advised him to change his name, and went in to the psychic surgery for a healing. What I realized later, when I was making notes in my journal about the encounter, was that at no time throughout my interaction with Mike Michaels did I have any recurrence of my paranoid fantasy. I had demonstrated to myself that I could hold my own reality, see his situation clearly, and not get the two confused. It was a profound healing—more effective in its own way, I might add, than my somewhat inconsequential visit to the psychic surgeon.

What an extraordinary teacher life can be! Patterns repeat in such odd ways. By contrast, the following two events, both dealing with fear, took place on exactly the same block, on the same street in New York City, and yet were separated by the time of almost exactly ten years.

On a warm spring day in 1979 I was sauntering down Central Park West on my way to catch a train to go out to Long Island to vist a psychologist friend of mine. It was a quiet Sunday morning, and I was just coming up to 88th Street when I heard some shouts and the sound of running feet coming from around the corner. As I drew abreast of the street, I saw a very large man rushing toward me, pursued by three or four others who were yelling for someone to stop him. He was about eight or ten feet away from me and coming at full tilt. I started moving toward him. He was clutching something in one hand and had the other tucked inside the lapel of his jacket. As can be imagined, it all happened extremely fast, but he growled something menacing, his face twisted into a mask of ferocity, and he did not slow down one bit.

Then the strangest thing happened: I found myself frozen in my tracks. All I could move were my eyes as I watched him thunder past me and rush off up Central Park West. I was still standing there when his pursuers, some thirty yards behind, also ran past.

I was bewildered. I had heard of "fight or flight" but never "freeze." It had occurred on a level beneath any conscious decision I might have taken. I was not even particularly frightened on any level of which I was aware, although, as my psychologist friend later suggested, I really should have been.

I puttered off down the street quite baffled by the whole affair and feeling thoroughly aggrieved that matters seemed to have been taken so completely out of my hands. It was some time later that I realized I had become hypnotized by fear, and I resolved to do whatever I needed so that such a thing would never happen to me again. Then followed the ten years more or less covered by the events in this book.

On a blustery late afternoon in the fall of 1989 I was walking down Central Park West on the way to the subway. I was halfway down the block between 89th and 88th Streets, avoiding the puddles, and about four feet behind a middleaged lady walking in the same direction only at a slightly slower rate. Once more I heard a commotion of running feet and looked ahead to see a bunch of young lads running directly toward us. A couple of them slammed into the woman, knocking her purse out of her hand and spinning her around. The bag skidded to a halt right in front of me, and one of the guys bent down to pick it up. Before I could stop myself, I thrust both of my arms out in front of me and screamed a primordial roar of challenge at the crouching man. I saw the fear cloud his eyes as we stared at each other over the purse. Then his feet scrabbled convulsively, and he was up and away. I picked up the purse and gave it back to the severely shaken but grateful woman and walked off to catch my train.

Once again, the action had come from well beneath my level of conscious awareness, but this time I did not freeze. My action was unhesitating and total. My entire personal power had been brought to focus and there seemed to be no residual fears left in me to blunt the clarity of the intention.

IO

Signs of the Coming Race

Our little female dolphin grows and dreams and moves fluidly through days of ease and abundance. Food is ever plentiful. Joy and compassion surround her, supporting her awakening and blossoming. She becomes more skilled, with practice, at using her multidimensional communication systems . . .

A few days after returning from Florida, I met Dr. Kamayani, a chiropractor from upstate New York who had become interested in underwater birthing. She lived and worked in a large religious commune, an ashram, at which two babies had been successfully delivered underwater—apparently the first known to have been born on the East Coast.

Underwater birthing—also sometimes called water birthing—was pioneered in Russia in 1962 by the shaman/midwife Igor Charkovsky. News of his extraordinary work reached the West during the seventies and has spread rapidly since then.

The idea of underwater birthing has appealed to me ever since I first came across it. After all, what could make more sense than flowing from amniotic fluid straight into warm and welcoming water? Good for all, I thought. But it was not until I received what I felt was a telepathic message from the dolphins indicating they wished to be included in the birth process that I found myself more personally involved.

Over the years I have been delving into the mysteries of spiritual intelligence, I have become aware that the parts of a large jigsaw puzzle are fitting together piece by piece. A story is being told and a vast plan is being revealed to those who are open to it. What I believe is being shown by this ongoing revelation is that our planet is to become home to a new form of being: quite literally a new and different species—a mutation to be sure, but one with the strangest and most intriguing qualities.

What I am being led to understand is that our human race is like the proverbial caterpillar, enclosed in its chrysalis before it becomes the butterfly—that we are incubating this new mutation, which will be as substantially different from us as we are different from the higher primates from which we sprang. Intuitively I know, too, that underwater birthing is a key to these astonishing changes to come.

Dr. Kamayani further strengthened this by telling me something of Charkovsky's observations regarding the sensitive brain cells in and around the crown chakra, which he believes get knocked out of action by conventional birth practices. These cells, he maintains, are kept alive by birthing into water, thus allowing them to be in place and ready for the development of cosmically conscious capabilities.

Even in Russia, where scientists seem to be more open to psychic and spiritual realities, the concept of cosmically conscious capabilities must be a trifle challenging. While there is little or no scientific evidence yet to support Charkovsky's claims—these are early days—there is, nevertheless, a growing body of anecdotal material that suggests waterbabies have unusually high psychic and paranormal skills. The chiropractor also mentioned that Charkovsky uses ice-cold water in the treatment of newly born babies. He frequently douses freezing water over the heads of the children, an act that, Dr. Kamayani told me, would rapidly constrict and then expand the brain cells.

Over the months that I came to know Dr. Kamayani, we found that we both had been given bits and pieces of information that have led us to believe we are about to witness the transformation of life on our planet. She told me of visions she had received of a species that drew from dolphin, horse, snake, and bird. I showed her an early message I got from the dolphins: that they wish to help produce, through cooperative effort, a conscious race of beings who truly represent the best qualities of the life forms on this planet.

There is little doubt that the dolphins, with what I believe are their very considerable biosonic talents, are involved with this process and possibly always have been, since the transmutation of a species is such a rare event. Information that I received from Joe, the Lillys' dolphin in Key Largo, certainly suggested that the dolphins have an ongoing interest in working with the biology of our species.

Are there, I wondered, any examples in history, that might suggest earlier delphinic experimentation? Of course Oannes came to mind. Mentioned as a historical fact—and not a myth—by the historian Berosus, the Oannes, or the five Annedoti, were large amphibious creatures who, over a period of some centuries, came up from the sea to teach the arts of higher living and ultimately to found the Sumerian civilization. Berosus tells us that the Oannes returned to the sea at night.

Was there some connection between all this and the singular personal experience I had with the Oannes when I first encountered the dolphins? It was a hard-won inkling, a glimpse into what I thought then was a mythic reality. As I emerged from the sea after a particularly exhausting swim with a pod of dolphins, I became intensely aware that I was being overlit. As I hauled myself up the long, sandy incline, I had the distinct impression that I was wearing a great ambling, scaled, bipedal body. For those moments, I was Oannes.

So who were these odd creatures? Where did they come

from? And what might have been their relationship with the dolphins?

I remained in good contact with Dr. Kamayani and it was she who told me about the Homo Delphinus conference that was to occur in New Zealand early the next year. It was to be held at the Rainbow Dolphin Centre and had been drawn together by Estelle Myers, an old friend who had originally reminded me of my interest in dolphins. An Australian filmmaker, Estelle sports a persuasive and driving personality and has probably done more than anybody to get Igor Charkovsky's work known outside Russia. Her devotion to the cetaceans is wholehearted, and at some point in her spiritual journey she had been led to create the Rainbow Dolphin Centre in Keri Keri, on New Zealand's North Island.

Although I did not have the money for the trip, I determined to get to the conference. Estelle had promised that there would be more than twenty water babies present at the event, and I wanted to meet them for myself and determine whether the information I had been getting from the dolphins had some truth to it. I used an approach that has served me well these last ten years: I put out to the universe and the powers that be that if they wished me to go to New Zealand, and it was for the best of all, then *they* could manifest me a ticket and expenses for the trip.

Manifest they did. Presents appeared unbidden, old loans were repaid, and unexpected business deals came through. There might have been a small tax rebate in among all the excitement, too!

And Michael Miller wandered into my life. An Irish American, he is the eldest of seven children. He was in his mid-thirties at the time with a medium-sized frame but strong, with slightly bowed legs that erroneously (he will tell you) suggest a background of horses. He had dark, short, curly hair and a face that looked then as if it might have been built from a kit. His eyes were unexpectedly blue and very expressive. When he arrived on our doorstep, however, there was a deep overlay of sadness that hung like a veil all around him. He looked like he had been on a holiday in hell.

It soon emerged that Michael had suffered a near-fatal ski accident a few months earlier and had had major surgery, including extensive facial reconstruction. Having heard that "floating" would be an excellent restorative measure and since my companion was at that time running a float-tank center in New York City, Michael embarked on a concentrated series, coming in every day for weeks at a time. He had a powerful desire to heal himself and consequently made rapid strides toward recovery. He also effectively treated himself for a galloping case of candida.

From our first meeting with him, there was always something a trifle unusual about Michael. Neither my companion nor I thought he was as he seemed. He appeared to have a remarkable memory of his previous incarnations and a driving need to release any karmic residue he was carrying. He was very intense and counterphobic to the extent of actively searching out his fears and confronting them. As his tank work progressed, therefore, it was not surprising when it came out that Michael considered himself to be a walk-in.

By the mid-eighties I had met a number of people who thought of themselves as walk-ins—personalities who have taken over, literally, the bodies and lives of the vacated former occupant. Ruth Montgomery extensively explores the subject in her book *Aliens Among Us,* and although there have been several well-publicized hoaxes, the subject remains something of an enigma. Claiming to be occupied by another personality altogether could be the result of a psychic or psychological disorder, a technique for avoiding an unpleasant reality, or a simple con trick. But the world is a far odder place than much contemporary thought will allow, and given the transformational circumstances in which we live and the interest we have evoked from our galactic family, it might not be so outlandish to assume that volunteers from other domains have found unusual ways of helping us. In the clearly authentic walk-ins I have encountered, I have found a profoundly transformed level of consciousness coupled with information that could be coming only from other dimensions of existence.

Michael's being a walk-in, however, was of subsidiary importance at that point to his immediate and lasting love affair with dolphins. Having done his fair share of diving in different parts of the world, he had his own stories of cetacean encounters. But he had not experienced the telepathic matrix until he floated in the tank. His progress was assured when he emerged joyfully one day having met a magnificent dolphin who made contact with him while he was in an out-of-body state. Michael was well on his way to healing.

We grew to know each other better over the months that followed. Michael came and went from the city a number of times, signing on at one stage as a crew member of a catamaran that took people out for dolphin swims in the Caribbean. His stories are many and varied, but two factors stay in my mind: whenever people went in to swim with the dolphins, Michael reports, the first thing the dolphins did was to excrete in the water (no prizes for working that one out); and whenever dolphins were around the boat, the sugar and coffee consumption on board shot up.

When Michael heard about the Homo Delphinus conference in New Zealand, not surprisingly, he wanted to go. He also, most generously—and unbidden, I might add—offered to pay the balance of my way. I thanked the universe and was off on another adventure.

New Zealand . . . what a joy it was to be there. The psychic atmosphere was spotlessly clean and the air itself clear and fresh. Certain aspects of physical existence, however, turned out to be somewhat more demanding, as Michael and I discovered after only a few hours off the plane. Winterbound, sun-starved New Yorkers, we threw ourselves down on a golden sand beach, fell asleep in what we thought was mildly overcast weather, and promptly nearly burned our backs off. We later discovered that it is one of the more recent peculiarities of the dwindling ozone layer in these southern climes.

On first impression the New Zealand countryside looked like a beautifully tended garden. Everything seemed new and fresh. But as we wound our way up and around one extinct volcano after another, edging our little camper—a tortoise of a hut on wheels—along the narrow, winding country roads of the North Island, another and deeper knowing altogether arose in me: that the place was utterly ancient. And there was an intuition I had never experienced before: that the land had been loved and cared for continuously over hundreds of thousands of years. I could feel the truth of it in my body.

Climate and geographical conditions changed constantly as we careened around broad rocky vistas one moment and into tiny enclosed valleys the next. Yet every tree and meadow, every mountain and waterfall, was precisely in its correct place—all was perfectly positioned. The garden metaphor came to me again, and my spiritual vision deepened. I saw the entire countryside as a massive feat of geomancy, the most sensitive landscaping I had ever seen—a touch of Lemuria. It created an immense and palpable feeling that never left me throughout my stay in New Zealand.

Michael and I took turns driving while we caught each other up on what we knew about water birthing to date. What appealed to us both was the feeling of slipping from the amniotic fluid directly into warm, familiar water. The umbilical cord could then be cut with no undue rush and the infant lifted to the surface for its first breath—a wonderful, deep, sacred first breath, glowing with prana. Without a doubt, it was a most benign and far less traumatic entry into this world than most of us have had. We speculated that in earlier and more rough-and-tough ages, a harsh birth might be seen as an appropriate start to an even harsher lifetime, the traumas inculcated possibly serving some sort of evolutionary function. But surely now they have become counterproductive. Contemporary Western hospital birthing practices often take little account of the mother and child's emotional and psychic states, and it is more than probable that such insensitive methods contribute directly to the angry, fearful state of much of modern life.

The dolphins, with their nurturing, creative natures and their evident interest in helping us through this difficult transition in human history, have more than a flipper in the whole matter of underwater birthing. We had both heard that

Charkovsky noted the calming effect dolphins have on mothers giving birth and, in one of his home movies, the dolphins can be seen swimming around in the background while tiny babies, nearer the camera and apparently totally unafraid of the water, are paddling their little legs off.

By the mid-eighties, there were, to our knowledge, at least three places in the world that were actively pursuing water birthing. Of course, a far larger number of women are using Jacuzzis and tubs, primarily in the United States, New Zealand, and Australia, and apparently somewhat less in Europe. Medical authorities have been reluctant to endorse or encourage the spread of underwater birthing, although we had both heard of a few courageous doctors, like the French M.D. Michel Odent, who have pursued the craft. This unwillingness of the medical establishment to give water birthing a fair hearing has predictably driven interested parents underwater, so to speak, and has resulted in a quiet network of those who have simply taken it upon themselves to arrange matters and allow the results to speak for themselves. Nowhere has this network flowered more effectively than in Australia and New Zealand, where a steadily growing number of children are being delivered in this gentle manner.

There are two quite different approaches to spreading the information on underwater birthing. One suggests that it should be moved quietly into social acceptance on a grassroots level, making as few waves as possible and avoiding any direct confrontation with the powerful vested interests of the medical establishment. The other insists on presenting underwater birthing as a fait accompli, maintaining that sufficient evidence is in—the Russians are doing it, why not us? In juggling these two different approaches, I knew Estelle Myers and the Rainbow Dolphin Centre had been vigorously attempting to get underwater birthing accepted by the public as well as the medical establishment, but with very limited success.

At the time of this writing, the Rainbow Dolphin Centre has been closed for a few years and Estelle has gone on to make the beautiful and powerfully affecting video *Oceana*. The center was possibly a little ahead of its time. Very wisely, underwater birthing practitioners have decided to keep a low profile, and the concept is now sliding naturally and easily into place. It is clearly not being allowed to become another fad—the stakes are far too high. If parents—especially the mother, for obvious reasons—have a genuine desire to give birth in this way, then have no doubt that their guardian angels or spiritual guides will direct them toward the relevant people.

II

Meeting the Maori

Our small female dolphin starts to be able to read the ocean. The delicate scents of mineral traces in the water, the exudations of other creatures of the deep, the warm streams and the cool currents—all this and more constantly present her with a never-ending display of who and what might be out there, way beyond the effective range of her echo-recognition . . .

Arriving at dusk, Michael and I found the Rainbow Dolphin Centre perched on the crown of a wonderfully curved, rocky headland. Its location could not have been more superb: a coastline both wild and beautiful, with the sea on three sides turning blue to violet and broken only by the animal humps of sleeping islands.

Estelle Myers was in her customarily ebullient form, greeting the new arrivals as we tumbled in from all corners of the globe. She quickly filled us in on the lastest happenings. By her account, the last year or two at the center had not been at all easy. Estelle felt that some of her actions had angered a number of influential people in the medical community, and although miracles had been strewn on the founding of the place, funds had never been plentiful enough to achieve her ambition for it to become a birthing center in its own right. Her publicity efforts had paid off in a number of full-page newspaper stories that, while generating a lot of interest, predictably had not enamored her to the medical establishment.

Since she felt she had been led to the spot by the dolphins, she had had high hopes that they might have intended to be more in attendance in the bay at the foot of the cliff upon which the Rainbow Dolphin Centre was built. But this had never really happened either. Dolphins are so notoriously slippery, like Zen saints, especially where human expectations are involved, that it might seem more than a trifle unrealistic to base the location of such a center on the hope that they would appear on the doorstep. But Estelle had hope and faith in boundless measure—and what could be a more pragmatic result of her untiring energy than the Homo Delphinus Conference?

The door began to open, and the candles flickered as more and more people arrived. Old friends, surprises: "Good heavens! Are *you* here?" Hugs, bright eyes, all happy to get in from the evening rain. "Help yourself—it's over there": fresh food and caring in abundance. We settled into the easy chaos of it all.

After dinner was cleared away, Estelle's eyes were sparkling in occult humor. She could hardly contain her good news. "Guess what?" she said. "We're not going to meet here at the Centre, but on a Maori *marae!*"

The Maori are the indigenous people of New Zealand. Estelle went on to tell us that the word "marae" not only means a Maori settlement as a whole, but also the large meeting hall that serves as their tribal focus. Apparently the local Maori had heard about the conference, and the concept of underwater birthing had so interested them that only weeks before the scheduled date of the gathering they turned up at her front door and suggested the meeting be held in their sacred space.

The privilege was not lost on Estelle, since the Maori, somewhat like the North American Indians, have carefully guarded their sacred truths and their natural wonders over the years. Never before had they opened their arms in quite this way.

We slept peacefully that night, our "tortoise" parked out in a field and surrounded by sheep, lulled by soft sounds of the darkness and the distant throbbing of the surf far below us.

Next morning found a convoy of some seventy-five people driving the twenty-odd miles to Maori land. It was misty and wet, the sun breaking through intermittently to light up a countryside that was both utterly unfamiliar and insistently reminiscent of England's county of Somerset—or Sumerset, as a wise woman of my acquaintance once re-minded me.

We arrived to discover the marae cupped in a small valley and rimmed by a sheltered bay whose mirrored, turquoise surface was broken only by the dark, hunched backs of volcanic rocks. We disembarked. After milling around self-consciously and searching out familiar faces in tentative anticipation, we were guided to line up on the edge of a large and beautifully tended lawn, on the opposite side of which stood the marae—the meeting hall—with its yawning entrance doors. We formed a long line, two or three people deep, and stood in the light mist awaiting our next instructions. The night before, Estelle had made the point very forcefully that on no account were we ever to set foot on this large, grassy rectangle. It was regarded as the most sacred part of the entire settlement, having something arcane to do with the Maoris' buried ancestors.

In fact, there were quite a lot of specific rules of conduct that we were all keen to observe in this rare meeting with what was essentially a thoroughly alien culture. For example, when we were inside the great meeting hall, we were warned never to walk over another person's body—sensible enough in terms of not disturbing their aura. And since we were all expected to bunk down together for the nights we were to be spending there, we should also be most careful not to sleep with our feet pointing at anyone else's head. By the second night this last caveat was enough to give most of us a mild case of spatial dyslexia!

Once again we milled around as the thin rain gave way to

the first tentative rays of sunlight. The next thing we knew, we were all being asked to walk slowly over the hallowed turf toward the marae. *Walk* over the holy of holies? Was it a trick? Did one of our people get the wrong message? We hung back, kicking our heels, dreadfully confused and wondering perhaps if this might not be some sort of test.

"What about the buried ancestors?" I asked.

"Shush!"

It was at this stage, I believe, that I started to slip—first mildly, then inexorably—into an altered state of consciousness. The cognitive dissonance between the two quite different perceptions of the sacrosanct lawn, must have pushed my authority buttons in some way and opened me up to other states of awareness. I wondered if this might not be the intended effect. The Maori, as we were soon to find out, were extremely sophisticated in the psychic and spiritual realms.

As I vacillated backward and forward, caught between the proverbial rock and a hard place (heaven forbid that I might insult our generous hosts before the conference had even started!), the psychic turbulence struck. The Guardian of the Threshold reared up. And as I, along with the others, overcame my reticence and placed my suddenly very Western feet on that sacred grass, over me fell a stark vision of enormous natives leaping out of nowhere: hundreds of 'em, spears flashing, teeth gnashing, drums crashing—something out of a childhood memory of Movietone newsreels, with Her Majesty the Queen looking stoically into the middle distance trying to deal with it all.

This palpable vision, of naked men hurling themselves at us for the pure splendor of it, came and vanished, leaving me blinking in surprise and concern across the lawn at the Maori tribal elders, who were now lining themselves up with their backs against the marae. Not leaping, prancing warriors, of course, but people just like us. They were a little older, and in some cases wearier, but mostly with sparkling, bright eyes full of humor and relentless wisdom.

We walked slowly and reverently across the grass as the senior elder welcomed us (in what we found out later was the key point in the ceremony) and formally invited us all to join their tribe. He spoke casually but rhythmically, skillfully modulating his voice. His open-hearted resonance reached into my spirit, and as my feet seemed to find their own way across the space in between us, tears of joy started rolling down my face. Others around me were having much the same reaction. We were starting to realize, perhaps, why we were all called there to be together. Beneath the elder's words, which wound on in the way of simpler people and echoed in the rise and fall of the round, volcanic hills and the quiet, wind-eroded valley in which we rested, it came to me that we were all being welcomed back to Paradise. The wise old voice ringing in our souls, we walked proudly forward, filled with light and happy license, stepping—just this once!—over the forbidden green rectangle.

To be welcomed by a people—by an entire tribe: what a rare and blessed experience! I closed the intervening distance, and all I could see were their smiles growing broader and their wide-open arms more expansive. I felt as though I were dying and my loved ones were coming to greet me. In that moment my spirit soared like a great hawk, and suddenly, for a quite distinct but fleeting instant, I was looking way over the line of elders and the marae's timber facade with its enormous, lizardlike carved ancestral figures to the smaller houses and workshops beyond—and further beyond them, to the quiet, mysterious water. The hills, softly molded by time and erosion, lent the vision the quality of a kingdom, once lost in the mists like Avalon, yet now seeping back into this reality, shepherded by the love and caring of the Maori people.

When we gathered inside the marae, we fell naturally—or were we guided?—into two large concentric rings. We visitors were on the inside, and the Maoris were spread out around us in the wider circle, standing back against the walls. Behind them reared the curious, powerful carved figures of their sacred ancestors, standing nine feet high and supporting the roof. In a primordial way, these carvings' reptilian bodies were oddly reminiscent of something I could not quite grasp. The moment, however, became consumed with the greeting.

Now, *this* was meeting people! Slowly we circled around,

honoring and in turn being welcomed by each member of the tribe, holding forearms and then bending over toward each other and touching noses—first one side, then the other. To a jaded city boy, the intimacy and purity of it was like a cool mountain stream.

After three or four noses, winks, blinks, and mutual knowings, I caught on: we were drawing in the breath of each other's spirits. No hiding or trickery here, I realized. In the presence of these scrupulously honest and openhearted people, we were all expected to be *who we truly are.*

More noses, new wisdom, and then an old woman with eyes of lapis lazuli faced me. "We've seen *him* before!" she said, followed by a weirdly familiar laugh while she looked deep into my soul. I stared back astonished, recognizing in her eyes one whom I have always sought. I knew then that I was among manifestations of the Divine Mother and that this indeed was holy ground.

Once again I threw myself in, a willing participant in the sacred game, moved beyond words. It was the most complex of joinings—literally a merging of realities—a mutual revelation taking place person by person, mounting in waves of newfound ecstasy, with most of us weeping unabashedly. Then, when we had been washed into a circle of stillness by the strength of our emotions, individual Maoris publicly took their opportunity to welcome us. We replied with warm little speeches, good-hearted in spite of stilted deliveries. What a fear of public speaking our culture has!

Our Maori friends, obviously more used to tribal gatherings, were masters of the short speech, filled with verbal feints that made the listener think the talking was going to be endless: words lurched and snapped and sparkled until you realized you were hypnotized and caught in their web. Then the speaker would bring you back into the quiet clearing of your known self, refreshed and tingling with joy.

When the greeting was over, the conference guidelines were discussed in this new atmosphere of freedom. It was agreed—and all credit to Estelle for encouraging it—that the four days should not be planned out but everything allowed to be loose, openly informal, and Spirit guided. And indeed it did seem as if the meetings and encounters moved with the swell, gatherings changing in size and passion with the wind and the tide, as the group soul was refined and harmonized. It was quite evident that the conference was going to function on a number of levels—I had already experienced some of them—and that this occasion was to be more of an emotional/spiritual experience than an academic or intellectual exchange.

Looking back, I can see that as the group soul was brought into harmony, we were all taking significant leaps of consciousness and that we were being upstepped jointly, as a unit.

No Carlos Castaneda, I. All I found myself able to scribble during that first break was: "Ah! The wonder of it! ALL together again in the whispering sunlight."

Afternoon found us gathering back in the marae, each person expressing what she or he would like to see accomplished, both personally and as a group, during this four-day period of closeness. Everybody was encouraged to speak from the deepest place, and as you might imagine, it took a very long time. But somehow, really listening with full attention to others' visions and aspirations must have subtly changed our bodies' inner rhythms, slowing and quieting them. I found myself slipping into a timeless state, and as I did, I started to experience a direct level of contact with the group soul. It came to me through listening. I started hearing *everything at once.* It had happened before in much smaller, more intimate gatherings—possibly a dozen times in my life. The sound made by everything-at-once starts forming into a communication, a metalanguage that I have thought of as a precursor to certain levels of telepathy. Although the psychic mechanics of what was happening may not be well understood in our culture and were certainly beyond my conscious comprehension as a participant, I was sure that our collection of more than two hundred women, men, and children—visitors and Maoris alike—experienced an undeniably unified state of soul. Whether the others heard what I heard, I shall never know. I have blocked out completely what the group soul said.

Like most indigenous people, the Maoris were more

skilled in the ways of group telepathy than we and consequently seemed able to sink back into the matrix, the psi field. They acted, at the conference, rather as facilitators of the effect and were always totally present when we needed them.

This palpable sense of unity continued well into the evening and manifested in different degrees throughout the conference. But in any gathering that involves a personal depth of honesty and integrity, not to mention the introduction of entirely new realities, there are areas in all of us that simply have to be brought out and expressed. Fears, anger, hurt, repressed emotional pain, and other egocentricities, like closed coils of recording tape, have to be unwound. Our ego frameworks and status investments, the delusionary webs we have all created to maintain our personas—all these have to be honed down, refined, and brought to consciousness before we can enjoy the exquisite harmony of a full, telepathic, group-soul experience. What I (and who knows who else) heard in those tender twenty seconds was itself possibly a herald of what we can expect in the future as our race moves more fully into the telepathic dimension.

12

Birth of a New Species

Our dolphin finds, as she sweeps the bottom of the shallow, coastal waters with sound, that certain shells and small sea creatures light up in the most delicious manner. She tightens her echo-recognition beam and focuses in on a sea urchin, for instance, and finds a whole delphinoid history encoded within its living protoplasm . . .

During the next two days of the gathering in New Zealand, it was as though we had all become part of an elaborate dance, a conspiracy orchestrated on a metalevel by the group soul, designed to allow the stronger egos among us to strut their stuff.

I have often observed that dolphins tend to draw toward them people with powerfully formed egos, as well as those who have learned how to move in and out of an ego state. I have wondered whether the dolphins, with their delicately balanced group soul, might not be studying what must be for them our alarming level of individuality.

This releasing process, which took the best part of two days, was extremely gentle and loving, and nobody was made to feel foolish; yet one by one, with the help of our Maori friends, we were able to shuck off the rigidities and barricades of "civilized" life. As we started pulsing more closely with one another, and as we progressively trusted the Great Spirit to guide us into being at the right place at the right time, so also was the wonderful mystery of *Homo delphinus* revealed to those open to receive it.

In the gathering oneness of the telepathic dimension, I felt we were being asked to consider some strange and truly magnificent possibilities: What if the evolutionary processes on this planet are far more dynamic than we have been led to believe? Supposing the structure and form of the various species—cetaceans, humans, and others—are not the ultimate flowering of the life forms on this world as has been generally thought? Is the mutation of consciousness that so many of us are experiencing—from third- to fourth-dimensional awareness—in fact leading toward the physical development of an entirely new species? A new phylum? Might it be conceivable that we are about to be presented with a mutated being, a new order of intelligent life, perhaps as far removed from us as we are from the reptiles?

These were the concepts raised by the group soul in those moments of intense collective resonance, and surely each of us perceived our own pieces of this awesome possibility. For me it came as a euphoric confirmation of my earlier thoughts and my talks with Dr. Kamayani back in New York, serving to bring into new focus some of the more puzzling gestalts I have been receiving from the dolphins over the years.

It struck me that this transformation of life on our planet is a blossoming of the new energy that is manifesting all over the world. Wherever love is, wherever there are open hearts and strong spirits, there also is this sublime energy. Could this extraordinary harmonizing, synchronizing, expanding energy be the precursor—even the creation of—a creature even more capable of expressing this unconditional love energy than we? Might it indeed be the entity described so elegantly by Raphael, channeled through Ken Carey in *The Starseed Transmissions,* as being amphibious, equally at home in each element and yet also able to live and travel in outer space? A telepathic entity, in constant harmonious contact with all parts of itself is, in a sense, a group creation and certainly one through whom our fumbling attempts to master the unlimited potential of the group soul might be more fully articulated.

"This being might be born through the womb of woman—or it might come through the womb of a dolphin!" I found myself blurting out at some point in this gentle flow of events to Jacques Mayol, the French diver and inspiration for the movie *The Big Blue.* I have no idea how much he appreciated of what I was saying, but he looked a little shaken by the possibility.

I should also add that while all this suggested a very strong link to the dolphin world, there has never been any suggestion in any of these revelations that the mutated phylum might result from interbreeding between humans and dolphins. Rather, it would be an entity born to either one or even *both* species!

At another time, the remarkable Oannes, the fishy teachers of the Sumerian culture, came waddling back into my consciousness. I wondered how these creatures would be received today if they appeared on the Florida coastline and if they got through the police, the press, and the politicos what they would teach us. In the longer cycles of the evolutionary process, five or six thousand years is barely a heartbeat. Was something happening in the watery depths of the third millennium that was itself a prefiguring of what was about to occur?

Up to this point I had favored the supposition that the Oannes were most likely to have been associated with an extraterrestrial mission from Sirius, since a somewhat similar story emerges from the Central African tribes, the Dogon and the Bozos, and within much the same time frame. In that case, the mysterious aquatic visitors certainly hailed from the double star system of Sirius.

Now, prepared by the group soul for a deeper truth, I was being asked to contemplate a different scenario. If it were possible that such a being, this new species, might choose to express itself through both cetacean and human wombs, then surely there is a far more intimate relationship—a far more profound entwining of the branches of the great tree of life—than we have hitherto allowed. And might it have been precisely this transformational miracle that had drawn the Sirius mission to our world in the first place? There was also something immensely humorous about it all—with a sense of divine fun that I have come to associate with our Creator—as though having to cope with this new race of superintelligent, amphibious little monsters will keep us all busy and well out of future mischief for a long time yet!

Before we came together for bedtime, and while the psychic and telepathic ambience of the group soul was fairly humming along, Estelle played a message of good wishes from Igor Charkovsky that he had recorded and sent especially for the conference. In his five-minute address, filtered through an interpreter in halting English, the Russian shaman spoke out strongly for the process of meditation. He called for the proliferation of meditation centers, suggesting that all of us focus on both "our extraterrestrial brethren" and "our invisible friends."

The message came at the perfect time, of course, once again demonstrating to us just how widespread the effect and manifestation of this new energy is becoming. Finally, exhausted from the excitement and the unusual psychic crosscurrents, we found our places to lie down, made certain our feet pointed at no hapless other's head (a longer process than might be imagined), and curled up for the night. More than one hundred people—women, men, and a lot of children—clumped down together like a bunch of happy animals, perhaps to dream further of these magnificent new vistas.

I lay awake savoring the pleasure of a more tribal life, listening as the breathing slowed down and the small disturbances ceased. I had found myself so transported that I had been scarcely tempted into my rational, left-brain, note-taking way of being. Now, as I write, it seems odd that I have so little memory of what actually went on between all these very different people. And Michael Miller, what of him? He was there, and yet I cannot recall seeing him or spending any time with him throughout the first two days. When I look through my journal, all I find is:

> Refreshing breezes against the damp cool of a memory,
> the first blue sky in days
> opens the doors to another time and space.
> Wisdom. A resonance with natural ways,
> and ancient trees rearing up over grassy mounds.
> ALL shivers with anticipation
> as secrets held for centuries
> sparkle and crackle through
> the homely aether.
> The sun at last
> joins us in broad, beaming wonderment.
> Silence roars amid the childlike babble
> to a background of surf and quiet hills,
> bringing to this auspicious occasion a Vision that,
> with almost unbearable tenderness,
> seals a new rapport between the worlds.

It was indeed a pleasant night—a night of flying dreams and meetings with one another and with stranger beings still. We revived our ancestral memories of all being together, remembering the dolphins' world of easygoing, playful relationships with none of those authoritarian separations of our more "civilized" cultures. No child cried that night, and everybody seemed to awake enlivened in our new sense of oneness.

Looking back, I can appreciate now what I could not see but only feel at the time: that while we were being incrementally upstepped and our consciousnesses synchronized, a choice was always available to us individually as to whether we wanted to jump further into the group soul. For me, there seemed to be a series of hints, presentiments of the Great Mystery, continually drawing me in, beckoning me on. *Homo delphinus*—what could it all mean? A new phylum? An unheard-of species? Beings who might be as strange to us as the first two humans must have been to the primate family who reared them? For evolution is far more likely to be discontinuous, as modern science is now starting to discern—punctuated, I believe they call it. Mutations happen extremely fast, possibly over one or two generations, rather than through the interminable durations of the Darwinian paradigm. Then there are the long periods of stabilization and assimilation. Could this be what the interlocking pattern is starting to reveal? Have we been gathered together in this fairest and most benevolent of universes to comprehend, to choose, and, possibly, to sanction the advent of this unique manifestation?

As you might imagine, we spent a lot of time at the conference meditating on this whole issue. The overriding impact of the group soul and the different effects the upstepping of vibration was having on us all became more important than the information exchanged on underwater birthing and the other matters that had acted to bring us together—in spite of the fact that films, workshops, and presentations were available to those who wanted a bit of left-brain stimulation.

And, of course, there were the children: more than thirty of them, between the tiniest newborn to some eight- to ten-year-olds all born underwater. You will recall that water birthing has been actively practiced in the West only over the last decade—with the majority of these children now in the two- to five-year-old bracket. While I am no expert on children, each of these youngsters, without exception, appeared sturdy, highly responsive, and very bold and adventurous, while at the same time, they were singularly graceful and well behaved. Surely, under the circumstances, it is unheard of to have had four days of such intense inner communion without the constant disruption of young children—and yet, in retrospect, not one such disturbance echoes in my mind!

Each child with whom I interacted had her or his spirit firmly in place and was fully present throughout our encounter. However young, not one of them had that numbed, vacant, stoned-out look that so many babies have in our culture. I was able to photograph a six-month-old girl, laughing and triumphant, standing upright on her mother's outstretched hand after the mother had been whirling the baby around by her feet!

I later learned that this redoubtable woman had five children and that the last three had been born straight into the warm seas of northern Australia. Oddly enough, and almost without exception, the waterborn children at the conference had fair hair and the bluest of blue eyes. While this may have been the result of the racial and genetic predisposition of their mainly New Zealand and Australian parents (and the sampling itself was admittedly small), it might also be an indication of an exciting genetic possibility: the advent of some more "violet blood" (see appendix F).

When looked at from the perspective of a widely inhabited and seeded universe, the various races of humankind, each with their own unique genetic endowments, might well be regarded as part of a large breeding program. As we would hybridize a rose, selecting for those strengths we most valued, so, surely, would those whose function it is to nurture and cultivate the human species work toward an advantageous genetic mix. Lest this sound a little detached and inhuman, I should stress that here I am talking only about the nature of our bodies—our physical vehicles. We who inhabit these profoundly complex pieces of bio-mechanical equipment are as perfect or imperfect as our experience and our wisdom allow; it is merely our bodies that are progressively refined in the twistings and turnings of the bloodlines through history.

According to the angelic communicants of *The Urantia Book,* at a certain point in the growth process of a planetary race of human beings there is an infusion of off-planet, high-energy, genetic material from sources that could be called extraterrestrial but that are more precisely intraterrestrial. Under normal circumstances, this rich, quintessential genetic endowment, known in the cosmic gene-splice biz as violet blood, would have radically shifted the overall consciousness of our species when it was originally introduced some forty thousand years ago.

Unfortunately, if we are to believe most available planetary histories, life on this world could never be described as flourishing under normal circumstances. The mission to introduce a new, higher-vibratory gene had to be aborted, and with very few exceptions the violet bloodline has not made its presence strongly felt on this planet.

But times, they are a-changing, and the major political reconciliations that have occurred recently in our sector of the universe have permitted our planet to regain something of our rightful heritage prior to moving on into the galactic community.

Could it be that some of these water babies are bearers of a new infusion of this violet blood? They seem peaceful, yet fearless; adventurous, but generous—and, of course, they are simply children as well.

Among the little-known characteristics of this bloodline is that bearers of it, like certain of the Egyptian pharaohs and the Merovingian kings of France, are reputed to be telepathic with each other up to a range of some seventy miles. I wonder now, as I write, whether the strange effect that was starting to come over me at the conference might not have been an indication of this very capability in action.

Over the days of the gathering, I found I had the growing feeling that these kids—these clear-eyed, wise little beings—were, in some supremely effective way, instrumental in forming the psychic intimacy of the group soul. While I have no clear experience to indicate that this was true, I remain with a strong intuition that the children were involved. Doubtless, most children are mildly telepathic to some extent, but this was a sensation of an entirely different order. It was subtle, but there were times I knew with an inner certainty that the group soul was being telepathically orchestrated by the water babies, who were reaching out and affecting all of our lives.

Dawn on the third day was a beauty. It spread over those quiet, rounded hills until there was no question in our minds that the weather had broken. We hoped it reflected something of our inner states! Freewheeling workshops and discussions drew us together on the beach, the outermost people in the circles being lapped by the gentle surf. The sun was with us for the remainder of our time together.

Not surprisingly, most of the group had had some form of

contact with the invisible realms. We were able to talk about them freely, exchanging our experiences with angels, nature spirits, and extraterrestrials without any embarrassment. Many present also had swum extensively with dolphins and found, when they compared notes, that they were able to perceive their encounters in a far deeper and more meaningful context. Mostly, however, there was simply sitting in silence and touching heart to heart with our Inner Source and the tender sweetness of sun and sea.

Who could say which presences accompanied us during those spirited discussions and long silences? And perhaps it was best that we did not know—such things can render our species a tad self-conscious! But I fancy there was not one of us who did not feel a tangible sense of higher-dimensional involvement. Igor Charkovsky's message of the night before, with its open acknowledgment of matters angelic and extraterrestrial, alerted us to what must be of vital interest to our galactic family. And among "those who watch" are doubtless some of the very beings who were originally responsible for seeding life onto this planet in the first place—observing, I dare say, with a particularly passionate detachment.

On the afternoon of the third day, one of the Maori elders led a group of four of us off to the nearby kauri forest—for the Maori, amongst their holiest of sacred places. While we drove over there, I had a chance to admire the Maori relationship to matters mechanical. The car itself was archaic: an English saloon from another era, badly beaten up and rimed with the dirt of country lanes. These roads were not paved but were studded with potholes and large rocks—New York City could have taken a lesson. And yet, more like a hovercraft than an automobile, the car just flew along! Sitting in the front seat, gliding fluidly over those improbable roads, I felt yet again that I was a fortunate participant in another small miracle, albeit of a rather everyday variety: when we arrived at our destination, therefore, it was with a somewhat heightened sense of wonderment.

We got out and walked slowly into the forest. As the air grew cooler in among the great trunks of these most ancient of the world's trees—some kauris have lived for more than three thousand years—the psychic atmosphere tangibly broadened and deepened. The Maori have revered their forests for so long that the trees look as though they have taken on all that extra sweetness. Everything was exquisitely tended, and the smooth bark of the kauri trees glowed from the loving touch of countless generations of hands.

In the way of forests, the air and the spaces between the enormous trees had a gelatinous quality, almost a slow-motion effect, as if the birds, butterflies, insects, us—all short-lived phenomena!—were preserved in the finest, most lightly golden mist of amber and hung quivering in the afternoon sunlight. After the intense excitement back at the marae, our time in the kauri forest was a serene and consummately grounding experience.

On the last day of the conference, there was a lively discussion regarding the nature of the water-mammal function (a reflex that automatically closes off the windpipe underwater in all water mammals, including, oddly enough, our species), as well as the ability to swim, which all newborn children appear to possess. Igor Charkovsky has been able to demonstrate that the reflexive motions that babies make with their arms and legs is, in actuality, an example of their natural inclination to swim and not merely random, arbitrary movements as has generally been thought.

These actions closely resemble an adult's breast stroke but, if anything, are even more perfect. The adult has had to learn to swim, Charkovsky points out, but the baby has never forgotten. With appropriate training, water babies have been able to hold their breath for up to eight minutes. Now, that is certainly going to interest the dolphins! Jacques Mayol, who can now dive to 105 meters without an aqualung, has trained himself through breath control and yoga to hold his breath for an astonishing four minutes. He talked about going through the fear and panic points by using a self-disciplined will, ensuring that he surrendered into relaxation the moment the fear started making itself felt. This is stern stuff considering the powerful terror that our species in general has toward the sea.

I am still trying to master the panic reflex my body goes through if anything touches me unexpectedly in the water! Whatever the creature from whom our bodies evolved all those millions of years ago, it may well have had very good reason to forsake the perils of the deep for drier prospects.

Around four o'clock on the afternoon of the last day, I found myself recording rather portentously in my journal, "HOMO DELPHINUS IS BORN!" I realized that by the end of the conference, a sufficient number of people had at least a conceptual reality of what a mutated being or a new species might mean—its extraordinary impact on the life of our planet. Perhaps this conference, I thought, would allow the next stages of the Great Work to unfold, whether it might occur in our lifetime or further down the line.

The invisible realms, I reasoned, are always eminently fair in presenting us with freedom of choice on any significant issue. For something as far reaching as the introduction of another sentient—indeed, supersentient—species on the planet, they would want to make sure that we know exactly what we are getting ourselves into! I had the impression that the people present at the conference, drawn as we were from all over the world and from every walk of life, were a seed group whose function it was to midwife the concept into the world mind as a preparation for its introduction into the womb.

Whether everybody understood and assimilated these revelations is less important than the experience of being there. I am sure there was much more going on than any of us could consciously register and convey, but at the same time I am certain that each of us attending this august gathering was allowed our own unique, miraculous glimpse of what could lie ahead in the coming golden age. On a more down-to-earth level, the conference confirmed for many the viability of underwater birthing as a process, and it encouraged people to exchange confidences with parents who have given birth in this way.

A number of younger midwives came from different parts of the United States, Australia, Europe, and New Zealand, and fine, spirited women they are. These ladies really mean business—they are at the bleeding edge of guerilla midwifery! One formidable young woman told me she was planning to drive a mobile birthing center—a pool in the back of a Winnebago—all over Australia, going wherever she was needed. She is probably out there doing it right now!

As fellow attendees David Goodman and his new, pregnant wife (the ubiquitous Roberta Quist) pointed out to me, most of the water babies have rather unusually shaped heads: large craniums and slight bumps on their foreheads. Nothing very obvious yet, but it could be the start of something—just the tip of what we might be witnessing over the next three or four generations. Of course, it is far too early to establish any kind of accurate overview of what actually might be happening, but there can be little doubt that the extreme stresses and strains our planetary culture is currently undergoing must be attracting spirits of considerable age and experience to take on the challenges of further growth. And we certainly know that stress enhances the possibility of mutation in the natural world.

The Homo Delphinus Conference was one glimpse of what we as a species might be growing into. By the end of our brief time together, I was able to intuit glimmers of this new level of consciousness in all the water babies I met. It was a very familiar feeling, as if it has always been happening, or about to happen—full of humor and knowing. In a scarcely surprising way, it has something of a delphinic quality about it as well as the supreme delight that is the stamp of higher orders of beingness.

Without really knowing it, we are gearing up for the wonders ahead. As underwater birthing becomes more widely practiced, I believe we will be setting the stage for the appearance of altogether new levels of wisdom. And with the present momentum, I do not doubt that the water-born are already evidencing some pronounced manifestations of higher consciousness—gifts and talents that will make metal bending and firewalking look like the parlor games they can tend to be.

Chris Griscom's son Bapu, whom she writes about in her book *Ocean Born: Birth as Initiation*, is certainly an excellent example of these higher faculties in action. If the revelation and manifestation of this new phylum are indeed true, then how magnificently humorous that such a planet as this, long thought of as near the bottom of the barrel among inhabited worlds, should receive the rare cosmic privilege of hosting the birth of an entirely new species!

13
Nonhuman Intelligences

Our little female dolphin learns through delightful experience that other dolphins have long been beautifying their underwater paradise by overlaying the slowly growing shells of certain sea creatures with sonic holograms. She moves through these gardens of knowledge as we might wander through a field of wildflowers, seeing them bursting into rapid bloom as her supersensitive intelligence picks up every note of every melody . . .

My various actively telepathic encounters with dolphins seem to have led, quite naturally, to a deeper appreciation of other nonhuman intelligences. Once cetacean intelligence is acknowledged, the floodgates of sentience seem to open up. It becomes suddenly and peculiarly obvious that we live at the bottom of a well of intelligence every bit as much as we do a well of gravity. My experience so far suggests that nonhuman intelligences comparable to or higher than ours or the cetaceans' can be subdivided into a few broad categories.

Extraterrestrial. These are mortal human beings like us, some aquatic but mostly bipedal and bilaterally symmetrical, and visiting from spheres more advanced in light and life. In 1975 the Pleiadians estimated and told Swiss contactee Billy Meier that 105 different civilizations were keeping us under observation. With the extraordinary acceleration in world events in the past few decades, today there may well be many more.

Interdimensional. This is an equally large category that includes beings from other planets who have dimensional access to us, including time travelers, future selves, spirit guides, and other denizens of the fourth dimension.

Angelic realms. Though, strictly speaking, interdimensional, the angels hail from *inner* space, and this is such a vast domain that it deserves a category of its own. I have personally encountered numerous types of angels: guardian angels; angels of the future, of progress, of education, of entertainment, of nations and nation life, of health, of the home; seraphim; supernaphim; a couple of Trinity Teacher Sons; and, of course, our friendly Beings of the Violet Flame—the Midway Creatures of the Urantia cosmology. Angels could be said to be the mistresses of the fifth dimension.

Devas and nature spirits. These are of very different but certainly comparable intelligence to ourselves. They are all the spirit workers who guide, nourish, and maintain life on this planet. To the more contemporary scientific imagination, the devas can be seen as the morphic patterns which inform all living Systems.

Mysterious and unknown. And just to be on the safe side, a category for all those wonderful beings who do not fit into any of the above pigeonholes.

I started with dolphins because they are more accessible. At least they share the joys and hazards of this dimension with us. We can touch them and swim with them, even if it tends to be completely on their terms. But for all the adventures I have had with dolphins, it was really a training, an opening up to vistas that I had previously filtered out. Indeed, it was the dolphins who made it clear to me at a certain point in this journey that I needed to focus my attention in another direction. "Quit being so interested in us," I felt they were saying. "Dig deeper and you will find the angels. Work more closely with them. Get to know *them* better."

When the angels revealed themselves to the small group of us in Toronto, what had been an idea in my mind—barely a belief system—flowered into a full-blown reality. I had acknowledged that there must be angels prior to this encounter, but there was a great deal of difference between thinking about them in an abstract way and the obvious, pragmatic reality of their existence. Toronto changed my life. I *knew* angels were real.

I found, as I got to know them better, that angels exist in their own reality, just as we do in ours. Their vibrational frequency resonates just a little more rapidly than ours and therefore interpenetrates our reality. They are literally inside us, sharing our space, and yet paradoxically their reality also enfolds ours. They can see and feel us, but under normal circumstances we cannot perceive them with our five senses. Of course, they can be felt or experienced with our higher sensiblities, our finer feelings. I have no doubt that it is *feelings* we are here to learn about in this incarnation, and getting to know the angelic realms allows us to develop and perfect finer and more subtle intuitions.

One of the keys I have received from the angels is the warmth of their desire to have us know them better—to enjoy the happy wonderment of working more closely together. They tell us they have received encouragement from their higher sources to make themselves more known to us. Angels do not want to be worshiped or treated as a substitute for divinity. They say they are drawn to minister to us because they can see the light of the Creator burning in each of us—even if we cannot see it ourselves! It is this that they serve and not, strictly speaking, ourselves. The more we identify with the indwelling God, however, the more we are permitted and encouraged to work with the angels. This is the true meaning of magic.

Naturally, there are many different kinds of angels, from

the extremely intimate guardian angel to the universe-spanning nature of an archangel. We, being at the bottom of the intelligence well, tend to throw them all together. There is an essential oneness to angels, but given the enormity of inner space, there are angels beyond angels beyond angels. If there are layers of angels and angelic realities encompassing and interpenetrating each other, then there must be a group of angels who are the nearest to us and who resonate within a frequency range more or less compatible with ours. I am not talking here of guardian angels—or, companion angels, as they prefer to be called these days—who stay in very close contact with us through our multidimensional inner sensorium, but of another species altogether, one that might well coexist with us in our reality yet remain largely unperceived by us.

In looking through our planetary literature with this in mind, many examples emerge throughout history of the intervention and involvement of a species with quite definite powers and apparently superior knowledge—who are also invisible and who claim immortality. Although we moderns might dismiss them as mythological archetypes, as if we could bracket them as mere inner phenomena, the old gods were very real to the ancient civilizations. They might well be very real to us, too, if one popped into our lives. But something radical has changed, and whatever the reason, for the last couple of thousand years we have not had to deal with the constant encroachment into our reality of gods and goddesses with very definite opinions as to what should or should not be happening in the realms of humankind. Archetypes or angels—life has become considerably more simple.

Who are these beings and what are they doing here? *The Urantia Book* suggests they might be called Midway Creatures, or Midwayers, because their field of existence is midway between the human and the angelic levels of fifth-dimensional vibration. I prefer the name "Beings of the Violet Flame" (BVF), which is starting to be used colloquially among those who have experienced their presence. *The Urantia Book* goes on to say that although there are currently very few of these beings with us—a few thousand at most—they are of great value to the angelic "overgovernment" because, under certain conditions, they can manifest in our reality. This means they can also effect physical changes in matter. Since these BVF are virtually immortal and are stationed on the planet for enormous lengths of time, they could also be seen as the true residents of the sphere upon which *we* are the visitors, spending our four-score and ten before moving onto higher regions.

"Planetary custodians" might be a better way of understanding them, since their function covers two most intriguing areas. First, for hundreds of thousands of years they have been storing away all the very best works of humankind: the finest pieces of art, the most precious of objects, great and inspiring ideas, and all that moves a fledgling race of godlets toward light and life. *The Treasure of Eldorado* is considered to be a coded reference to these extraordinary caches, which will be revealed when our species is deemed sophisticated enough to savor their true value. And second, by all accounts the BVF monitor and coordinate all the extraterrestrial and interdimensional traffic we are starting to attract.

As might be imagined, these are some kick-ass angels! Since human affairs are guided in a far more comprehensive fashion than contemporary culture allows, this particular group of angels is naturally involved with anything considered to advance the higher aspirations of the human race. Consequently, I have no doubt that underwater birthing, with all its profound implications, is of great interest to them. By the time I arrived in New Zealand, I had had a few brief interactions with the BVF and one quite extended encounter with a specific angel who had been assigned to guide my companion and me on an early journey through Europe. It was a tacit lesson in letting go of a personal need to control, and it showed me in no uncertain terms the decaying nature of much of the old reality.

On our trip in our tortoise up the North Island of New Zealand, as well as during our time spent at the conference, I felt very strongly that we were once again being accompanied by one of these angels. Michael Miller certainly felt its presence, although neither of us caught even the slightest glimpse of it. In this game, I am learning to trust my intuition, and even if it all turns out to be rubbish in the ultimate analysis, it yields a wonderfully interesting way of living. Beings of the Violet Flame like to stay anonymous—it makes their job easier. So I cannot say that Michael or I ever got to know our friendly BVF in any real sense, but its presence and counsel were available to us throughout our travels in the Southern Hemisphere.

Although the conference was over, the Maoris still had some tricks up their collective sleeves. I have no doubt that they recognized the spirit in me. All through the conference, on their land and in their sacred places, I had certainly come to deeper levels of self-recognition and self-acknowledgment. And I am sure this was true for each of us.

The parting ceremony, orchestrated and produced by our Maori hosts and hostesses, was profoundly touching. They asked us to take our places in the marae in the exact positions where we would feel most comfortable. I cast around for my power place and found it beneath a tall, carved, slightly reptilian piece of sculpture that I later learned represented a particular prophet/preacher who had lived four or five hundred years ago. He was holding a Luciferic pentacular star and a half-moon—always provocative symbols!

Maori speakers affirmed the importance of the whole area of underwater birthing and told us how much they had appreciated the truth and beauty of the conference. Masters of the great web of feelings that had come to join us all together, the Maoris then started juicing up the psychic atmosphere. It was becoming so charged that I found myself, almost unwillingly, starting to fall back into the old lizard prophet behind me—feeling distinctly at one with him.

The ceremony moved along fluidly and joyfully and was closed by the singing of the Maoris. It was a divine a cappella, masterful and ineffably beautiful. After a time of such intense emotions and self-revelation, their singing became as relaxing, satisfying, harmonically delicious, and soul stirring as a plunge into a clear waterfall on a hot summer's day.

We emerged into the fresh, sparkling sunlight, and I went quickly back to the tortoise to pick up a couple of books I wanted to give to the Maori elders. Michael was already in there with an old lady, Alice, who was the wife of David, one of the senior elders. Both had missed the last part of the ceremony, preferring the exchanges that are possible one-on-one. They appeared to be deep in communion.

I crept back out and sat on a bench outside the marae, struggling to bring my rational mind in enough—my poor old left brain—to get it together to write a meaningful, if illegible, message in each of the books. My eyes were brimming with tears, and I was feeling generally a bit wobbly.

Glancing up, I saw a strange-looking man standing a few feet away. He was staring at me with a remarkable intensity. Every bone, sinew, and muscle was taut, focused on me. He was in his mid- to late sixties but with the vigor of a man in his full power, of medium height, and slim but emanating a wiry strength. He was dressed in an old, dark suit with an open-neck shirt, and he carried a cane. He was naturally distinguished. He also wore a pair of wraparound dark glasses, much in the style of Ray Charles—so much so that I wondered briefly if he might be blind.

We must have stared at each other for ten seconds in frozen astonishment. I had not seen anything of him throughout the conference, and his intensity was a complete surprise to me. Now, as I look back, I see him in my imagination as a man who might have just phased into this reality—Captain Kirk of the Starship *Enterprise* has something of this quality when he gets beamed down. I must have appeared quite a sight, too: face burnt by my first-day foolishness with the sun and tears squishing out of my eyes, smudging what I was trying to write.

Then, when he had sized me up, his whiskery old face broke into the most glorious smile. His teeth were hideously broken, but that seemed to mean nothing to him. His was the broadest, happiest, and most encompassing smile I have ever seen.

He came and sat beside me, putting his arm around me and holding his cane with his other hand. It quite amazes me now as I recall it, but he smelled absolutely marvelous, like fresh flowers. With all those bad teeth, it could have been frightful! But no, it was a pheremonic miracle.

A sense of such utter familiarity fell over me that I was able to completely relax against his arm. I felt waves of love coming from him and was consumed in the fire. It was the love of a father for his son that I had never enjoyed through my earlier years. I learned his name was elder Don, and that it had been his wife, Millei, the one with eyes of lapis, who had recognized me at the start of the proceedings.

Whether we talked then, or whether it was an inner, more telepathic dialogue, I have no clear memory, but I emerged knowing that elder Don was their local shaman, wise man, and sorcerer. I felt a kind of Castaneda's don Genaro trickster projection from him, but I am sure he can be a stern teacher when it is required.

I gave him the remaining copy of my book and managed to write a heartfelt message of gratitude in it. I guess that was a bit smudged, too.

But he had not finished with me yet!

Lying back against elder Don's arm, the late afternoon sun flooding us both with light, my eyes are closed and I am sobbing gently in joy—old pains are dropping away in the face of this all-consuming love. Suddenly, there arise all around me the most beautiful sounds I have ever heard: voices singing eight-and nine-part harmonies; sweet tenderness mixing with a deep, earthy pulse. Is this a movie, or am I dying again? I have the good sense not to open my eyes. Music of such poignant memory washes over me that I have no choice but to surrender to the new levels of rapture washing through me.

I have little idea how long the music goes on, but I finally open my eyes after a great crescendo to find ten or twelve Maori women gathered all around elder Don and myself. Their eyes and their smiles are glowing. They are of all ages and radiantly beautiful. They shift easily from foot to foot as they sing, setting up a curtain of fluid movement that surrounds us. It is a benediction, a catharsis, a blessing on levels that as I write I have no access to.

I have also forgotten entirely how the encounter ended. The last I recall, I was swooshing around the cosmos in total, unfathomable God-consciousness. When we came to compare notes afterward, Michael had something of the same kind of encounter with Alice, but we found we could not talk easily about the time we had spent—these matters are very poignant, especially when they are fresh and not yet assimilated. All I could be sure of was that the conference and everything else that had happened were life-changing events for me—and they certainly appeared to be for Michael as well. I can only assume this was also the case for the others who were there, both Maori and "Pakei"—their name for the rest of us.

An important piece of local lore with which Michael emerged concerned the Maori belief system regarding the whereabouts of their spirits when they die. According to Maori legend, the spirits of the dead return to Hawaiki, their ancestral homeland, and on this journey they travel to the Bay of Spirits, to a particular sacred tree—called the *pohutakawa*—on Cape Reinga, at the northernmost tip of New Zealand.

Not so well known, Michael had been told, was that when the spirits pass down the exposed roots of the pohutakawa into the ocean, they become dolphins. And it is as dolphins that they make the three-to-four-hundred-mile swim to the Islands of the Three Kings. They then spend time doing whatever newly dead spirits do, before taking off for higher climes.

"You mean an actual tree?" I quizzed him. "A real Bay of Spirits?" I was captivated. We had time on our hands, our little tortoise was ready to take us anywhere, and we were just waiting for a sign to suggest a direction. The Bay of Spirits it was.

Before we set off, however, a small group of us gathered at the Rainbow Dolphin Centre to discuss some of the practical outcomes of the conference. There continued to be a tremendous sense of excitement in the air, and ideas were flowing.

The Maoris apparently had offered a small beach house to a Pakei couple intending to have a water birth and were expressing a great thirst for knowledge about underwater birthing. They had not yet told anyone why. They certainly spent much of their time with the water-born at the gathering—I saw one Maori girl of around sixteen with the same tiny water baby for almost the entire four days.

There was talk of the Maoris setting up a birthing center on their land on the marae: a perfect location, and one that was tucked away neatly from the interference of Western medical vested interests. There was also talk about creating a new sort of indigenous school teaching Maori ways and that Pakeis would be welcome to attend. A concerned local schoolteacher wholeheartedly greeted this one! A whole new line of Maori/dolphin jewelry was mooted—a potential cottage industry. The elders had told us of the blight that had drawn most of their young people away from their maraes and into the cities. The Maoris are, however, extremely dexterous, good designers with a bold, flowing, primal line about their work. Dolphins are evidently very much in their lore, and jewelry featuring dolphins was just coming to the fore at that time in the United States and Australia.

The talk swept on, ebbing and flowing, gathering momentarily on one concept or another until we came together finally, in a small circle, holding hands and quietening ourselves. We grounded our energies and in our imaginations created a pool in the middle of the circle. Then we put all the ideas, concepts, and speculations into the middle and surrounded them with light, each one of us asking the invisible world to support and help make possible that which is for the best of ALL.

It was an appropriate ending to the Homo Delphinus Conference. We bade Estelle and all our new friends goodbye and trundled off in our tortoise to find the Bay of Spirits.

14

The Bay of Spirits

Life for our female dolphin is perhaps more like a great song: a vast concerto of meaning, in which each dolphin has her or his own unique destiny within the glory of the dolphin oversoul . . .

Te Rerenga Wairua, the bay that is the parting place for the spirits of the Maori people, is a nine-mile-long, sweeping golden beach that lies deep in the heart of Maori land. That they allowed us to go there at all was a wonder, but there was even a campsite huddled on a meadow in the bluff of the great headland.

Michael and I arrived one afternoon, sighting the headland from a long distance away. It looked for all the world like an enormous dragon, its vast head not yet obscured by the elements and its body snaking away to form the mountains and valleys farther inland. We rapidly made camp on the all but deserted meadow and started off for the beach and the rocks.

I fancy we both saw it at the same time. Michael was certainly looking up at it when I turned to him in surprise. Half-hidden by a large tree and about three hundred feet up the cliff was a colossal human head: a large rock, surely—we could both see that from where we stood—but standing poised on a small neck. Unlike the balanced stones in Utah, Arizona, and New Mexico, this seemed in some strange way to be all one rock. It had a small, delicately pointed chin, a quite evident nose, and two large, deeply shadowed eyes. There was something undefinably feminine about it. The head must have stood eighteen to twenty feet tall. It stared benevolently down the beach that the spirits use to make their way to the pohutukawa tree for their final plunge into the dolphin world.

After some time, we passed beneath the gaze of this astonishing simulacrum and on out to the rocks. Here the lava had cooled on its impact with the water and flattened into terraces at the base of high but accessible cliffs. Pools had been hollowed out in the terraces by rocks stirred around in constant friction.

Michael and I both had the same picture at the same time. Birthing pools, of course! Remarkably, they were at different levels, thus allowing for more constant use. With very little modification, they could be made highly functional for waterbirthing. Granted, this did not allow for the participation of dolphins, who are incidentally numerous in this area, but when we came around the headland sometime later, we saw a channel of calm, shallow water separating a small island from the volcanic headland itself. Michael promptly named it Turtle Island, after his totem of the time, and because it did look inordinately like a turtle crouching in the water. Beautiful, clean sand lay at the bottom of the channel, and there was plenty of room for dolphins.

It was all perfect. As the days passed, the concept grew in our creative imaginations of a thriving holistic birthing and health center: a place for underwater birth in a variety of natural conditions that offered sea birthing as well; a place that could function as a perfect environment for conscious delivery and conception, as well as allow extended time for the family to be together after the birth—a place for women and children first.

Since this was a child of our imaginations, the project soon expanded to include an interspecies study center with hi-tech computers, satellite video conference capabilities, and an educational faculty that could teach some of the knowledge acquired through the interspecies connection. We also expressed our concerted agreement to collaborate as closely as possible with the Maori, to work alongside them, and to help them develop their skills and artistic enterprises. What a setup that would be! We wondered if we would see it manifest in our lifetimes.

Our first night at the Bay of Spirits was intense—and seemingly not just for Michael and me. After once more gazing up at the massive and mysterious head, we returned to our camp and found Roberta and David, as well as Jacques Mayol and a woman friend of his. All had had the same idea to explore the bay.

We met for a simple meal, each party bringing and sharing their food. During the meal the wind picked up and soon was howling around the tortoise, with the rain yammering on its thin tin roof. We spoke about the holistic birthing and health center, and the wind and the rain noticeably abated, giving the occasion a sense of grace. David and Roberta added their concept of an interspecies traveling roadshow as an outreach project of the center, and we all speculated happily and wildly on whether the Maoris would ever build us large, oceangoing canoes and whether the dolphins would accompany us. Off we would go, continent to continent, bay to bay, harbor to harbor, bearing with us the wonder of the whales and dolphins; the latest in extraterrestrial innovations, appropriate technology, Earth magic and mysteries; an ecological clearing house and information center; the technology of light, sound and fun; entheogenic initiations and ceremonies; and all the news of importance that misses the media. This dream was something well nigh inconceivable now, yet held firmly in the hearts of creative people, we all agreed that it would surely manifest when its time had come. With this evocation of the Creative Spirit, we parted company and attempted to settle down for the night.

It must have been around midnight, and the heavy rain of earlier had been blown away more thoroughly by a new and gusty wind. Michael and I walked down to the beach by the intermittent light of an almost-full moon. The Dog Star, Sirius, and its dark companion hung directly overhead. Mystery was in the air. "If you see the Oannes, invite 'em back for tea and cookies," I called to Michael as we separated.

Michael decided to stay out for the night, so he told me later, to confront the last of the fears that he had found in his new human vehicle. One of the first tasks of the walk-in, you will recall, is to work off the encoded fears and pain of the body's previous owner. I went back to the tortoise to shiver through a few hours of psychic and spiritual turmoil. Even Jacques, not a man given to indulging his imagination, told me the next day that he had never felt such powerful emanations as he experienced that night. He assured me that he was not normally "sensitive to such things."

For me the turmoil began mildly—I imagine with a bout of self-doubt or some such silliness—but before I could stop it, it had built up to a wave of pain and terror that continued to sweep over me. Fortunately I was no newcomer to such horrors so I knew there was no fighting it off. I just had to sit there and witness this thoroughly unpleasant psychic storm.

Now, as I write and piece it all together with the advantage of retrospect, I can see that this whole event may well have had something to do with our friendly Midwayer, our BVF, who was still traveling with us. I know now that in any encounter with higher-vibrational intelligences, the lower frequency will be upstepped by the higher. The results of this in the lower frequency life form is often panic. The fear circuits encoded into the body on a cellular level are activated by the vibrational increase, with what can be terrifying results.

Looking through my journal, I see signs that I may have once again blown my cool and pestered the poor creature to manifest. The desire sometimes overtakes me, it pains me to say, for a definite proof of the existence of these other levels of life—an event that I can experience with *all* my senses. I knew the BVF had been instrumental in guiding us here, and earlier in the evening I had asked it to keep me free of the many mosquitoes, a small but important task that it carried out excellently. Perhaps it would decide to manifest tonight, my dear old mind thought. Maybe that is why we had been brought to this strange and isolated place.

Of course, nothing like that happened. If and when it ever does, it will probably be when I am least expecting it. But my expectations, and my mind, sometimes get the better of me, and I start thinking about all those times the BVF must have appeared to other human beings. Why not now? Why not to me? Not a squawk. In fact, for my troubles, I got a stream of horrifying and fearful images layering over me, which must have continued for hours.

The odd thing about the images was that they did not seem to be mine. Having been born into a war and my first memories being fearful, and having spent a lot of time taking on my terrors and facing them, I have a good idea at this point what my own fears are, what they look like, and how to deal with them. But this was something different. I wondered if they could be hells of others' making, perhaps?

When the psychic turbulence finally lifted and my mind had cleared enough to be able to handle a pen, I saw that I had written: "The world mind has within it fear-trapped thoughtforms just as you do, and it is these that you are in the process of releasing."

Thanks a lot!

I did not sleep that night and stumbled out early to a new dawn. How perpetually astonishing and happily sobering it is that after a night like the one through which I had just shivered, a new day should arise. The self-importance of fear! A violet glow suffused the air over the dragonhead . . . Ah, the bright dawn of clarity. Darkness vanquished again.

I met up with Michael, who had had an equally horrible night sleeping out on the beach, and together we climbed up the cliff to the Maori burial caves. We went barefoot in appreciation of the holiness of the land and found to our delight that each footstep was cushioned by the welcoming ground. This sense of total safety, of no particularly vicious thistle or any other deadly little critter—nothing to stand in the way of a full and deep knowing of the Earth—continued throughout our time in the Bay of Spirits. User-friendly countryside, I remember thinking at the time.

We found the burial caves, ancient and no longer functioning as a graveyard, to be perfectly formed hollows, evidently created by the sudden expansion of the gasbubbles in the lava. These were joined by small volcanic gulleys that had been shaped in part by hand.

About halfway up the cliff, the slope fell away beneath us in a gentle curve of meadows, broken by large outcroppings of volcanic rock, until it reached the lapping surf of the Bay of Spirits. This was sacred land, and in the half-light of dawn it looked supernaturally beautiful, pulsing with radiant promise.

We caught our breath while the world changed color around us. Once again we let our creative imaginations run free, and we quickly saw that the bubblelike holes of the burial caves must go all through the headland. If this were so, then the entire complex of buildings we imagined could be built into the mountain itself—and done in a way that would bring plenty of light into the rooms.

This removed our last reservation—of spoiling the landscape with our human-made structures. At their most ideal, the two can augment one another, and we wished nothing but the finest for our collective dream.

We continued on, snaking our way up and around the cliff. I was in front of Michael when, rounding a bluff, I came into the presence of the giant head. Here it was. It stood about fifteen feet high—an enormous cranium molded onto an absurdly small neck. All the features were there, just as we had seen them from the ground, seemingly carved out of a single large conglomerate of lava and mixed rock.

If it was made by human skill, then what an exquisite piece of Earth art, but I could see no indication that it had been worked. Possibly it was a natural feature that had been helped along by some ancient hand, the tooling now veiled by erosion. But how wonderfully enigmatic was its slight smile and how immensely peaceful—the work of an extraordinary artist!

Yet neither was this the head of a creature who knew gravity. The neck belied it. We watched and wondered as we gazed up into its huge face. Was this what our BVF had wanted us to see? Was there perhaps something of the BVFs' own creative juices in this? I have no doubt that this species molds natural features to their design, using the elements and the immense time spans of nature to create their wonders. I have seen their vast, sculpted pictograms on the sheer walls of the Gorge of Samaria in Crete and an apparently natural stone circle on a beach in Israel, as well as in other places in my travels. The Australian Aboriginals are well aware, for instance, that their *wandjinas* formed many aspects of the landscape as they moved through dreamtime. Could this enormous head be another of *their* works of art?

Michael and I spent the next few days exploring the area. As in every place of power, we found ourselves at the receiving end of a run of delightful synchronicities. It seemed that everyone we met knew something or somebody we needed to know. When we descended from our first morning's climbing, we came upon a family group of three Maori women with their children sitting beside the track. One of the women was old, well over eighty, and we stopped for the customary salutations. They had evidently been waiting for us—had seen us climbing and wanted to know what we were doing. No aggression, just simple curiosity.

When we started telling them about the underwater birthing conference and water birthing in general, they became extremely agitated—and also very interested. After some talk among themselves in their own language, one of the younger women turned to us and blurted out that it had been known as quite natural for a Maori woman to go off alone to a creek and bear her child into water. We were astonished! In all our time with the Maori, there had never been the slightest suggestion, to my knowledge, that they included water birthing in their traditions. This would certainly account for the intensity of their interest!

When the old woman started talking, the others became silent. "I remember now," she said, quite evidently recalling for the first time, right there in front of us, "that my grandmother told me that her great-grandmother was born into water." That might give us a time fix on when it was discontinued. I knew that the Maoris, communally, had decided to accept the teachings of Christianity, and water birthing was barely likely to have met the standard of propriety encouraged by the wives of those staid old missionaries.

The old lady confirmed it. "It was the missionaries who taught us these new ways," she said, with some rancor in her voice. "But why are you both so interested in this?"

"Because we're sensitive to these issues," Michael told her. "We're sensitive people," I said, rather unnecessarily, and she apologized gracefully for suggesting that we might not be.

We talked some more about the natural wisdom of many of their old ways, and I could see as they were talking to us that they held a deeply buried passion for what they might have lost. They glowed at our genuine interest in the Bay of Spirits, and we told them something of the psychic storm the night before. I thought I glimpsed a quick look exchanged between the two younger women but I felt it discourteous to question them about it.

The conversation soon drew to an end. "I wonder," I found myself saying as we parted (although now I am a little embarrassed by my smugness), "if it'll be people like us who will help you remember the wisdom of some of the old ways."

Over the days at the Bay of Spirits, I had been getting to know Chuck Morton and his wife and family of four children. I had heard guitar music coming from one of the very few tents pitched on the site. Following the sounds one evening, my own guitar tucked under my arm, I came across a young Maori sitting back with a big old Martin steel-string and coaxing out of it some of the most exhilarating music I have ever had the pleasure to hear—the guy was a natural master. I sat down in wonderment, his family making room for me with gentle smiles. He saw my guitar, beamed with delight and nodded for me to join him.

We started fast. My fingers were good from a few months of constant playing, so he let me set a spanking pace, easily moving around me, drawing back, then rippling ahead of my rhythm in a fabulously fluid descent, bending the notes in the air and letting them dance between us. I moved to other rhythmic patterns, and he instantly changed with me, like dolphins flicking through sunlit water, setting up cross-rhythms that pattered and bounced off each other, that echoed the night sounds and the surf beyond, that moved with me and yet gave me the space to move. This was the soul of the music I loved, the sounds and feelings of completely freestyle improvisation. This is what I have come to know as Bozon music—the music of complete honesty and reckless courage—and the virtually telepathic linkage that tends to clear away any ego considerations on the part of the musicians. If each player truly listens, first to the spirit and then to each other, it is as though each one is soon played by the same hand. The feeling is glorious. Bozon music—anyone can do it!

It was like that making music with Chuck. He was fabulously proficient and always completely flexible in the styles he could play, with a tender but strong sense of melody. He loved the freedom and challenges of total improvisation. Somehow, though coming from very different cultures, we clicked musically and were able to meet one another on the mutual terms of pure sound.

Chuck was not only a superb musician but also a fine example of how well adapted a Maori person can choose to become to modern urban society. His wife and family were a delight to be with, languid and laid back but genuinely happy, moving easily with the flow of events. I had seen the family out in the bay, on the beach and in the dunes, picking and digging up and catching their food, moving over the landscape as one being, the parts joined by invisible filaments.

Chuck's problems were those of any musician struggling to make a living in a relatively small city. He confessed, after we had gotten to know one another better, that he, too, was becoming more interested in the old ways of his race. He said that coming here to Maori sacred land with his family and spending time in nature was part of his path; this was how he was getting back in touch with his roots and his heritage.

He told me that at the time of the first missionaries, and after the independent and courageous Maoris had decided they could not win against the unstoppable weight of the European colonizing forces, their wise men and women had gathered to discuss what would happen to their traditional ways. After many arguments had been presented, they came to a consensus on what proved to be a most unusual and farsighted policy. The Maoris knew their ancient traditions well, good and bad. They had brought their knowledge with them halfway across the Pacific only a few hundred years earlier. They were confident their old ways worked. What they did not know was whether this new god Jesus Christ would also work. If he did, then it would surely strengthen their people, and possibly in time they would be able to regain their land and their dignity. Or he would not work, and they could return to the values and traditions of their ancestors. So doing, the elders threw in their lot with the Christian missionaries and, for the last 180 years, they have been making up their minds. I loved the lucidity with which it had all been perceived.

"Are you a Christian, Chuck?" I asked him in one interlude from the music.

He considered the matter before replying, and when he did I could hear his heart speaking. "I would have to call myself a Christian," he said. "I know Christ. I've met him," he said shyly, pointing to his heart. "Inside, I can feel his love. But there are things about Christianity, the religion itself, that make me sad to consider myself one."

I was thinking he would give me the standard objections: church living in plenty while the congregation remained poor; all the wars and killing done in Christ's name. But he was taking a much deeper slice at it. "I don't believe Jesus Christ is the only son of God," he told me, looking straight into my eyes. "We're all sons of God—that's what Jesus himself told us. Then the church came along and turned Jesus into an unattainable figurehead. They made him the one and only Son of God and then tried to manipulate our guilt because we're not as good as Him. It isn't like that at all! Jesus didn't die for our sins—that's another story made up by the church. We are each responsible for ourselves. We each have to live with our own sins until we forgive ourselves. I know that's true because I can feel it."

What a remarkable analysis, I thought, and I asked him if this was a more generally expressed idea among the Maori people. "More and more of the ones my age feel this, if they don't reject Christianity altogether," he said.

Is this the time, I wondered, when the Maoris will decide which way to go on their spiritual journey as a race? They are a formidable people with a deep level of contact with the Spirit. I recalled the intensity and the passion of the Maori singers who surrounded elder Don and myself, and the strange old man's wisdom and quiet confidence. I thought of the generosity and curiosity of our Maori hosts on the marae, admiring their ability not to reveal their own past of water birthing. I believe I realized, in those moments, the degree of clarity indigenous people can bring to bear on belief systems that have supported so much of our Western culture's shortsightedness.

Chuck returned to Auckland with his family to continue his nightly gig at one of the big hotels. We got to see him on the one night we were in town. Although he played with great energy and consummate skill, it made me sad to see someone of his extraordinary talents playing in a piano-bar trio for a small group of generally unappreciative tourists and businessmen. Not for long, I trust.

Michael and I spent a fine day with a fisherman—or, *the* fisherman, as he quickly told us, who had captured the two bumbling French Navy frogmen who blew up the *Rainbow Warrior*, Greenpeace's flagship, which had been attempting to halt France's atomic testing in the South Pacific. An easy catch, he roared with laughter, because they had attempted to disguise themselves as locals in a place where everybody was related to everybody else.

We went out on his boat into Parengarena Harbor, an

enormous natural bay with protected warm waters set against golden sand and black lava. When we asked the fisherman about Maori legends of dolphins in the area, he rather amusedly told us about an old woman who, some years ago, used to regularly ride a shark across the bay.

After you, Michael!

The spirit tree, the pohutakawa, turned out to be somewhat of an anticlimax: just a regular, rather scrawny and weather-beaten old tree, its roots spread wide in search of purchase. Neither of us had any idea of what we might have hoped to see or feel in its presence, but apart from wondering whether the strange night a few days earlier could have been a bunch of newly dead spirits hotfooting down the beach, neither of us had anything like the reaction to Cape Reinga and the spirit tree as we had to the great headland at the other end of the bay. Often the true centers of power in a sacred landscape are occulted, hidden near to the ones that are generally thought to be the main centers. If these hidden loci of power can be located, then the leys—the meridians which connect all these places of sacred telluric energy—can be once more activated by the human creative imagination.

15

A Curse on the City of Sydney

There is very little difference between what lies inside our dolphin and what lies outside of her. She is like a point of consciousness floating in a sea of sounds, of echoes and forms. When she reaches out to another dolphin in help or support, she is reaching out to herself. She feels another's emotions much as she feels her own. Another's pain or joy is simultaneously experienced by all through the giant web of infrasound. Not a nuance is lost as it reverberates in the glistening hologram . . .

"**T**here's a curse on this city!" Michael Miller had stopped walking and was looking at me with a gleam of prophetic certainty in his astonishing blue eyes. We had been in Sydney, Australia, for all of twelve hours. What did *we* know?

Granted, our accommodation could not have been more stylish: the miracle of modern travel; from the Bay of Spirits to Tinsel Town; from a tin tortoise rocked by wind and rain to a magnificent duplex, glitteringly new and overhanging downtown Sydney. How strange it all was! Yet Michael's comment had expressed for both of us our feeling of malaise, of some frightful horror, of some malingering and unfinished business.

We had both felt this dreadful state of despair fall over us within hours of arriving in the city. We had talked about it without really giving it a name as we spent our first evening walking—soaking in the energy of the place. We were fresh and open, having been gently tumbled into new levels of consciousness by the conference and later by the spiritual depth and reality of the Bay of Spirits. Both of us were about as psychically aware as we had ever been.

Michael was telling me about a film he dimly recalled seeing—*The Last Wave,* he thought it was called. Now if I were an obsessive researcher, I would have rented the video and gotten all my facts straight. But I do not own a TV set, let alone a VCR, and my policy has always been to take matters as they come—which is perhaps for the best, because it allows me to approach this ticklish issue without too many preconceptions.

What Michael had remembered of the movie was that it dealt with the city of Sydney and its possible inundation by an enormous tidal wave sweeping in from the Pacific. He also recalled that it featured a tall, fair-skinned, gray-haired, blue-eyed man who somehow had become caught up in aboriginal legend and either saved the city, or not—Michael could not remember which.

I wondered, as Michael was telling me the story, whether this might have colored his feelings toward Sydney, but there was no denying the atmosphere. It lay over us as tangible as smog—a stifling, collective schizophrenia that forced everyone to exist on the surface of their lives while underneath, deep in the caves that honeycomb the hills of the city, madness and horror awaited.

I had seen something of this before: Paris in 1982. My companion and I had found ourselves almost completely swamped by the weight and density of all those centuries of ingrained rationalism and the soporific lifelessness it produced in both of us. Then we had changed the psychic atmosphere, at least for us, by locating the main power center of the city, Notre Dame Cathedral. We climbed the main spire and asked the angels of the place to help us dissipate and release the accumulated layers of fear-trapped thoughtforms. If nothing else, it sure made us feel better. Might the same approach work here, I wondered?

Arriving back at our apartment for the night, I settled down to my journal and a conversation with my guardian angel, Joy. I had been writing some general notes about the city and the various manifestations of the discomfort we were experiencing. I knew we would have to take on these feelings—not resist them but allow them to soak deeply into us so that we could ground and hopefully release them altogether. I also became intuitively aware, as I wrote, that there was something of the Beings of the Violet Flame in all this. In the Bay of Spirits I felt that we were working through some of the psychic overlays of this group of angels—their collective karma—at least to the extent that their actions in the past still resonated in the world mind. I understood that if we did this, it would allow the BVF to be more effective within their realm, since they are required to abide by human choices. In the changes to come, we will doubtless all be laboring together in more open cooperation, humans and angels alike, but for now our two species need to reconcile our differences as best as we can.

When Michael had asked me over dinner who was present with us in Sydney, I found myself telling him, without thinking: "One of the Melchizedek Brethren, a BVF, and our angels and guides." Yet we both knew the initiative had to be ours.

It was at this point in my meditation that Joy's voice came through: "Greetings. Know we love you and are with you in all the work you are doing. You are indeed becoming more conscious of our combined functioning." (I fancy I might have been moaning about having to figure it all out myself. I sensed that it amused her to see me wrestling with these matters—*she* knew I was getting stronger for it!) "And it is right that it should be so. We are weaving a magnificent new reality, full of the collaborative designs of humans and angels. To know one another more intimately is to make the overall fabric that much more fascinating. It is therefore perfectly holy to call on us.

"Your intuitions regarding Sydney are indeed accurate," she continued. "There are deep levels of activity that have been covered up over time. The city feels profoundly superficial, as you had remarked, because, as a reality construct, it rests uneasily on the reality matrix of the previous peoples. You have already taken in that the Aborigines are a very superior people in many ways. Their sense of natural integrity makes them a race from whom much can and will be learned. You have observed, too, how little they figure in the Sydney Arts Festival." (We had spent some of the afternoon looking around the festival, held out of doors in Hyde Park.) "This is symptomatic of the way they are regarded. Unlike the Maoris, who have chosen to integrate their culture—and therefore their reality construct—with yours, the Australian Aborigines have chosen to move farther into the desert hinterlands of the continent. In this way, they can still practice their immensely useful psychic capabilities—of special value at this point in time since the human race is moving toward practical telepathy.

"The Australian Aborigines know more about telepathy and psychic communication than any other race alive on the planet today," Joy went on. "They will become your teachers in the times to come, as you are able to integrate them into the new global culture. By raising the curse and formally releasing the negative thoughtforms, you are effecting a release for them that has been long held. Continue along the lines you have been receiving. Ask for help, and you shall receive it. Find the power point, and you shall be joined by a third. I wish you all the affirmations of my station. May our Beloved grace us all."

Taking Joy's admonition to heart, and by following our own natural cycles, Michael and I soon found the city's main power spot. A combination of intuition and asking three of the local cognoscenti led us to the Archibald Fountain. However, as with many active power centers, the actual spot was a bit removed from that generally thought to be the place of power. We decided to scout out the location, then do some research in the museum before returning at dusk for our ritual. The Archibald Fountain, when we found it, was in the middle of the aforementioned arts festival. Although an obviously imposing structure (if a trifle pompous), it did not feel to either of us as if it possessed much real power. Apart from that, it had been festooned with a number of life-sized cut-out figures, hideously painted to represent a tableau of city lowlife. Whatever sacred powers the fountain might be imbued with on a good day, the degrading images destroyed them.

With gratitude to the unknown artist for making it so obvious, we continued our walk along an avenue of enormous spreading trees, until there, on the right-hand side, gurgled another fountain. This one was far more modest in proportions and, according to its plaque, was a gift from British royalty in commemoration of King George V. Sunk a few feet into the ground, it was a circular pool with twenty-four individual fountains of water—not an insignificant number, we agreed. But what drew us both were some beautifully flowing aboriginal designs that were tiled on the bottom of the pool and flickering up at us through the dappled water. We could see two snakes circling another figure, which looked as though it might be a turtle. The telluric "hit" was immediate and undeniable: this far more laid-back and magical place was in actuality, at least right then for us, the true center of the hidden powers of Sydney—and one that, in a city as troubled as this, combined the best of both cultures.

Having found the fountain, we made our way to the Australian Museum to see what information it might have on the Aborigines. I had not used a museum in quite this way before, but I soon found that by going around and participating in the exhibits—a stone mortar and pestle, for instance, that a visitor could grind away at for a minute or two to get the feel of it—I was picking up psychometrically some things that booklearning would never permit.

The story, as it unfolded, was a bitter and sad one and not unlike the fate of the American Indians. The Aborigines, however, with few exceptions, were hardly an aggressive people. Nomadic, they had split during their forty thousand years of continuous oral tradition into more than five hundred tribes with as many different languages. Collectively, they are a people who love their land with such an intimate intensity that they literally *become* it, are inseparable from it. There can scarcely be an outcropping of rock or a stand of trees on the whole continent that is not named and sung. As is now more generally known, they preserve their web of traditions in hugely complex songs, which then serve as sacred milestones on their journeys. They "sing" the landscape as they move through it from waterhole to waterhole, sacred place to sacred place. They are in such harmony with their surroundings that even now it is hard to recognize an aboriginal encampment the day after they have moved on. Everything is returned to its correct place.

Their traditions tell of *wandjinas,* most generally interpreted to mean "spirit ancestors." "The wandjinas came from the north in Dreamtime," said a museum pamphlet, "and wandering over the area, they created some of the physical features of the landscape. Each wandjina wandered until he reached the place he was to die. After painting his image there, he entered a nearby deep waterhole, making that his permanent home."

But the wandjina does not necessarily die, my intuition tells me: it lives on to guide the Aborigines in their explorations of Dreamtime. And Dreamtime, I suspect, is none other than an alternate reality, the sorcerer's *nagual*—a fourth-dimensional stepping stone to the fifth-dimensional reality.

The immediate problems of the Aborigines are still numerous, but the larger Australian awareness is on the move. In spite of their surprisingly scant showing at the festival, it is largely through their art that the Aborigines are accomplishing this, and at such an early stage in the great transformation, I have little doubt that we are seeing only what our Western culture is currently able to handle and assimilate.

We felt something of the potency of aboriginal art later on that afternoon, in an upmarket gallery on top of Grace's department store. I have never felt in art such a power and immediacy as was hung on those walls. Michael, with his vivid imagination, told me later that he had found himself in the desert with Uluru—the enormous red rock in the center of the continent—rearing up in front of him. I did not doubt it: art this energetically evocative has the capability of recreating the environment in which it was conceived and created.

On a number of paintings, the dominant symbol portrayed was that of *Njaljod,* the Rainbow Serpent, and as often as not, there were two serpents going in opposite directions. It came to me that this was a clear indication that the Aborigines know time flows in two directions at once—a concept with which even the most progressive Western physicists are only beginning to struggle.

We arrived back at our fountain as the sun was setting. The newly mown lawns around the circle cast a scent of natural simplicity over us as we relaxed and waited for the departure of a small group of Japanese, intent on being photographed one after another, flash bulbs crackling in front of the fountain. The damp grass felt good to our bare feet, shoe bound as we had been again for a day of city life. We settled into the deeper atmosphere, meditating together until we felt the Holy Spirit join us. When we opened our eyes, the Japanese had left, and the twenty-four individual spouts of water were bobbing and quivering, seemingly in constant conversation with one another.

As I came out of my silence, my senses slowed and opened. It was as if I could hear and identify each and every one of those twenty-four voices; and in those moments I knew—through happy numerical correspondence—that the esteemed Council of Elders stood together with us for the time of our ensuing sacred ceremony.

Michael and I walked together slowly, counterclockwise, three times around the pool. Blossoms of the red and white flowers, planted in regular rows in the borders enclosing the fountain, glimmered in the crepuscular light while the general hubbub lessened, leaving, in that way of cities, a sudden stillness, as if every living being were simply listening at the same time.

We evoked the spirit of the land, the devas and nature spirits, the appropriate angels, and any extraterrestrial or interdimensional beings who might happen to be listening in. We asked for the cooperation of all those of the human races who might wish to be involved on a soul level and also the dolphins who, if they were half as telepathic as we now believed, were probably tuned in to every nuance of what was happening.

We came to rest after our circumnavigations, one on each side (north and south) of the circle. I found myself drawn to address a first prayer to the Trinity. I thanked and sent out the love of my heart to the Creator Father, Biami of the Aborigines, the First Source and Center, a prepersonal shard of whom lives in each one of us. And with that, I threw into the pool a stone I had been carrying from American Indian sacred land in New Mexico—a water stone from the Pecos River near Santa Fe. The fountains seemed to gurgle joyfully

Next, I prayed to the Great Mother Spirit, Eternal Creatrix, the mater, or matter, of us all; and I placed in the water a small piece of kauri bark that I had brought with me from New Zealand. It bobbed away into the downspill of one of the fountains.

The light was dimming fast, and standing quietly by the pool, I breathed away any remaining doubts concerning the sanity of what we were doing. We had been in the city only twenty-eight hours, and here we were presuming to attempt a reconciliation between races that have been locked in disharmony for hundreds of years. Pretentious? Absurd? Of course. Yet we are assured by the angels that if a problem such as this can be presented to the universal authorities and help asked for—a right that we all have—and that if such a petition should be granted, then it assures a positive outcome for the best of all—the best of ALL. "The act is ours, the consequence is God's," we are told, and this was no time for a crisis of faith.

Last, I prayed to the Infinite Spirit: the active principle of the Creator, whose life force we breathe and who sustains us in the light. I offered our deepest gratitude for the gift of life and consciousness, and I asked for help in the reconciliation to be achieved between our two races. I let drop into the water a small white feather that I had picked up earlier on the streets of Sydney. It spun for a moment before being buffeted by minute tidal waves into the center of the pool.

A huge silver moon, almost full, slid up over the trees, bringing a renewed sheen to our rite of urban geomancy

. . . . Now it was Michael's turn. He addressed the Supreme—the very best of us ALL, a god in the making. He called upon the Supreme to come forth in the actions of all those, aboriginal and white alike, who are involved with the real issues of coexistence. Saying that, he threw into the water one of his most precious possessions, a small malachite turtle that had represented for him divine protection.

We turned as one and joined each other on the west side of the fountain. As we stood together, we expressed our profoundest sorrow at the crimes and cruelty of our people, both past and present, and we asked the Aborigines of today to forgive us, if they could find it in their hearts to do so. Such excesses will never happen again, we felt sure. Besides, the True Age, I have no doubt, will put an end to all that foolishness. We know that these have been desperately difficult times for everybody—those of all races and places. Indeed, those whose function it is to classify and compare life on other planets tell us that our small sphere is third to worst—that is, third to worst out of the ten million inhabited worlds of this local universe!

Until now, of course. Because now everything is changing. The planet is transforming itself, and we are being drawn along with it (some of us complaining) all the way. The spirit of reconciliation is sweeping the land, and it is in the release of the energy so long trapped in conflict that the true power lies.

"All things are made anew," our supernaphim, Shandron, had told us in Toronto. Whether *we* knew it or not! Whether we *believed* it or not! And in this newness, can Aborigine and white coexist in a vital, creative, growing, deepening relationship to the mutual benefit of all? With open hearts and an intention to succeed in the endeavor, might it not be possible to find a path of mutual respect in which both races could share their knowledge and their resources in harmony with each other? Would not the spiritual coming together of these two races become the basis of tremendous hope to others still locked in strife? Tremendous hope.

Surely every Australian of every race and cultural group

would feel that much more joyful, more relieved of ambient guilt and hatred, more deeply elated to know that a peaceful, harmonious, co-creative future was sought and wished for by all. Although it seemed inconceivable to us as we stood in the moonlight, the twenty-four fountains murmuring silver thoughts, the two serpents dimly seen wriggling within the ripples on the water, we prayed passionately that sometime soon it would indeed be so.

16

The Artist and the Shaman

Because of their extraordinary sensitivity and also the particularly conducive electrical qualities of large bodies of saline water, dolphins are privy to all those signals that pour into our planet's electromagnetic envelope from the sun and other close solar and planetary bodies. Our young female dolphin receives a continual flow of information that cascades down to her from the galactic core, down-stepped through the constellations and finally whirling out from the sun itself . . .

"**N**etwork of Light" is a term many of us have used—long before George Bush Sr. ever extolled his "thousand points of light"—to cover the wide-ranging matrix of people who are awakening to the great changes that lie ahead. As a network of people, this loose-knit group is just getting to know itself, and those involved are finding themselves progressively more thrown together. We are drawn surely, from every background, every national or racial group, but as I am sure you are discovering, there are clear signs of cosmic complicity that shine through all our differences.

The Network of Light is not a computer hookup; neither is it a newsletter, a society, nor a club. There is no membership;

there are no rules, no dues. So far our members are small—some sixty million worldwide, so my angelic sources tell me—but more are awakening to their spiritual destiny every day. Most are still not aware that they are linked to this circuit, except possibly in dreams, or the strange feelings they experience under certain circumstances. Many have not yet fully awakened to their position in the network, but they will—as in time, all will.

Over the next ten to twenty years, all of us will have the chance to experience an extraordinarily rapid period of growth. As the planet transforms, so will we, and vice versa. We are being given the chance to work collaboratively with angels and extraterrestrials; to become recipients of all the knowledge so long hidden from us; to be able to re-form our ideas of an inhabited universe and what it might mean to become part, once again, of our cosmic family.

These are the areas that are being pioneered by the Network of Light, and with these realizations come certain, rather weighty responsibilities. The highest of these responsibilities is to be who we truly are. Each of us is an active participant in this network to the extent of our level of self-recognition, not in the sense of self-aggrandizement but with the reality of having experienced, and made our peace with, the indwelling God.

This process of assimilating God-consciousness can take twelve years or more, suggests R.B.Bucke, after the original transformation breakthrough, to ground itself within the psyche and the physical body. His splendid book, *Cosmic Consciousness,* is of immense value in presenting a series of signposts through this long and strange period. Bucke was among the first to identify what could be happening to consciousness on the planet and to weave it into an evolutionary context. At this point, in the early stages of the global transformation, the task of grounding the conceptual possibilities of fourth-dimensional consciousness into the world mind is being taken on by those who have been trained through many lifetimes to fulfill specific roles. It is a very large plan and certainly encompasses all of human history. There is also no halting it.

To those contemporary thinkers like Umberto Eco, the hero of whose delightful and humorous book *Foucault's Pendulum* expends vast efforts wondering if there is a grand plan, the answer is probably disturbing. Not only *is* there a grand plan, but there are at least *two* that I know about and quite probably others as well. Doubtless the upcoming events are of sufficient importance as to be most carefully shepherded along. But the plan of the Network of Light is written in our hearts, and since it is also of the Kingdom of Heaven, it protects itself naturally from power manipulation and unscrupulous behavior. It is also the Holy Grail, which is surely not only an object but a state of consciousness open to all who purify their hearts. The Great Work is the grounding—literally, the earthing—of this state of consciousness into the world mind and soul of the planet. It marks the arrival of the True Age.

Of course, we have immense aid in this, since it is a task of vital interest to beings of the inner and outer spaces, many of whom are here specifically to help us along. Beings from the star system Arcturus in the constellation Bootes and several groups from the Pleiades have already made themselves known to us, as have other races in less obvious ways. What they all tell us supports the view that we are about to go through a quantum leap in consciousness. They know it because they have undergone it themselves. The Arcturians claim that it could happen any day now, but I suspect that they, too, are a little overoptimistic in their timing.

The Network of Light functions like most natural progressions of critical-mass change. It is the straw that breaks the camel's back and the much-maligned hundredth monkey munching on her yam. Up to this point in time, those in the Network of Light have been buried in the fabric of our cultures the world over. We are the moles of cosmic espionage. Our influences stretch out to include every aspect of life that will survive the transition. As we raise our own energies, and as the vibratory frequencies of the planet herself ascend to new levels, so also are our reality constructs being drawn up with us. We are the nursing mothers of this new reality, the very vehicles through which the great transformation is being accomplished.

I have been very fortunate and privileged to meet a number of these participants in the Network of Light in different parts of the world—I seem to be guided to them. Whether in Peru or Paris, Britain or the Bahamas, California or Calcutta, New York, New South Wales, or New Mexico, they all have one thing in common: a wonderful glimmer of knowingness in the twinkle of their eyes.

Bali was to be no exception.

Michael and I had never intended to stay very long in Australia, and as he had begun having a succession of vivid dreams and waking visions featuring the Balinese volcano Mount Agung, he wanted to go and see what it all meant. A little extravagant, I thought at the time, but since Michael was taking care of the tickets . . . Thus, we arrived in Denpasar, the largest city on the island of Bali, on a delicious sultry day in late January.

We both loved the spirit of the island as soon as we landed. A powerfully strong presence made us welcome and beckoned us further into the island. We were so excited we almost fell into a beaten-up old cab, which humped and hooted its way through the crowded, narrow village streets until we reached the intensely green fields of the southern lowlands. Water buffalo turned to watch us lurching along as we kept our eyes open for a good place to stay the night. When we reached Peliatan, a small village just outside the town of Ubud, we both had a sense of happy recognition: it just felt right. The driver wrestled his cab to a stop. We paid him the astonishingly small fare and made our way into a courtyard compound advertising itself as Mandala Cottages. Perfect.

Cottage number seven was available. We followed a winding path past heavily scented, flowering shrubs; under stone archways; around a large open-air stage upon which stood the musical impedimenta of a full gamelon orchestra, polished and glowing in the late afternoon sun; and finally arrived at a beautifully crafted little hut. Its thatching curved up on subtly shaped wood rafters, and a large, superbly carved and painted garuda bird stood over the doorway. It was a warm and elegant welcome.

The Ubu/Peliatan area turned out to be the main center of the artistic enterprises of the islanders. Although the villagers have had no choice but to cater to the increasing number of tourists deposited there by tour buses, they have managed to preserve something of the integrity of the spirit so prevalent in Bali. The gods and goddesses of Hinduism and Buddhism seemed ever present. Temples dotted the landscape, and sacred sculptures with small sacrifices of food beautifully arranged at their feet can be found in almost every street. Each bridge had its sculpted protectors, as often as not wrapped in curious checkered sarongs that to our uninitiated eyes appeared to be the sort of tablecloths found in a French bistro. Together with the Buddhist and Hindu cultures, there was also a flourishing group of Moslems in certain parts of the island. With very little strife, they all managed to coexist in a remarkable degree of harmony.

A story passed on to me by the family that owns and runs Mandala Cottages serves to convey the essence of the spiritual atmosphere of the place. By all accounts, through the 1960s and early seventies, the Balinese had collectively allowed their spiritual and religious observances to slacken to a point where the impact of Western culture was far outweighing the importance of spiritual values in the minds of most islanders. Apparently, this culminated when a particularly sacred ceremony was delayed expediently so that it could be combined with another more frequently celebrated ritual—it was simply more convenient.

Then came the night of the volcano. Entire villages were swept away by rivers of molten lava. Tens of thousands were killed and never found, buried under twenty feet of magma. The gods had spoken. The Balinese could read the signs. Once again all the offerings were made, the ceremonies were correctly observed, and the people turned back to their spiritual heritage. So the situation now stands, as the small island continues to absorb more and more travelers and tourists every year. No place occupied by human beings is going to be entirely devoid of problems, but the Balinese are confronting the rapid change with great dignity, a lot of humor, and a built-in sense of grace.

Our hostess and host, Siti and Ri, were fine examples of these very Balinese characteristics in action. Somewhere in the middle of their lives, they were both physically quite beautiful. Siti was small and compact, with a perfectly composed face and almost fiercely aware eyes. Ri, as large as Siti was small and with the balance of a dancer, was infinitely patient and kind. They both had the bearing of royalty, and it turned out that the vast extended family living within the compound were all part of the oldest and finest dance group on the island—and the compound had indeed once been part of a royal palace.

I suspect that the Balinese like their emotional lives to be somewhat complex because every generation, from greatgrandparents to the smallest newborn of a third wife's cousin, seemed to dwell in one or another of the small cottages that dotted the compound. All the elements of a first-rate soap opera were present, yet Siti and Ri presided over the ever-shifting tapestry with continuing aplomb and remarkably good humor.

As with almost all Balinese, our hosts' sense of place was so exquisite that little was ever added or subtracted without immense thought and care. That first night I sat out on our spacious veranda, a torrent of tropical flowers all around me, and watched as dusk fell with unaccustomed speed. Small lights were lit and perched—perfectly placed as perhaps they had been for generations—on walls and among the trees. They sputtered and throbbed in the new darkness with the sounds of the nearby forest. Two geckoes danced up the white walls on padded feet, to hang as still as death on either side of the carved garuda bird. The air was moist and strongly scented, and the pyschic atmosphere was thick with activity.

What was it that gave Bali its almost electrical psychic charge? I turned inward to Joy, who said to me, "Greetings, Beloved. You have been drawn here to witness the product of much experimental work by the BVF. Here you see the fruits of their labors and people who quite consciously await the coming of the Supreme."

Then she turned me over to an unnamed Being of the Violet Flame, who informed me in a clear voice, "Greetings, brother of the flesh. We are strongly here with you. You will see our hand very directly among the people you encounter. These are people who have kept their openness to our contact by experiencing our support and cooperation. A Balinese knows that we are effective, even though he or she might perceive us as household gods—somewhat similar to the tutelary deities of the Cretans, the Greeks, and the Romans. In answer to your unspoken question as to how you can be of most value to the overall situation, I will say that it is merely your presence here that will create the desired effect. There is no need to say or do anything [out of the ordinary]; you will be recognized, and the situation will progress accordingly."

I thanked the BVF and turned in for the night.

Although Michael's health had improved immeasurably since he had first appeared on our New York doorstep, he was still far from well. And he knew it—so much so that I wondered whether among his more unconscious reasons for coming to Bali was the hope of encountering one of the island's indigenous healers. Our first visit with Gusti confirmed this.

Gusti was a young Balinese artist who had a gallery/studio in Ubud. His work, to one not yet versed in the island's art, was both intricate and expressive, as well as very symbolic. When I came to know the style better, I soon realized that it was a visual affectation trotted out by virtually every painter in the area. But as we sat there in the small brick room, surrounded by paintings of all sizes, sipping tea served to us by Gusti's beautiful young wife, a tiny child perched on her hip, I was struck hard by the Escher-like precision and the controlled flamboyance of Gusti's canvases.

The artist, however, when he found out about our interests, became far more concerned with telling us about his meditation teacher than with presenting his art. As I came to know him better, I understood how depressed he had become at reaching a creative impasse in his painting. He knew that his spiritual truth lay in his artistic journey, but somewhere along the line the responsibilities of a wife and children, or possibly the ease of a readily known and easily accomplished style, had stultified his vision and made it impossible for him to grow and blossom into what he could well become: a painter of real genius.

As Gusti described his teacher, a certain Mr. Ketut Cutet (his last name pronounced, appropriately enough, "tutor"), and enumerated some of his many spiritual attributes, I became aware that the artist was trying to convey another factor for which he could not find words and that possibly he did not want to spell out too clearly anyway. Mr. Cutet, it seemed, was something of a rebel and not a member of one of the rigidly delineated priesthoods of the island. He did very much what he thought best, and in a place where custom and tradition were all important, he was quite predictably shunned by the orthodox priests. We were to see more of this later. The best news, however, was that Mr. Cutet was a healer of singular power and skill. Gusti suggested that perhaps Michael would like to go and see him.

A time was decided, Gusti enthusiastically volunteered to interpret, and a couple of days later found us crushed amiably into a Balinese *bemo,* an old VW bus with seats along the side walls. Michael, our intrepid walk-in, was definitely somewhat trepidatious, laughing and joking a little too loudly with the other Balinese occupants.

Mr. Ketut Cutet lived some three or four villages distant, and when we had to dismount from the bemo, it was to walk through a small village not as accustomed to odd-looking foreigners as Ubud or Peliatan. We picked up our token group of small staring children, stamped through the puddles of a recent tropical deluge, and finally found the teacher's compound down a long lane, the enclosing walls of which glowed green with moss on venerable stones.

We were met by Gusti, who had already arrived, and led into what we took to be the healer's reception room. Half a dozen other Balinese sat around the dank little chamber with its small, grubby coconut mats on the floor. Michael must have felt some momentary misgivings that any good could come from such dilapidation.

After ten minutes of fitful talk, the holy man himself came to join us. Small, strong, dressed in nondescript clothes, his face and head brown and incredibly smooth, Mr. Cutet looked far more Tibetan than Balinese. Most remarkable were his eyes, which, when he finally took off his Sukarno-style dark glasses, appeared to be intensely animated, dark-brown pools of vital energy. Surely these were windows to a strange but caring soul.

Michael explained about his left eye, which had never recovered from the impact of his ski accident, and Mr. Cutet listened patiently to the translation. The healer then bowed his beautifully polished head, gripping his own temples on either side with the forefinger and thumb of his right hand. I could see the skin of his face whiten under the pressure he was exerting. After a few minutes of this concentrated silence, Mr. Cutet announced that Michael was "ill all over"—a diagnosis that came as no surprise to Michael, since he had been told by a radionics practitioner back in the States that his blood was in very poor shape and that this had resulted in a systemic malaise. However, Mr. Cutet also told Michael that he could heal him.

I was interested to note that when the subject of fees came up, the healer merely told Michael to give him "whatever he thought it was worth to him." Clearly he was no charlatan!

Michael sat with his back against the whitewashed wall while Mr. Cutet worked first on his feet, then on his knees and thighs. The healer appeared to be manipulating pressure points on the main meridians, because poor old Michael started sighing and grimacing in agony. The other people in the room, although obviously fascinated by what was going on, discreetly turned away from his pain.

Then Mr. Cutet was pushing and pressing into all the blockages in Michael's stomach and chest, finally tapping hard and rapidly on my friend's thymus. Michael was starting to get the look of a punching bag, rocking under this barrage of carefully aimed blows.

Going around behind him, Mr. Cutet then struck the base of Michael's spine three times, extremely hard. I could see by this time that Michael was wondering what in heaven's name he had gotten himself into, but there was more to come.

Next, the head—seat of so much mystery. Thirteen billion brain cells, each with upward of three hundred connections. Star stuff. Incomparable biocomputer, the result of so many million years of evolutionary design . . .

Mr. Cutet, however, evidently came from a rather different school of thought. He spent some time cupping Michael's head in one or another hand while emitting all the while a low, buzzing sound. Then, as suddenly as had come the thwacks to the base of the spine, Mr. Cutet was blowing hard into Michael's ear. I mean *really* hard—a lesser man's brains might well have shot out the other side.

Much to my surprise, I found myself experiencing an intense rush of energy while Mr. Cutet was delivering these final blasts of prana. I knew, in those moments, that the shaman was in actuality driving out the fear-trapped thoughtforms—Mr. Cutet would have probably called them demons—from Michael's poor, wrecked body.

This whole process, which lasted about twenty minutes, left Michael coughing up reservoirs of mucus he did not know he possessed and spluttering in pain and surprise. Mr. Cutet gathered us all around in a final prayer and a short meditation, and when that was over, he moved rapidly on to his next patient.

When we emerged into the soft sunlight and the unexpected scents of the compound, I had to admit that my friend looked much more alive and vigorous than I could remember seeing him, although I recall wondering whether it might not have been the relief that comes after so much pain. However, after two more sessions over the next couple of days, it became clearly evident that Mr. Cutet had initiated a very real healing, and Michael appeared, all in all, a new man for it.

I also accompanied Michael on his second visit, but this time I chose not to become involved with Mr. Cutet's healing work. From the sounds I heard while I sat drawing the cottages in the compound, it was even more strenuous than the first. As I finished my sketch, which I later gave as a present to Mr. Cutet, one of his sons approached me, saw what I was up to, and asked if he could show me his paintings. They were exquisite, not at all in the convention of Balinese painting, but passionate and beautifully crafted. For a boy of sixteen or seventeen years old, they were truly masterful—as was his guitar playing. I knew in my heart that I had been casually guided to see and hear one of those amazing prodigies who appear only once every so often in any culture.

After the furor in the hut had died down to a gentle burble of conversation, Michael appeared. He looked a lot sicker this time, but he assured me that it was only a healing crisis and that he knew he was well on the way to full recovery.

He had also made the point of telling Mr. Cutet something of the dolphin reality, getting across as best as he could through Gusti's willing but haphazard interpretation the amazing possibilities of dolphin telepathy. He soon found out that he had to fight through the Balinese entrenched dread of the sea. They have been taught that the oceans are replete with demons, a belief system that generally holds them in a panic of insularity.

Mr. Cutet, by training and inclination more courageous than most, seemed to be able to grasp the main issue of what Michael was telling him. He insisted on putting us in contact with an old friend of his, a sea captain from the nearby island of Lombok, who he said would agree to take us out to where the dolphins could be found. Thus, when we were least expecting it, the dolphin journey opened up once again.

17

A Strange Full Moon Ceremony

Dolphins are constantly in touch with all manner of wave forms. They sail free of gravity, and yet what secrets they could tell us of all the scents and colors and melodies carried by those great, long, slow gravity waves—waves that sweep out from the galactic core carrying information of a kind greatly valued by advanced societies. Our young dolphin would know all about that. Her growing is her mastering of her ability to comprehend the enormous amount of data continually pouring in . . .

"**I**t is suggested that you use MDMA for the full moon ceremony" was the last statement I had received from my BVF friend when I was trying to get the angelic view of Bali. Now, some might think that getting counsel from an angel to do substance is simply a highfalutin' justification for taking a trip, but it happens rarely enough that I am always happy to give it due consideration.

One reason that MDMA, or Ecstasy, as it is known colloquially, proves to be such an interesting chemical is that it enables ego-bound patterns to be gently shunted aside, allowing them to be replaced by genuine heart-to-heart communication. In its all-too-brief career as a psychotherapeutic tool, according to the professionals who used it with their patients, it helped to produce many rare and wonderful breakthroughs. And, since it is an empathogen, it seems also to permit the psi field of the user to upstep the localized vibratory field of those with whom she or he has come into contact. It is therefore a substance to be taken with great care and attention; sometimes, when a person's emotional and psychic field becomes rapidly or unexpectedly accelerated, the dross will be the first to surface. Like chicken soup over a stove, the scum has to be lifted off before the soup becomes clear and palatable. If this is not known and understood, the ecstatic sense of inner joy can easily be shattered by the mayhem created in others. But the angel must have suggested it for a good reason, so I chose to trust that the consequences would also be good.

Participation in the full moon ceremony had been offered to us by Siti and Ri when they realized that Michael and I were sincere men of the Spirit. It would also be a chance for us to get to meet our hosts' teacher, Adi—everybody seems to have a teacher in Bali—who lived on the other side of the island. Meanwhile, we explored Ubud and the surrounding countryside.

In the manner of sacred places, everyone we needed to meet or to whom we wished to talk would appear suddenly around a wall or be standing on a bridge, seemingly waiting just for us.

We spent much of our days before the night of the ceremony clambering over the landscape. We would make our way down to a holy junction of two streams of clear water, one female and the other male, which joined to make a third, and then climb up and over the massive ridge shaped like the head of a vast reptile, swaying in its coat of bright green elephant grass. This was quite evidently sacred landscape, since no one had built anything but a temple on the back of the dragon's kindly head.

We also went for twilight walks into the backwaters, the rice paddies with their custodian flocks of ducks, and the steep watercourses and gullies carved deep into the volcanic soil.

Moss is ubiquitous in the rainy season, lending many of the small alleys and cobblestone steps the look of being underwater. Such a soft green haze would fill the air, especially at dawn, that it would have us both jokingly reaching for our diving masks.

As the night of the full moon approached, I noticed a certain tension growing in the Mandala Cottages compound. It was clear that Siti and Ri were regarded as the spiritual bulwarks of the family, somehow holding it all together. As such, they tended to live under an extraordinary amount of stress. Quite naturally, this had a way of increasing with the waxing of the moon.

Ri's father was the primo dancer on the island. He had a reputation of being the one who took Balinese dance to America. However, he was in declining health, and all was evidently not happily balanced between his five wives, four of whom lived within the compound. This thoroughly complicated situation was not made any easier by the psychic shenanigans of David, a Westerner who was studying magic on the island and who was hoping to be admitted any day to the rituals of the highest caste available to him. Magic is very real to the Balinese, both the black and the white, and since it is required of the acolyte that he study first the black variety, the vibes in the compound were getting progressively more discomforting. I could see that the two days put aside for the ceremony and the long trip across the island were going to come as a welcome relief for both our charming hosts. They were looking forward to it as an oasis of spiritual peace.

Setting off in the early afternoon of the full moon in Ri's spanking new VW bus, we were accompanied by Marj Munro, an Australian schoolteacher and an old friend and business partner of Siti's. Only half an hour after leaving Peliatan, we stopped at another small village. We were to pick up a priest friend of our hosts' who was to accompany us to the ceremony. The place looked vaguely familiar to us as we got out and walked along a side street and up to a most impressive house on a small hill.

Gunko and some of his family greeted us. He was an old

man and evidently highly placed in the Hindu priesthood because he stiffened noticeably when Michael told him about his healing from Mr. Ketut Cutet.

"Ah! Yes! Mr. Cutet." Gunko winced when he said the healer's name, and it suddenly dawned on me that we were in the same village. Mr. Cutet lived just down the lane, right on poor Gunko's doorstep.

We set off again after tea and some slightly forced conversation all around. The atmosphere was noticeably cool, and I was aware of Gunko eyeing Michael with a mixture of suspicion and righteous indignation. The VW bus climbed up through the foothills with their terraced rice paddies curving gently around the contours of the soft, green valleys. Streams were rushing everywhere, carrying the rain down off the mountains; deep chasms opened up to us briefly with glimpses of white water heaving among the rocks at the bottom. Mount Agung towered up on our righthand side, the lip of its crater torn away by the massive eruption that so recently had brought the Balinese back to their ceremonial senses.

I fell to mulling over what my angel had told me the day before while I was trying to get some insights about the upcoming event. The gathering was obviously important—she had told me that it was the central reason for my being on the island. She had also emphasized that I should be true to myself at all times. This, as I thought it through, might well turn out to be more challenging than I had imagined. It was also not going to be made any easier by Gunko's obvious resentment that he showed in regard to our interest in Mr. Cutet, a professional envy felt by many priests the world over toward the more intuitively inclined shaman.

When we arrived at Adi's compound, darkness had already fallen. Michael and I were deposited rather unceremoniously in a small room kept for visitors while nearby we could hear the animated voices of the others—no doubt discussing the tricks of the impossible Mr. Cutet. I took the enforced privacy as a sign that it was the right time to drop the MDMA, seeing that it takes about forty-five minutes to come on, and we settled down to wait for the next act to unfold.

After about twenty minutes of nothing happening we decided to push through the etiquette of the situation. We let ourselves out of the waiting room and, following the sound of voices—which dropped off at the unexpected sight of our faces—we soon found ourselves in another slightly dank and dilapidated room. Bamboo mats were strewn on the dirt floor, and it was open to the courtyard on one side. About twenty people squatted or sat cross-legged, most of them outside the room itself. With the exception of Siti and Marj, all the others were male and Balinese.

Space was courteously made for us, and we settled into the proceedings. From what Siti was whispering to me, I gathered it was a combination discussion and encounter session. Three of the men came forward consecutively to present their problems and ask for advice. What surprised me, though I did not understand a word of the interchanges, was that the questioners went on and on—eight or ten minutes of long, rambling, presumably he-did-this, I-did-thats. Yet Adi, Gunko, and a young man somewhere in his late teens all listened solicitously before entering into even longer replies. What could they all be finding to talk about?

I had plenty of time to observe their interactions. Adi was undoubtably the teacher, yet, oddly, every once in a while he would defer a question to the young man who sat to his right. Siti murmured to me that the boy was Adi's grandson.

I watched the young man in action. He was superb. Even though I had little comprehension of what was going on, I could see how the others bowed to the wisdom of his answers. As I became engrossed in this, it dawned on me that I was in the presence of a very high spiritual consciousness. I could feel the spirit beaming through him, even though he looked like he was doing his best to conceal it. I knew in those moments, with the MDMA breaking over me, that I was in the room with a true master—an incarnation. I could also see that Adi and the others were not aware of this. While there was little doubt that the boy was Adi's pride and joy, I could feel, with that lucid edge the substance allowed me, a mixture of wonder and unease in the grandfather—and a certain level of incomprehension.

The talk veered on. One by one, the questioners moved back into the shadows, nodding their heads with new resolve. After Siti had told the assembled company what she knew of us, Adi turned to face me. Slight movements of adjustment went on in those around him. Siti translated: "And you. Do you have a question?"

"Yes," I replied without a pause, the question drawn out of me. "Is God inside us or outside?"

A murmur went around the room when my question was translated. Some of the men around the edge laughed, I thought, a trifle nervously. Adi, Gunko, and the grandson looked at each other before Adi answered.

"God exists outside the self, of course," and then he continued with a long explanation of the nature of Brahma and the Brahman.

"Then who is the Spirit that dwells in our hearts?" I asked when the translation had finished. I noticed the grandson leaning forward with intense interest. I must have been peaking on the MDMA at this point, because I felt a tangible stream of love connecting the two of our hearts as Adi tried to answer the unanswerable. He explained that they did not believe God existed within human beings but that we had to reach upward toward God.

"If God is inside us, then why do we need temples to worship in?" Adi then asked me. An obvious trap.

"Because it's good to revere God among friends," I replied without missing a heartbeat. There *had* to be some jobs left for priests (and priestesses).

More questions followed full of theological tricks and feints, amid laughter and a generally good-humored ribbing of the crazy foreigner who thought that God was inside him. But I saw that Adi's grandson did not join in the banter.

Adi motioned for silence. "Is the air inside the *kapoc* [a floating cotton blossom of the island] or all around it?" he asked.

"Both," said I. "It's inside it *and* outside it." Simple an answer though it was, it seemed to stir up a tremendous amount of chatter. But I could feel there was no taking the matter any further. My question had been answered.

Midnight was approaching fast, and we were shown our designated places in which to settle ourselves. Michael and I shared a tiny room with four other Balinese, among whom, significantly, was Adi's grandson. We made ourselves comfortable and meditated until dawn. The angels were with us.

"Just be yourself; be your Self," Joy had told me, and I had followed my Spirit without hesitation. It was also evident that I had become something of a local laughing stock.

I fancy merely standing up to the priest had caused its own reverberations. Gunko, however, did have the generosity to tell me that I was a "very strong meditator," while we drove home to Peliatan the next day. I asked Siti what he meant by "strong," and after some to-ing and fro-ing she translated it as "sitting very still and upright so you can move up the chakras to where God is." And, remembering the kapoc, we had all laughed between ourselves about "outside, inside, or both."

I could feel that Siti, with her woman's intuition, had been able to see more of the truth of the encounter the night before. This was borne out subsequently by a number of invitations to meditate with her and others of her family in the small temple adjacent to their compound. The truth, however, did not become as clear to me until I talked once again with my guardian angel.

"Last night was crucial," Joy wrote through me, "in that it opened up what will become a heated discussion, particularly between the young and old. The ramifications of the meeting will take the appropriate Balinese time to filter through into the larger matrix; however, the points not only have been made, but have been demonstrated, too. It is this latter that makes the difference because it shows the young ones that what they are feeling can be accepted and allowed to be."

I asked what Adi had learned from the encounter. Had he been able to see? "Not fully," Joy responded, "[but] by actually witnessing the presence of God in you, albeit with his slightly dormant spiritual vision, he was greater able to understand more of his grandson. Although he knows the child well, there are continuing depths and wonders emerging that he has not previously witnessed. Astrologically, his grandson fits the avatar model so perfectly he has never dared to tell him, taking it upon himself to wrestle with the reality of having a young god in his family.

"And herein lies the quintessential situation on the island, and in Hinduism in general," Joy continued. "They do acknowledge the Atman [the indwelling Spirit], but it is not with much conviction since they have made it so extremely hard for themselves to actually experience it—and thus demonstrate it. Adi's grandson largely has avoided this issue due to the rapidity of the acceleration over these last few years. The Hindu proclivity for immensely long cycles has prohibited their sages from becoming aware of the transformation so close at hand. The child will be one of the ways this experience of inner divinity can be reintroduced, thus allowing large numbers of young Hindus—and possibly the old, too—to follow suit and awaken. Among these are many of your sixty million."

So, the Network of Light again. And in such hidden ways do we light each others' fires.

18

Healing and Black Magic

Our female dolphin, now growing rapidly and joyfully, is no longer reliant on her mother or the immediate family pod. She can turn to seek telepathically the help of the Watchers, the wise old dolphins who have mastered the Web, the great sonic hologram in which all live and find their sustenance . . .

Mr. Cutet looked happy. He had an impish smile on his smooth, brown face as he passed on to us the news that his friend, Mr. Oko, the sea captain, would be pleased to escort and guide us to the island of Lombok. He added that Mr. Oko had told him of the astonishing phenomenon, observed every year in May, of millions—literally *millions*—of dolphins congregating in a small area of sea in the Straits of Lombok. (By all accounts, they gather for three or four days at a time when the Dog Star, Sirius, is directly overhead.) While January was not exactly the right time of year for the convocation, Mr. Oko would organize a small boat and take us out looking for wild dolphins.

We had wondered when we would see Mr. Cutet again. No doubt he had his own full moon ritual because it was some days later, as we passed Gusti's gallery on our way into Ubud, that we heard the by-now familiar call from its dark interior. Sure enough, Mr. Cutet had just returned from his negotiations with the sea captain, having gone all the way down to Dempasar on his motorbike to set it up for us.

After the timing had been decided and all the details finalized, a long and marvelously complicated process in this culture, I suggested that we meditate together again. The healer agreed eagerly, and offerings were prepared and laid out in Gusti's small studio. We settled into our meditation with Mr. Cutet huffing and puffing up a storm in the manner of a shaman from these parts.

I allowed the energy first to ground me and then to enter my heart. As I did this, I felt a tremendous wave of love for the healer, which was matched equally by a beam of vital energy from his fourth chakra. This ecstatic blast joined and intermingled with my own feelings before coalescing and moving up through my chakras. It was the most palpably discernible energy flow that I have felt in twenty years of group meditation, close and singularly powerful, and I am sure that it linked us in ways I could scarcely comprehend.

We all came back at the same moment and sat open-eyed with happy surprise at what we had just experienced. Mr. Cutet was curious to know how Michael and I meditated, and he became very animated as I described the progression up through the devic realms, ascending from mineral, vegetable, and animal realms to the heart and the higher angelic domains.

In reply to his questioning about the mineral kingdom, I produced my gilded crystal wand, which I had first dreamed of and then had made some ten years before. It was a natural quartz spur about four inches long with gold leaf covering all the surfaces except the two ends, which were laser cut and highly polished. Of all those to whom I have shown my curious artifact, no one has handled it with such loving care and curiosity as this Balinese shaman. Peering at it from every angle as he turned it around in his long, brown fingers, he asked me what it was for. I told him, somewhat humoriously, that under certain conditions I could look down through it into a candle and get glimpses of the future. He seemed to grasp its significance because he ordered up a candle right then and there. After a few grunts and much blowing, he peered down it with what appeared to be considerable interest. Whatever he saw he did not say, but I have no doubt that the possibilities it aroused in him were endless and varied. I could think of no finer resting place for my sacred object and gladly gave it to him.

"It is Michael who is ill and you well, and yet you have given me the drawing—and now this," Gusti translated. Mr. Cutet wanted to know what he could give me in return.

I found myself telling him about the Network of Light, attempting to communicate the reality of a far-ranging, global network of people to someone who had in all likelihood never left his small island, who certainly did not watch television or read newspapers, and who might well have had a very hazy idea of what lies in the great out-there.

But he understood perfectly. Would he consider, I asked, when he meditated in the future, consciously linking up with the network and adding his own very considerable spiritual energies to the matrix? He agreed with manifest pleasure.

Knowing that we were to leave Peliatan at the end of the week, Gusti and his exquisite wife most generously offered to throw a family feast on the night before we departed. We hoped Mr. Cutet could take time away from his busy healing schedule and that we would be able to have a warm, quiet evening with those we had grown to love. However, expectations of that sort are seldom likely to bring the intended result, and the feast turned out to be no exception.

The food, quite naturally, was wonderful: Balinese delicacies, carefully prepared and offered with fragile elegance on a low table in the center of the artist's gallery. We sat around with candles burning, the conversation flowing considerably more fluently with the help of a new friend, American artist Barbara Laughing Water, who had been studying dance in Bali long enough to speak the language well. With this advantage I was able to discover that Mr. Cutet's method of meditation, which he called "going up through the numbers one to seven," was remarkably similar to the approach taught us by the angels. Little wonder that we were led to him! We also related, much to the healer's amusement, the events of the full moon ceremony with Adi and Gunko. He could barely contain his mirth, punctuating the story by poking our noble translator in the ribs and leaning back with a what-did-I-tell-you? look on his face. With Mr. Cutet, the inner divinity had never been an issue since clearly he was very much aware of this energy within himself and had courageously carved out his own path in a culture steeped in priestly traditions.

As we were talking, a small movement in the shadows at the edge of the room caught my eye. I stared into the gloom and soon made out the unhappy presence of A——. We had seen her previously around town: one of those unfortunate souls sometimes met while traveling, most probably an ambulatory schizophrenic, burnt out on drugs or social rejection, and who brought chaos with her wherever she went. Siti and Ri had unwillingly, but necessarily, moved her out of Mandala Cottages, and now poor Gusti had given her sanctuary because, as it turned out, he had thought she was a friend of mine!

I motioned her out of the shadows and asked Mr. Cutet if he would have a psychic look at her. After some head squeezing, he pronounced her very ill.

"Can anything be done about it?" I asked.

"Only if she wants it," the healer very sensibly replied.

I asked A——, and she agreed somewhat reluctantly to a treatment. The table was moved aside and Mr. Cutet laid her down on the floor between us, starting on much the same process as he had used with Michael, although more gently in this case. Evidently a skillful showman, he also had all of us involved, positioning us at A——'s various extremities and encouraging each to do our own thing.

Michael, having already undergone the procedure, appeared to be taking on some of A——'s negative energy—and hopefully releasing it—because he spasmed violently every once in a while. I focused on pouring heart energy into the healer, while Marj and Barbara participated as they saw fit and observed Mr. Cutet's astonishing performance. They agreed later that it allowed them a far deeper perception of the culture to which both had been so drawn.

It was hard to imagine that Mr. Cutet could have hoped for a complete recovery. A— was certainly out of the reach of conventional Western medicine. But that did not stop him from throwing himself totally into the task of healing with all the strenuous vigor that his craft demanded. There was also no doubt that A— appeared to be lighter at the end of it all, and she touched her forehead to the ground in recognition and gratitude before getting up.

Next morning, as we were saying our good-byes, Gusti whispered to me that A— seemed considerably better—that she was far less intrusive and could even be heard singing while she worked. I look forward to the time when such healers as Mr. Cutet will be welcomed by Western medicine, their methodologies studied without fear or bias, in the spirit of genuine, cooperative research. We have much to learn from them.

Mr. Oko, the sea captain, joined Michael and me in Dempasar, where the three of us caught a ferry together to the small, predominantly Moslem island of Lombok. He was a compact man, and he must have been well over sixty years old since he had retired from his captaincy some years earlier, and yet he radiated the vitality of a far younger man. He smiled easily and spoke passable English. This would make arrangements a trifle less torturous than they had been with his friend and teacher Mr. Cutet.

Bonnie and Clyde, dubbed in Indonesian, screamed down at us from a flickering TV set mounted on a ceiling bracket in the forward passenger lounge. Two young Balinese haltingly picked out Mexican ballads on a pair of tuneless Japanese guitars. The child in the seat next to mine started throwing up, and I surreptitiously laid on hands, much to the surprise of her mother. The boat rolled in the heavy swell. While Warren Beatty died in a hail of bullets, Mr. Oko regaled us with his exploits at sea. Fortunately, it was not a long crossing.

We did not see much of Lombok. Mr. Oko wanted simply to drop off a suitcase at his house, and then we caught a bemo to the other side of the island. There, an outrigger canoe with an outboard motor lashed to its wooden flank took us over to an even smaller island, Gilli Air, where our guide felt sure we would see the dolphins. As if to tease us while we were making the crossing, a large fish leapt high into the air off the starboard bow. While obviously not a cetacean, this fish apparently was called dolphin hereabouts. We chose to take it as a good sign.

It soon became clear that Mr. Oko, although most enthusiastic, was scarcely in his element. I suspect that he took on the assignment as a favor to his teacher, without really considering what it might entail. Whatever boats he might have captained, they were not small outrigger canoes. Moreover, as we were to find out over the next few days, the ancient Balinese terror of the water soon emerged in him, and he confessed, rather shamefaced, that he was unable to swim. Standing on the bridge of a cargo boat was a very different experience from being whirled along two inches from a heaving ocean full of demons.

Gilli Air is a beautiful little tropical island, quiet and unspoiled, and it has some of the best coral reefs in that part of the world. It was altogether a strange and unlikely place in which to receive the shocking lesson of that first night on the island.

The three of us checked into the only *losman*—a small lodging house—on Gilli Air and spent the late afternoon exploring the white beaches and snorkeling among the clouds of vividly colored fish. We ate simply and well.

Electing to avoid the losman's idea of a convivial evening, we decided on a good night's sleep before setting off in search of wild dolphins the next morning. Having slept fitfully through the party's early stages, I was awakened around midnight by the drunken roars of two Swedish lads, whom we had noticed before turning in, settling into the local brew. Possibly they were no more than typically noisy drunks, but somehow the contrast of the quiet beauty of the island served to exaggerate their cacophony.

The awful row, and the rank insensitivity of it, ground down on my nerves. They were much too far gone to have appreciated or complied with my telling them to quiet down, so I lay there stewing on it, getting more and more angry. Before finally dropping off to sleep, I recall a dim memory of hatching up some insane plot to finish them off for good. I would torch their bungalow with them inside it. That'd fix 'em. The plan must have satisfied my addled mind, because it was the last thing I remembered.

I had a particularly vivid dream that night, which I recorded when I awoke. "I am in a large and spacious bus in New York City," I wrote. "A spirit of weirdness fills the air. I see my mother on the bus, and she is annoyed about something but I can't tell what it is. I look around the bus at all the vaguely familiar faces. Happiness and this feeling of weirdness prevail, and people are bantering with one another. Outside the bus, everybody is at each other's throats. We discover, bit by bit, that we are being tested—all of us. Dramatic tests of skill, humor, and faith. One such test, near the end of the trip, involves swinging down an incredibly worn, rusty, and dilapidated metal ladder high above the ground. My mother is near the bottom of this ladder, and I have slowed down for her. The ladder is in an even worse condition now because of all those on the bus who have already climbed down it. I climb down past her in order to test the ladder for strength, and I can hear her concerned cry in the background. My cousin Christopher elects to go behind her. I remind my mother as I am swinging down that it is a test of faith. I even imagine that parts of the ladder will give away in my hands—but, of course, they don't.

"At the bottom, someone tells me to simply follow the Beings of the Violet Flame to where they direct. I listen internally, and within moments I am inside a beautifully appointed restaurant. I discover that I am among the first half-dozen arrivals in spite of holding back for my mother. People dribble in for some time, happy and greeting one another effusively. The tests are over, and it is time to have fun. Everybody agrees that the ladder and the climb down is the worst one. We laugh and exchange experiences. All is well." That was the end of the dream.

The next morning, as I was sitting with Michael and Mr. Oko, having bowls of fresh fruit and good, strong coffee, the Swedes appeared, looking predictably hung over but also very shaken up. I could see that one of them had bright red burns all over one arm, and he was pointing at them in dismay. He had no memory of how he had gotten burned. I thought little of it at the time beyond a rather malicious "serves you right for getting so sloshed"—which, of course, I did not say. The burns were painful, but there was no question that he would recover.

It was not until much later that afternoon, having returned from a fruitless search for dolphins and while I was taking a cold shower under a perforated steel drum, that it suddenly struck me I conceivably might have been responsible for those burns. Until then I had not connected my hypnagogic reverie with what happened to the young Swede.

Next time I saw him I called him over to our hut. "I did that to you," I told him straight.

"Yes," he said, with no surprise, as if he had known it all along, "to keep me from shouting."

"I'm sorry," I told him, and carefully smeared aloe over his burned arm, "but please don't keep me awake again tonight." He nodded in agreement and left quickly—happy, I imagine, to be out of my villainous presence.

I went down to the white sand beach, and there, sweeping across a clouded sky, was a magnificently radiant rainbow. It came to me in those moments how very carefully I needed to guard against the worst excesses of negative thinking. Although comparatively harmless, this lapse of attention had all the makings of a nasty little piece of black magic.

We had our first encounter with the dolphins a day or two later, after we had moved on to the even smaller and more remote island of Gilli Meno. It was by far the most peaceful and the most beautiful of all the islands we visited, perhaps because none but the most intrepid ever bothered to go there. Mr. Oko, true to his word, had organized a canoe for us with a young, rather excitable captain full of orders and slightly bemused that anyone would be interested in going out simply to look for dolphins.

They were some sixty yards away when we first spotted them—a small pod of about twelve spinners, or so we reckoned by the wonderful, whirling breaches of some of the smaller ones. They were feeding when we came upon them, roaming over the densely populated coral reef between the two islands. They kept their distance while playing their own subtle games with us.

Everybody felt their presence. A Scandanavian girl, Helen, whom we had invited along, cried quietly while the three fisherfolk, relatives of the captain and whom he had insisted on bringing aboard, all yelled *"lomba-lomba!"* (the Balinese word for dolphins) at the top of their voices, in evident delight that their captain had fulfilled his curious mission. Even Mr. Oko conquered his fear sufficiently to stand up in the prow and make the kind of noises he doubtless imagined would bring the dolphins nearer to us. Not surprisingly, in the light of this dreadful din, they wheeled and turned away, keeping what I have come to accept as the nominal seventy-five yards of ocean between them and us.

After trying to keep the noise and the general excitement of the fishermen to a minimum, I suggested that we all concentrate on visualizing the dolphins swimming around our craft. Whatever the boatload of clamorous people might have made of such an idea, it did seem to have a temporary effect. The dolphins turned briefly toward us and looked momentarily as if they were going to comply. But they soon became more interested in the fish again.

Michael, Helen, and I quickly slipped overboard, somewhat to the horror of the local folk, and swam toward the feeding dolphins. Michael reported later that they had swum right beneath him—he could feel their sonar playing all over his body—and although I never got near enough to see them underwater, I could hear their marvelous, high-pitched whistles in the distance.

I realized, as we puttered back to Gilli Meno, that I had

somehow known that we would encounter dolphins today. It had been a quiet conviction, a subtle feeling that I am starting to recognize simply does not enter my mind if they are not around. Like all delicate feelings, it is hard to pin down, but looking back through my notes, I can see that I have seldom been wrong about it.

We decided on our next venture to hire a still smaller boat, thus cutting down the number of people who could find a reason to clamber aboard, and one with a considerably less excitable skipper. We saw the dolphins again, but for some unaccountable reason, neither of us felt any strong desire to approach them. I put this down to a greater relaxation that both Michael and I were starting to feel about getting up close to them; as a result, we were both more comfortable with giving them their space and accepting their inevitable games of hide-and-seek with more equanimity.

The quiet, misty beauty of the little tropical island was working its magic on us. The pinks and mauves of the evening clouds etched against the remains of a duck-egg blue sky; the great twin peaks of Lombok's massive volcano still seen in the far distance over the palms of the intervening islands; the doe-eyed heifers and young goats calling softly to one another after a day's contented munching; the slight evening breezes stirring the palm thatching and swaying the tiny outrigger canoes in the warm swell—all contrived to create in us a feeling of such supreme contentment that the excitement of the chase, of spending time up close to our beloved dolphins, became increasingly less important than the pure joy of just being there.

We spent days hanging in pellucid water over the rare and intensely blue coral outcroppings, watching the myriad fluorescent tropical fish. This induced in me a strong ambivalence of awe and vertigo. In many ways, it was as if the water had not been there at all and I was flying, arms and legs outstretched, in the warm, yielding atmosphere. It was almost too beautiful a sight to sustain its massive improbability for very long, and I was grateful for all those flying dreams that had inadvertently trained me for such bliss.

On our last day on the island, Michael and I again took out the tiny canoe, heading this time for the open ocean, out past the last of the small islands in the chain. Although we glimpsed not the slightest sign of lomba-lomba, perhaps in the spirit of divine compensation we were privileged to see one of the more unusual spectacles that either of us had ever witnessed.

It occurred, significantly enough, when we had just about given up on catching even the briefest sight of our shy friends and were releasing the inevitable frustrations that can build up when dolphins do not want to be noticed. I was gazing into the water on my left-hand side when, at exactly the point at which I was looking with such dejection, the sea fluidly parted and a large stingray, silver delta glistening in the sun, leapt high into the air in a resplendent, double-back somersault. And not once, but twice. It was the most delicate and eminently graceful vision I could possibly imagine.

Then, in answer to my unspoken question as to what might provoke such an extraordinary maneuver, about thirty feet off the port bow there started a sudden and violent churning of water. It was as if the ocean were boiling. And there, seemingly within arm's reach, was a school of sharks.

Quite unlike the dolphins we had seen, who cut through the water with scarcely a ripple, the sharks appeared intent on beating and crackling up the surface of the sea. Whether they were attacking the acrobatic ray or this was simply their way of being noisy and aggressive, it was an electric reminder of how vulnerable we were in our minute outrigger, the ocean slopping only an inch or two from its wooden edges.

I fancy that our new captain—Mr. Oko had left us by this time, to return to Lombok—an uncharacteristically grumpy young Balinese lad, must have been terrified by the incident since he was most reluctant to gun the outboard toward the frightful melee for the closer look that both Michael and I wanted. But, then again, perhaps he knew something that we did not!

On our way back, between the islands and in the lee of Gilli Meno, another odd and rather magnificent sight greeted us. Thousands upon thousands of small fish suddenly started leaping out of the water all around us, a veritable magic carpet of undulating silver flashes. They crossed and crisscrossed our path, much to the excitement of another canoe that we were just passing at the time. Nets went overboard in a flurry of activity, and I guessed that the fishermen were after whatever it was down there that was creating this mass exodus.

While this was happening, I received an intense blast of predation, of vicious, wickedly toothed mouths snapping and tearing at the small fish as they were fleeing in the only direction left to them—right up out of the water. As I watched this and felt all the accompanying fears, it came to me that our own dimly distant ancestors must have bolted out of those primeval oceans and onto the land in much the same terrified manner.

Little wonder that we have, deeply coded into us, such a horror of the monsters of the watery depths. However, I was not to realize until later in this continuing adventure the lengths to which our species might go in our unconscious projection of this very terror. We have indeed emerged from a fearful past. I wondered, in those moments, whether we would ever survive it.

19

Lives of Willing Sacrifice

The intermingling of the dolphin pods constantly changes as they follow the tides, the currents, the fish, and the composition is always appropriate to their needs. Our female dolphin herself now has a young one and pods with an entirely new group, getting to know the new scents and sounds of other seas and other rhythms . . .

If dolphins have this magnificent intelligence, why are they choosing to die by the millions? This is something I am asked constantly as people become more aware of the cetacean "mind in the waters." It is not an easy or straightforward question, any more than the question of why so many of our own species choose to die in the variety of plagues, wars, and natural disasters that seem to be our lot. While it is evident that oceanic pollution, both physical and audio, has been progressively wreaking havoc with their ecosystem, as spiritual beings of high intelligence, dolphins and whales must also be exerting their free choice. In the spiritual domains, there are no victims.

During May of 1990, within a few weeks of one another, two small groups of dolphins had swum up, respectively, Manhattan's East River and the River Thames in London. It does not seem altogether coincidental that in each case they tarried for a day or two outside the apparent seats of power of both cities—the mayor's mansion in New York and the House of Commons in London—before dying of diseases that were most probably caused by pollution.

I am becoming convinced, as this story unfolds, that dolphins—and presumably whales, too—have a very different concept of death than we do. This is in no way to diminish their quite evident love of life or our responsibilities in the terrible carnage, for instance, left by the tuna fleets, yet the contradiction remains: If they are so gifted with wisdom, why are they allowing themselves to be decimated?

It was during one of the spate of many beachings that occurred in the early eighties that I caught my first glimpse of this different understanding of death in action. I was in New York City at the time, and the six o'clock evening news programs were showing in-time action footage of a pod of about twenty bottlenose dolphins on the Florida coastline—all of them were throwing themselves up onto a sandy beach, appearing utterly intent on self-annihilation. The images were too agonizing for me to look at for more than a few seconds—I had to turn away in horror.

Later that same evening, as I was pondering the whole dreadful event and my emotionally charged revulsion to seeing it, it became clear to me that I had allowed the fear of death to get the better of me. The images were so raw that I had let this ubiquitous negative thought form dim the awareness formed in the course of my own near-death experience, which had all but removed my personal fear of death. But my guard was down, and TV can be a wretchedly hypnotic medium, so the old fear and horror swept in amid the persistent mental images of the dying dolphins. I decided that I needed to more fully experience the reality of the dolphins' death, to know and understand it, as well as to challenge my own sentimentality in the face of it.

Setting the TV set up so that I could meditate in front of

it, I adjusted my consciousness, centered and grounded my body, released the nervousness I was feeling, and waited for the eleven o'clock news people to show the film again.

Show it, of course, they did, and this time it was a longer and far more detailed clip than in the earlier program. There were those pictures again: enormous, sleek forms hurling themselves out of the water, throwing themselves as high up on the sand as they could. Around them struggled concerned human helpers attempting to lift the stricken dolphins back into the sea, slipping and sliding, dropping their burdens as often as not, and when succeeding only finding the dolphins turning again and swimming straight back to the beach to cast themselves once more up onto the sand, under the harsh glare of the TV lights.

I watched with full attention while the dolphins turned and twisted in the apparent agony of their death throes—immense, powerful bodies of pure muscle slapping and flapping like the proverbial fish out of water. Except these were not fish, but air-breathing mammals. They were certainly not dying from asphyxiation. Then, as I looked still closer, I could see that the dolphins were trying to turn over on their backs so that they could force sand up their blowholes—and by their immense twisting and thrashing making it virtually impossible for the helpers to save them.

The camera focused in on one of the dolphin's eyes, and I saw it suddenly as full of intelligence and quiet determination—not at all the frightened or vacant eye of a being who was dying in fear or without purpose. I also realized that throughout this ordeal I had not felt one iota of the horror or fear that I had undergone earlier. It was as though it had been lifted from me. With the revelation of that beautiful, wise old eye full of peace and joy, I was being allowed to perceive what was happening in an entirely new light. I could see now that they were bending and twisting not in agony at all, but in the ecstasy of death. *They were deliberately killing themselves, and they were loving the whole process!*

A short while after my insight into the dolphins' superb

joy in death, there fell into my hands a photocopy of David Stewart's series of articles "Our Father Who Art in Water," published in the Australian magazine Simply Living. Much of the content of the articles is drawn from the work of the English astronomer Robert Temple, who became fascinated by anthropological studies suggesting that an isolated and remote African tribe, the Dogon of Mali, know facts about the star system Sirius that have been confirmed only recently by modern astronomy.

Sirius—the Dog Star—you will remember, is the brightest star in the sky and one of our nearest neighbors. Twenty-three times brighter than our sun, this giant forms a binary star system with Sirius B, a dwarf star that is invisible to the naked eye. It is also with Sirius that the dolphins are most frequently connected in history and mythology. Aristotle, for example, observed that "the dolphin actually disappears at the time of the Dog Star for about thirty days." And, of course, there is our own Mr. Oko's story of the vast convocation of dolphins in the Gulf of Lombok, when Sirius is directly overhead.

As Robert Temple comes to compare the sacred images of the Dogon, some of which show the spiral path of Sirius A and B orbiting one another, with his own contemporary calculations, he starts finding significant similarities. In addition, he indicates that the Dogon display an astonishingly detailed knowledge of Sirius B—this star is, in fact, at the center of their religious ceremonies. Sirius B was first photographed only in the early 1970s, having been postulated from observations made of the irregularities in the orbit of Sirius A. After years of meticulous research, Robert Temple was convinced from the Dogon's sacred teachings that at some point in their history the tribe had played host to an extraterrestrial mission from Sirius. He also became persuaded that these beings, whoever they were, had instructed the African tribe in certain cosmological principles.

The Dogon's knowledge is certainly most sophisticated and is by no means restricted to the Sirius system. They know, for instance, that planets rotate individually as well as revolve around the sun. They seem to know about Saturn's rings and

Jupiter's moons, and they also appear to understand the principle of blood circulation, of red and white cells, and the process by which food is assimilated into the bloodstream.

As David Stewart points out, the Dogon's knowing that it is the rotation of the Earth upon its axis that gives the sky the appearance of turning predates by 4,600 years our European forebears coming to terms with such a heretical possibility. Robert Temple, quite evidently a very straight astronomer, is predictably rather embarrassed by his findings, but he has the integrity to trust his research, widening it to include the Sumerian and Egyptian cultures. He even presents ample evidence to suggest that several cultures contemporary with the early Dogon also experienced an extraterrestrial visitation.

Temple's work is articulately presented in his book *The Sirius Mystery*, but great credit should also be given to Marcel Griaule and Germaine Dieterlen, the two French anthropologists who lived and worked alongside the Dogon through much of the thirties and who were first allowed to know the sacred teachings, some of which took a full ten years of trust to reveal. Their book is called *Le Renard Pale*.

In the Dogon belief system, amphibious beings calling themselves Nommo are said to have arrived in an ark. The tribe's stories and paintings still record the noise and drama of this vehicle's landing. They also tell that the ark itself descended from a larger ark, which remained circling the Earth during the time the Nommo were here. To the Dogon, the larger ark looked like a bright new star, and they make specific reference to the fact that it disappeared at the same time the Nommo left them.

The Dogon call their strange visitors collectively the Masters of the Water, the Instructors, or the Monitors. The Nommo brought with them a fairly complex cosmology, which has been filtered through the Dogon's intellect and handed down ceremonially for almost five thousand years.

What is evident, however, is that the Nommo regard our sun, and this planet in particular, as part of the Sirian system of stars. In fact, our sun, they believe, is the fourth star of their stellar family.

The Nommo taught the Dogon that human beings, too, are a part of their race and are known to them as Nommo Anagonno, or Ogo. They told the Dogon that there are four types of Nommo. The first is Nommo Die, or Great Nommo, the One or Great Mother, who stays on Sirius B, and it is she who is mother of all the spiritual principles of all living creatures, on Earth as well as on Sirius. She is linked with Amma, apparently the male principle, who manifests as the rainbow and is the spiritual guardian of all living creatures.

Second are the Nommo Titiyayne, who are the messengers of Nommo Die and carry out her great works. There are differing opinions as to how Nommo Tityayne are understood, but my intuition tells me that they must be angels, or beings from the fifth dimension. They are associated by the Dogon with Sirius A.

Thirdly, there are the O Nommo, also called Nommo of the Pond. These are the Nommo who arrived in the ark and who also seem to have a particularly strong association with our dolphins. The Dogon sacred drawings of the Nommo clearly indicate delphinic features: obviously air breathing, from the position of the waterline (see drawing); similar flukelike tails, horizontal to the body (unlike fish, whose tails

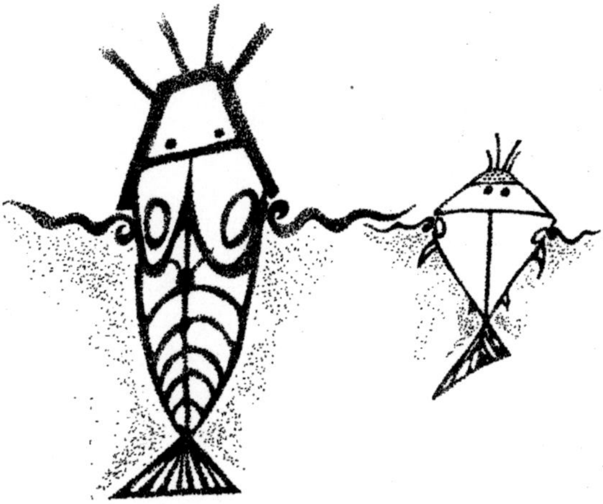

are vertically placed); and what looks in many of the drawings like a stylization of a blowhole.

The fourth type of Nommo is Nommo Anagonno, old Ogo the Fox, and this being is portrayed as the Disrupter. This, of course, is ourselves. The French anthropologists translate this Dogon passage regarding our humble beginnings: "As Ogo was about to be finished [being created], he rebelled against his Creator and introduced disorder in the universe." There appears to be a balance about the way the belief system is presented, however—an emphasis on the interdependence of yin and yang, an implicit acknowledgment that creation and destruction are equally important and interwoven. Most personally significant, too, is that here is another planetary cosmology that points to some sort of rebellion or upheaval in our dim and distant past.

Now comes the key to what I believe the Nommo were trying to relay to the Dogon and the factor that was to throw so much light on my acutely unsettling vision of the dolphins dying in ecstasy. According to Griaule and Dieterlen, it has long been the prophecy of the Nommo, and thus the Dogon, that the Nommo of the Pond, the third Nommo, will sacrifice itself for "the purification and reorganization of the universe." More specifically, the Dogon say that the third Nommo will sacrifice itself for the fourth, Anagonno, Ogo the Fox, namely us, the disrupters.

In recent years, self-sacrifice has become somewhat unfashionable in our thinking, being perhaps more frequently associated with the excesses of nationalistic or religious fervor, but as a practice it runs deep in almost all major belief systems. Exemplary lives seem invariably to be lives of self-sacrifice. The act itself seems to satisfy some deep inner need to do all that can be done. The traditionally romantic concept of "Greater good can no man do, that he gives up his life for a friend" can surge up surprisingly quickly in most of us.

Could it be that now, at this key point in history, the whales and dolphins are indeed sacrificing themselves so that we might wake up to the destruction we are inflicting on our home planet? Might this be one of the profound root connections between our two species? Might this explain something of what I saw in that beautiful dying dolphin's eye: the joy of willing self-sacrifice, the laying down of a life for a friend?

And after this sacrificial death, the Dogon record, the Nommo of the Pond will "rise in human form and descend on Earth in an ark, with the ancestors of men. Then they will take on their original form, will rule from the waters and will give birth to many descendants." Is it possible that this rising in human form might account for some of the strange feelings and experiences so many dolphophiles undergo? Could it be that some of us have been whales or dolphins in previous incarnations and have now returned to take our part in what Peter Shenstone, the Australian dolphophile, calls the force for freedom?

20

The Dolphin Tribal Adventure

Sometimes great convocations of dolphins will draw millions upon millions together to swirl and play and commune within the joy inherent in the massive biofield produced by so many, so close together. For days on end they lie there completely passive, in what we would call deep trance, their body rhythms quiet and slow, while Sirius A and Sirius B, the Dogon's Yasiji Tolo and mysterious Po Tolo, endlessly circle each other in the deep southern sky . . .

Peter Shenstone received the Legend of the Golden Dolphin in 1976, in a marathon ten-day telepathic experience with a cetacean consciousness. The encounter transformed his life, and the legend rapidly became . . . well, legendary. It is enormously complex and multilayered, taking a minimum of seven hours to reveal in its entirety and more generally a full weekend or longer.

From the time he received the legend, Peter has traveled all over, passing on the message of the dolphins to whomever will listen. It is always oral, in the old tradition. Because it is layered information, it is almost impossible to write down; to my knowledge, it has never been videotaped in its fullness, and yet it has been widely discussed. Some of the understandings have been coded into David Stewart's articles, and it was David who first introduced Peter to the Dogon prophecies some three years after the legend came through.

When I first met Peter, I quickly realized I had not the heart to ask him to tell me the legend, although I would have dearly loved to hear it—the poor guy must have recounted it a hundred times! Some years later, I could have kicked myself when he mentioned to me that he would have been delighted to tell us the legend.

We met in his native Australia, at Byron Bay, on the magnificent New South Wales coastline, a few days after ICERC's first International Dolphin and Whale Conference in 1987. Running into each other at a small outdoor cafe, we settled down to share with one another our gleanings of the dolphin reality. We sat at a wooden table in the warm winter sunlight, with the Pacific surf pounding away at the beach just on the other side of the dunes.

"For me it all started a few days before the birth of our second child," Peter began, "in a little attic flat on the point between Great and Little Sirius Coves, on Sydney Harbor. I was sitting for a midnight meditation. Jan and I had been practicing our own system of yoga in preparation for our first home birth. This bonding between Jan, myself, and the birthing energy had been building powerfully."

By this time, Peter's enthusiastic and magnetic presence had drawn six or eight other people, who had all gathered around us. "I'd been relaxing into my own form of tantric meditation for about an hour," he recalled, "when out of the blue—Bang! or rather, Ping!—I was filled with a singing, ringing, pinging, sort of dolphin/whale sound. It permeated my whole being—the room, the world, the whole universe."

Peter leaned back with his arms outstretched, a beatific smile on his warm, brown, bearded face; and each one of us around him, in our own way, picked up on the depth and intensity of the contact he had described. It must have been hanging there still, impregnated into his aura.

"I couldn't move," he went on. "It seemed as though the

whole universe consisted of this indescribable vibration. The booming voice continued, and I began to feel, rather than hear, the meaning coming through."

One of us asked him how long he had been into meditation when all this happened. "About ten years," he replied, "but I'd never experienced anything like this. I was transfixed. And for the first time in my life—and I'd been very doubtful about this previously—I started doing automatic writing."

Peter told us he thought at the time that he might be going a little crazy: "Slipping through the crack in the cosmic egg and scrambling my brains" was his heroic mixed metaphor. "I watched, half in awe, half in horror," he continued, "as my hand picked up a pencil lying nearby and began to write at a furious pace. The writing kept on going till dawn, and it went on every night for ten days, pouring out this incredible story about what was going to happen on the planet."

Peter said he was shown the massive cleansing that had to take place, together with the concurrent transformation of human consciousness. He saw the role the cetaceans would play in those events and his specific job as one of their messengers. He was told that he should share the legend with others but also that a new medium would be developed that could more appropriately communicate the wealth of knowledge encoded in the multidimensional story.

Peter continued: "I was specifically told not to sell the idea to anybody—and I'm a marketing expert by profession—but to allow people to find their own way into this new reality of cetacean consciousness—or, as my aboriginal brother Burnam Burnam calls it, dolphin dreaming." He looked around the group, seeing in our eyes that indeed each of us had found our way into the dolphin reality through our own paths.

"I was told that this would form the seed of a new global tribe of dolphin dreamers," he said, "a tribal gathering that would transcend the old barriers of race, creed, color, ego, fear, and alienation to become the new leaderless Aquarian network of free beings: the Force for Freedom!"

The Force for Freedom sounded so much like the Network of Light that I told Peter something of the beings—

cetaceous, human, and otherwise—that I had been meeting in my travels. His feeling was that many of these might indeed be among the prophesied "resurrected human Nommo," who he was told would be collecting from around the world in Australia. As the world's largest island, he says, it will become the beachhead for the return of Nommo.

Peter maintained he had also been shown that the dolphins, the Nommo of the Pond, having passed through the God-realization phase of evolution, had achieved a state of perfect balance with their habitat, and indeed the universe, many millions of years ago. "Choosing water as their perfect environment in which to enjoy this state of grace, their heaven on Earth, in which all their needs are met perfectly," he said, "what did they do? They discarded their hands." Peter stared at his own hands, turning them over in the sun.

"Once you realize that everything is perfect," he went on, "you don't need hands to manipulate the world or to make weapons to defend yourself by killing other creatures who share this perfect creation. And also, surely, the only real aim in life is to reach a state of mind development in which mind can realize its essence, its goodness, its oneness with creation. Having reached this point, the only way Nommo-dolphin can avert the threat Ogo-man poses for himself and the world is through the power of mind, the power of dreaming. The final showdown," he said with a flourish, "will be between Nommo's dream and Ogo's nightmare."

At this time, eleven years after receiving the legend, Peter was continuing to sit in meditation, plugging into his astonishing communication channel to dolphin dreamtime and awaiting further guidance. "The story goes on unfolding," he told us, "and each day brings a new piece of the jigsaw puzzle to light."

"And what about the legend?" one of us asked, perhaps half hoping we might actually get to hear it.

"We've started to live it—all of us," he answered, looking around our little circle of bright, shining eyes. "The Legend of the Golden Dolphin is simply a metaphor representing the spirit of freedom—our guide, if you like, through the reefs of time. All beings who enter into the dolphin tribal adventure bring their own unique contribution, and thus the legend grows and grows, and the dream comes nearer of a perfect family, a perfect brotherhood and sisterhood, a perfect life in harmony with one another and with the world and a perfect human/ dolphin tribe grows closer."

I met Peter Shenstone again in mid-January of 1991, at just the time when Ogo-man was preparing to duke it out over Kuwait. It was up in the raw beauty of the Blue Mountains west of Sydney, where Peter and his family had recently moved. The legend was very much alive and well, and the new medium, predicted in the story, had indeed come about.

CDI, or interactive laser disc technology, allows the participant to directly relate to the immense amount of information that can be stored on a CD. It encourages both a linear, goal-oriented questioning and a lateral movement, as though through a field of knowledge, allowing comparisons to be made between the scientific, the artistic, the mystical, the mythic, the political, and whatever other layers of information might be required. The legend, with all its multidimensionality, could have been made for CDI—which also, because of the way it is structured, encourages participants to build their own body of knowledge.

It was all starting to come together for Peter: the right people, in the right place, at the right time. He was making presentations to the government and to private companies. The project was taking off. So it looks like within a few years, we will all get a chance to interact with the legend. In so doing, each of us will doubtless bring our own unique contributions to the evolution of an ever-widening path of discovery.

Since I was moving toward completing my notes on dolphin telepathy, I asked Peter to elaborate on that first night he had heard the voice of cetacea and whether he had had any recent insights. "I've come to see how important that particular meditation was," he said, "using a point of light in the third eye to move through to a veil of light—a process of individuation first, then of an identification with the whole, and then back again. This sets up an oscillation, and out of this vibration comes a voice. It was like hearing my own voice, but it was telling me a story I didn't consciously know."

I asked him if there were any images involved. "No, not exactly," he replied. "It went on and on until dawn—and then every day for almost ten days. I'd had nothing really to do with dolphins up to this point, yet it was quite obviously a cetacean intelligence and it was using my voice to speak to me."

We also talked about the whole vast subject of dolphin and whale consciousness and what it might mean. Peter reiterated his own sense of the Nommo self-sacrifice and their scheduled reappearance in human form. He also made note of the historical fact that dolphins seem to appear more frequently when there are significant changeovers in human belief systems. I asked him whether he had a feeling that dolphins might have a different view of death from that of our race, and he replied that he believed cetaceans move more easily from the individual to the collective—literally, from life to death—and back again.

"I'll illustrate this by relating an experience I had at Monkey Mia," he said, referring to the now world-famous site on the shores of Australia's Shark Bay at which dolphins have been approaching humans for some years, "and this was with wild ones, mind you. What I saw with those dolphins in their natural element were highly individuated creatures who would come up to me one by one, look at me, and then look right through me: totally check me out, pouring sound all over me, swim all around me, and connect with me very personally. And yet, in an instant, when some other dolphins came by, they went into another kind of space. They were totally coordinated. It's like they acted out for me this whole process of individuation and then their collective. It's happening right there in front of your eyes. One moment you know you are dealing with a totally individuated creature that's one-on-one with you, and then the next thing there are three of them, and they're all moving around you in formation; they're obviously moving as one. When this happened, not just once but a number of times, I realized I was watching a being that was pulsing backward and forward between these two states."

And did he feel the dolphins could take information from their individual state to their collective? "I suspect they do," he responded. "They take what they've learned into group consciousness. But having said that, the pragmatist and the rationalist in me says, 'Well, if that's the case, some dolphin somewhere has realized what the tuna fishermen are doing, and why haven't they communicated it to all the other dolphins? Why don't they all just jump over the nets and save themselves?' You see, it's all very complicated. And yet instances of this sort have occurred. John Lilly reports the story of orcas collectively avoiding all boats with harpoonlike structures on their prows, after a single incident of an orca having been fired upon. So we don't really know, do we?"

I asked him if the Legend of the Golden Dolphin ever had an end. "A friend of mine defined a legend as something that never was, yet is continually happening," he said. "No, I don't see it as ever having an end."

"Why 'golden'?" I asked.

"Well, it's always been golden," he answered, "right from the first time it came in. I went through quite a bit of soul searching over that! I thought, for some reason, that it was related to the golden calf! But I dutifully called it the Golden Dolphin anyway, not really understanding what it meant. In the early stuff that came through, however, I got a very clear impression that, at some stage, a group of us were to go on a journey to the dolphins. And it so happened that in 1981, I was given money to take some people to Monkey Mia."

Apparently the trip had all come together with no preconceptions—just a group of people with whatever resources they brought with them. Peter remembers a film team joining them, that coincidentally was making a movie about dolphins. They all set out together in a convoy of vehicles, about thirty people in total, on the long, hard journey north to Sharks Bay. Having traveled overland for days, they arrived exhausted at dawn one day on the sandy shores of Monkey Mia to witness a miracle: a dolphin had just given birth to a tiny golden dolphin and was proudly presenting her to the small crowd that had already gathered in the water.

"I'd no idea that when a dolphin is born, it's covered all over with the finest layer of hair," Peter remarked. "This one was golden, and she shone like metal in the morning sunlight."

Well, I still have not heard the Legend of the Golden Dolphin, which no doubt rolls on. Peter tells me that everything revealed to him has so far come about and that if the Gulf War can be seen in the light of a cleansing, then whatever the outcome might be, it can only result in further exposure of the war god and the fear-driven reality.

Peter had talked, on the first occasion we had met in Byron Bay, of a mythic journey he felt many of us would be making together at some unspecified time in the future. He saw it as circling the coastline of the enormous island of Australia—a human/cetacean traveling road show (sound familiar?) with music, theater, dance, shamanic initiations, and hi-tech sound and light displays—and then coiling in a vast inward spiral toward Uluru, the great rock in the center of the continent. Mention of this seemed to evoke a powerful memory in me that I could not quite pin down. Perhaps, I thought, it is already happening in the state of consciousness that the Australian Aborigines call Dreamtime.

21

An Aboriginal Corroboree

The great day arrives: our female dolphin learns to fly. She has mastered the Web, experienced all the feelings and thoughts that hang as potentials in the glistening hologram. The Watchers lead her into new regions. She learns, with her consciousness, to lift free of that streamlined body, to fly into the inner realms of the collective imagination . . .

Australian Aborigines are unique among the peoples of this planet in that they can claim a continuing oral tradition of more than forty thousand years. In some cases I have heard Aborigines refer to uninterrupted habitation of a particular spot for at least 100,000 years. They are also very much a people of the heart. Their capacity to love and merge with the land and their oneness with the spirit of the Earth are characteristics of inestimable value to all of us as we weave our way through the great transformation ahead.

One of the main reasons for my return to Australia was to meet and spend time with Bill Smith and other members of the Komilaroi Tribe of the northern tablelands of New South

Wales. This particular group of Aborigines had been invited to participate in ICERC's second International Dolphin and Whale Conference, to be held at Valla Beach on the New South Wales coastline.

The conference itself was bound to be fun and intellectually stimulating, since the speakers were drawn from a wide spectrum of delphinic interests. Among them were scientists from different disciplines, dolphin dreamers, those working with dolphins and depressed people or autistic children, specialists in whale beachings, tuna/dolphin activists, divers and underwater photographers, water-birthers, ecologists and environmentalists, and a number of artists and musicians.

The gathering of some three hundred people at the conference center on Valla Beach burst alight, quite literally, on the first evening with the two enormous bonfires of the aboriginal corroboree, their tribal celebration. For a nomadic people, I realized the corroboree would have formed the center of much of their social existence as well as being one of the prime vehicles for passing on their oral traditions.

It had been raining hard all day, and I had seen people I took to be Aborigines moving around the dunes and the shore surrounding the main hall. These people were evidently following some ancient and arcane method of siting the correct place at which to hold a corroboree. Later, whenever I saw them, each was carrying a large load of dead branches and twigs. Each moved steadily, seemingly unperturbed by the often torrential downpour, walking with exquisite lack of self-consciousness, sodden yet determined. And all seemed drawn by invisible filaments toward the chosen spot, somewhere beyond my vision in the rain.

Kamala Hope-Campbell, the conference organizer, told me that the Aborigines had become very interested in the occasion after hearing that it was being held at that particular location. Apparently, hitherto unknown to the conference organizers, there had been an aboriginal dolphin dreaming site off the rocks on the point.

Until relatively recently, there was a tradition among certain of the coastal aboriginal tribes of fishing cooperatively and harmoniously with dolphins. This could be done either through dream telepathy or, more commonly, by singing the dolphins in. This was accomplished, in the main, by the women of the tribe, the dolphins reciprocating by herding the fish in toward the waiting spears of the male Aborigines. I have since learned from Bill Smith that the rule was "take only what you need," and it was one fish per family member—the remainder was always returned to the dolphins.

Although I have heard about this cooperative fishing in Africa and it is also mentioned in passing by one of the ancient Greek authors, here was an entire culture that accepted the existence of a relatively sophisticated level of friendship between the two species. I had read also that dolphins were represented strongly in the myths and legends of the coastal Aborigines of Arnhem Land and the Groote Island area. In their belief system, the dolphins were perceived as accompanying dead souls across the oceans to heaven—significantly similar to the journey that ushers in the Maori afterlife. By all accounts, there are still dolphin dreamers to be found living near Groote Island who can call in dolphins by telepathic contact.

Bill Smith, so Kamala told me, was a moving force behind the Komilaroi Tribe, one of forty to fifty tribes that used to live in the area now called New South Wales. He and a small group of aboriginal contemporaries were seeking to gather as much as they could of the remaining oral traditions of their tribe, the real learning accumulated through unbroken lines stretching down the millennia, and to keep this vital knowledge alive through dance, law, language, and ritual.

Needless to say, the rain lifted that evening—quite magically, as it turned out, since it was to pour unremittingly for the next five days. But not for the night of the corroboree. It was clear that the Aborigines were in synchrony with natural conditions. I was among the early arrivals, although others told me that the corroboree had already started when even the earliest had gotten there. There was a quality about the gathering that suggested it might always have been happening, an ancient memory rekindled.

The ground was damp and sweet smelling. About twenty-five people stood around in an irregular oval formed by the two large, blazing bonfires. The booming of a couple of didgeridoos and the arhythmic, snapping clack of the click sticks pulsed over the background surge of a stormy surf beating against the beach on the other side of the dunes. The bonfires crackled and spat sparks and thick smoke, lighting up two large men, very nearly naked and covered with ample amounts of what appeared to be ocher or white clay. Both were dark skinned and muscular, barefoot, and dressed only in working shorts, and between them they seemed to be carrying on a wonderfully intricate line of banter.

The older of the two I recognized as Bill Smith from his photograph in the brochure, although it was momentarily discognitive to associate the quietly respectable, besuited image presented there with this vision in war paint. The other man, perhaps in his mid-to late thirties, was radiantly fine faced and full bearded, and turned out to be Ray Kelly, Jr. (Watch for that name—Ray Kelly, Jr.—because if he ever gets his hands on white man's media . . . eh, look out!)

At first I could not quite make out what was happening. The dialogue was fast, and my ear had not yet grown accustomed to the accent. Both men were bounding around—sometimes upright, sometimes on all fours—while constantly keeping this line of patter going between one another. The small group of people were watching, feet shuffling, not quite knowing what to do, a little like embarrassed adolescents at their first dance. I wondered if perhaps I was going to be painful witness to that saddest of affairs, in which indigenous people perform their sacred rituals before the uncomprehending and patronizing eyes of their more "sophisticated" Western brethren.

I could not have been more wrong. I was simply not prepared for the true sophistication of the aboriginal worldview as it was to emerge through the course of the corroboree, or the degree of compassion and forgiveness, or indeed the pure sense of fun that radiated from these two men. Their leaping and gamboling suddenly started making perfect sense, and within moments I was swept along by the energy and the humor of it all. It was a multilevel dialogue, many levels of which I could only vaguely discern but not understand. Along with all the others, many more having joined us by now, I found myself drawn into a succession of teaching stories, one flowing naturally into another.

As I fell into the rhythms of the corroboree and learned to make out the words from the accents, it came to me that I was hearing the downright funniest, coolest, hippest line of patter I have ever encountered—well on a par with that of comedians Richard Pryor and Robin Williams—mostly from Ray Kelly, Jr. There was a weaving, too, of what were obviously, traditional stories, with a completely extemporaneous line of spontaneous repartee. It was very, very funny. In the kindest of ways, they put us all on; and while they were at it, they put themselves on, too. The whole occasion was a massive joke, and both of the men exuded a deep sense of joy and well-being. They were not mocking their own traditions at all but by frequently making themselves the victims of their own jokes, they broke down the barriers separating them from us, the spectators.

In aboriginal life there are few, if any, spectators. Everyone is involved, and I am told that each person in the tribe has something they do better than anyone else or knows a piece of information entirely personal to themselves. I suspect there are no passive survivors in the Australian bush. As I listened, I became aware of a larger picture emerging from the teaching parables and the fluid one-liners, of a people who have somehow managed to find ways of maintaining their spirit through the most inhumane of colonizations.

They told of how the old people of some sixty years ago had decided to pass on nothing more of the sacred traditions, so hopeless had they judged the situation to be. It was a deeply pessimistic time for all Aborigines in Australia, and it was scarce wonder that, after 150 years of virtual genocide, the old ones might have thought to give it all up. Now there are only a handful of older Aborigines still alive. It is to these that Bill and his younger friends are seeking to demonstrate a new breed: a people who want to reclaim their heritage and are proud of their ancestry and the wisdom of their ancient line—and who are also canny enough to coexist profitably with the prevalent conditions.

The fires were spitting great swathes of sparks, while curious night birds wheeled soundlessly overhead and the ever-present surf formed an embracing background to what was becoming a truly magical encounter. Ray was warming our hearts with his vision and intelligence, laced always with a marvelous wit. He drew us into acting out an emu story, and soon there was an eminent English doctor of biochemistry lying on his back on the sandy ground, his long, thin legs waggling about in the air to attract Old Emu's attention. Emus are inquisitive birds, it seems, and will stop, stare, and investigate the patently absurd sight of a doctor of biochemistry on his back with his feet waving in the air. At that point, of course, the waggler's mate strikes Old Emu with a spear from behind, and it is tucker on the table for everyone. The wonderful absurdity of this distinguished scientist, who was so taken with his part that he continued enthusiastically to paddle his feet long after Emu was dead meat, and even the implied metaphor for Western technocracy was not, I suspect, lost on Ray, who glittered with roguish delight.

Another story started, one that tells of the discovery of the European honeybee by the first Aborigines to encounter them. The indigenous Australian bees apparently have a negligible sting, so after 39,800 years of bushcraft there was considerable surprise and pain at stumbling upon this new species. Ray had about thirty-five of us out there in the center as a "gum tree forest," our limbs waving in the wind while the story unwound. It culminated in both Ray and Bill throwing themselves around in a frenzy of bee stinging.

I could see that whatever story they got into, they totally identified with the characters, whether human or animal. When Bill played a kangaroo, he *became* Kangaroo: sniffing, tense, watchful, with big, sad eyes. In the bee story, I could almost see the swarm of angry insects and feel the stickiness of the stolen honey. And in the emu dance that followed, Ray was uncanny. He became Emu so entirely that I all but saw his tail feathers. Soon he was beckoning us into the wide oval, the crowd having swollen now to some two hundred people, and there were soon two-score of us strutting spasmodically around, attempting to emulate(!) the stiff, jerky fluidity of what we imagined to be an alert emu.

It was all too much for the aboriginal women gathered at one end of the proceedings, who were howling with laughter. There were twelve or fifteen of them, some with babies in their arms, shyer than the men but being sure to keep a rhythm with the click sticks throughout the hilarity. A little later I spent some time together with them and found I was welcome to be close and included. We shared cigarettes and more laughter, and I was consistently overjoyed by their strong spirits. They were right there, fully conscious and in their bodies, and certainly appreciating the corroboree on levels to which I had no access.

One level I did see, much to my amusement: every once in a while Ray or Bill would come in for a pit stop, exchange a few jokes with the women, who would splash more of the ocher over the man's perspiring body. He would then take a slug of water, throw back his head, and howl a demented parody of a primitive war cry before dashing back into the melee. The women would then squeal in delight and feigned terror. Between all of them, they were working the energy like pros. I saw how this form of gathering—literally a sharing of tribal traditions—is sadly missing in our culture. Yet here was a way that two quite different societies could reach across their differences with respect and mutual fascination.

It became clear, as the encounter progressed, that the Aborigines were reawakening their own sense of the spirit of the land. Their visit to this dolphin dreaming site was evidently as important to them and their traditions as it was for us to have them. A bond of mutual purpose seemed to build between us: there was so much to learn. It was as though, in those moments of uninhibited expression, something of the intensity of the aboriginal reverence for the land washed over us—a sense of the sacred that English writer John Michell terms "the reenchantment of the land."

Then Ray called out anybody who fancied themselves a didgeridoo player. For those who have never come across this strange musical instrument—probably the oldest in the world—a didgeridoo is cut from a tree branch, generally about five feet long, hollowed out by termites, and modified slightly with a beeswax mouthpiece to produce a low, rumbling sound when blown. It is almost impossibly difficult to play unless you are brought up with it, and the Aborigines take great fun in the contortions we go through while trying to get a sound out of it.

Mark, a younger Aborigine who had already demonstrated his prowess with the instrument, handed out four or five "didges," blowing through them to show they were in good working order. A massive huffing and puffing started among the volunteers, and great humor was extracted from the profusion of Bronx cheers amid all the serious faces.

It is a feature of the didgeridoo that it cannot be played while smiling—the mouth becomes too tense. There must have been a few in that first half-dozen volunteers who might have thought themselves proficient players, but they had not bargained for the laughter. No one could get even the start of a decent sound out the didgeridoos amid all the hilarity, until, yes, there was our eminent doctor of biochemistry again, glazed out with concentration, not a trace of a smile on his face, his eyebrows going like a couple of caterpillars on a seesaw, puffing out the perfect tones of a well-tempered didge.

The women took up the rhythm with their click sticks, and a song emerged. Bill called for "Little Black Baby," and I noticed a certain flicker of uneasiness pass among the white Australians. It spoke of the dreadful compulsory separation of aboriginal children from their parents during the wholly misguided, forced assimilation policies in the early part of the twentieth century.

Although it was sung with full remembrance, and the words ripped into our hearts, I was also able to sense an underlying forgiveness. There was an astonishing lack of self-pity in their singing. Yet, in those moments, I was able to see the horror of this ancient people who, having stewarded the continent for so many thousands of years in such a simple and direct way, were suddenly overrun by a force quite beyond their comprehension: the implacable face of Western industrial materialism. I could feel the profound despair and disappointment of the older generation, who watched their language and culture so unthinkingly destroyed—those who could not pass along their sacred traditions because their young people were no longer capable of handling them.

It became obvious to me then that Bill and Ray, and all the other Aborigines present, were themselves seeking to gain the trust and respect of their elders, the last generation to have kept the knowledge. The corroboree was turning out to be far more than a cross-cultural wingding. It reached deep into the natural resource of self-empowerment that such ancestral cultures possess, and this group was determined to win back their heritage and to be seen as worthy recipients of the sacred knowledge.

The energy, both inside and around the oval cast by the light of the bonfires, intensifies. There are no more spectators. The spirit has us. Ray is calling for trees again, and a wave of people surges forward into the coruscation of the flames. Ray freezes us into position, our arms swaying slightly in the soft wind. The sky has cleared, and a full moon disengages now from the massive rain clouds of earlier.

We become a forest of trees. Ray takes one look at me and dubs me a ghost gum tree, much to the amusement of all the Aborigines within earshot; I take it there is a double meaning in there somewhere. Rooted to our spots we stand, reaching up our branches to touch the sky, to draw down the glistening mantle of the Milky Way, Sirius, and the Southern Cross. All the while, the Aborigines play around our feet, scuttling this way and that, being in turn all the animals in the bush. The performance goes on long after I think my arms are going to fail me, but instinctively I know that it is a well-calculated test of stamina, so I hang in there waving in the wind and gritting my teeth. Finally the music slows down, and we all gratefully unbend and fade back into the crowd.

Now Bill is calling for a sharing. He wants to hear more directly from us, the visitors to his land. There is a tentative silence before a young American woman with a pure, throaty voice starts a familiar chant. It is Goddess music, and the crowd quickly picks it up. I watch Ray and see him gradually assimilating the words as we go round on it a few times. He appears happy, but I find out later that there is no Goddess in aboriginal cosmology. There is only one Creator, Biami, the Maker of all the universe.

More chants follow, and then some heartfelt visions and intimate stories are haltingly voiced. At the fifth or sixth calling, I feel impelled forward into the circle. I have no idea of what I want to say, only that I have a deep desire to give them back something of the joy I feel at being among them. I find myself telling them about the recent reconciliation of the planetary rebellion that has been hanging over us for the last 203,000 years: that we have all, aboriginal and nonaboriginal, been living through millennia of spiritual darkness and that we are finally emerging into the light together. I talk about the help that is available to us now from the angelic realms and that any move toward the good, the true, and the beautiful will be amply rewarded by the Great Spirit.

The words are drawn out of me, and I am aware that there is a tremendous heightening of interest when I mention the 203,000 years. With their immensely long time periods it is not inconceivable that they may have some historical references to the rebellion and its appalling impact on the spiritual equilibrium of this planet coded into their sacred knowledge.

In the flickering light of the roaring bonfires, my hands trembling with emotion, the spirit continues to speak through me, telling them that their long waiting is over—that they have been carrying our shadow, bearing the brunt of our collective madness. As we struggle to awaken, I tell them, so can this karmic responsibility be taken back and acknowledged.

I talk about the ending of ancient cycles, and both Bill and Ray nod enthusiastically. Again I have the distinct impression that I am speaking in their language, directly to them. I sense that I am a messenger delivering a dispatch that they are half expecting or possibly even know about from their own sources. I tell them of the need to expose the war god, of the planetary cleansing to be expected over the next few years, and of the ensuing renaissance that will sweep the world and include all people of every race.

I am speaking the wisdom of my heart, and I can see that it is touching some place deep inside them. Bill and Ray both glow back at me as I thank them for their compassion and for the forgiveness they have shown by welcoming us to their beautifully tended land.

The voice stops speaking and I stand, still physically shaking in the long silence, until Bill rises to his feet, walks slowly toward me and enfolds me in his arms. He is so extraordinarily well grounded that it is like hugging a tree, but as we embrace, sweat fusing with sweat, I know the message I have come so unwittingly to deliver has been fully received and understood.

Before leaving the conference, the Aborigines participated in a number of the events, always adding a refreshing and clear-sighted perspective. I noticed that they were particularly interested in the underwater birthing presentations, although I did not get from them any indications that they had practiced this in the past. Mind you, anything to do with birth would most probably be women's business, and they would be unlikely to reveal such tender secrets in front of men.

I was also able to briefly meet one of the aboriginal elders, Uncle Lenny, and a formidable old man he was. Uncle Lenny's niece told me in an unguarded moment that her uncle could move down the songlines—the great mythic journeys of the ancestors, preserved in sacred song—at a rate of about eight hundred kilometers a day! I did not doubt it for a moment. The old man was as hard as a rock, and from what I saw of him (and from what I already knew of aboriginal magical ways), such feats of teleportation would not be beyond him. I recalled, too, the story I had been told by writer Marilyn Ferguson of the aboriginal elder to whom she had shown the now-famous photographs of the face and pyramids on Mars. He was surprised that we had discovered them!

Patience, I am recognizing, is the key virtue toward a fulfilling relationship with another culture—or, indeed, another species—and many a time in the past I have found myself reminded of this. The aboriginal elders, however, exuded such a sense of knowing containment that any residual impatience happily dissolved along with most of my questions. I saw in those moments that I was going to be making a lifetime commitment to this relationship: to be with my new aboriginal friends as much as I could over the years and to allow the natural growth of trust and respect to open our hearts more fully to one another.

Bill Smith and another aboriginal brother, Hector Edwards, took time before they returned to the northern tablelands to conduct a group blessing of a magnificent piece of land recently acquired by ICERC and that overlooks the dolphin dreaming site. After Bill and Hector had walked the land along with the rest of the group, they planted two small trees, drank some water (which they then sprinkled on the saplings), and Bill spoke the following prayer:

Blessed are You, Biami, Lord God, Maker of all the universe, Creator of all creation. Butta Waa GoYu (Big Boss), Maker of the sun, stars, skies, rain, wind, Earth, and all that lives within it: all glory and praise are Yours. Bless the people of this community. Help and teach us to live together in harmony, in our land, as one. Because who can own the land? For the land is our mother.

Biami is present in all creation. By His powers, strength, and spirit, there is nowhere on Earth within our land where you can hide from Biami. He sees us and knows our every thought. So take care, and let the spirit of the land breathe, for it is alive and breathing. He reaches out to His creation and helps us wherever we are.

Stop and listen. Be still. Be a part of your land; look after it. Nurture it so that it will bear fruit and become your home. It is yours only while you care and share with one another, as one with the land. We are only passing through; we are in Your hands, Biami. For who can own something that is part of us?

We welcome you to this land, our country. Our fathers' and mothers' spirits join hands with you. For we love you all. Our spirits are now one, and you are safe.

22

Underwater Birthing

Our female dolphin visits all those planets and constellations that she has seen on the Web: Arcturus, the 257 planets of the Pleiadean Alliance, the Sirius cluster, Orion, Ursa Major, Antares, the DAL Universe, and the far reaches of the Milky Way. At this point she can fly there as easily as she can swim. She can meet and meld with beings from a thousand thousand races who travel the highways and byways of inner space. She finds herself part of an immense and wonderful multiverse, thronging with vitality and interest and populated beyond her wildest dreams. Here are multiple levels of reality, each with its own learning and transformative experience . . .

It had not been easy for Igor Charkovsky, the Russian pioneer of underwater birthing, to reach the International Dolphin and Whale Conference in Australia. It was only his second time out of his country; in spite of new freedoms, the old bureaucracy was dying hard. When he went to the airport in Moscow, Aeroflot had lost not only his ticket but also his reservation. Finally getting out late the next day, he promptly found himself stranded in Singapore. The KGB was not above suspicion, he told us with a wry smile when he arrived on the fourth day of the conference, tired but indomitably enthusiastic.

Charkovsky's delay worked out for the best, of course,

since it allowed the rest of us undistracted attention on the more cetaceous aspects of the gathering and the many levels of interplay the dolphins brought out in us. If he had arrived any sooner, the extraordinary impact of his presence more than likely would have dominated the proceedings. As it was, I suspect that most of us were happy to have become as well-modulated a group soul as we were when he made his first presentation the next day. Had we been any less prepared, the power of what he had to say would probably have knocked us over backward.

In his early fifties, Igor Charkovsky was of medium height, with limbs that, even through informal slacks and an open-neck shirt, appeared massive and strong. His trimmed black beard was turning gray, and his face, marked by lines of worry and sadness, could occasionally break into a childlike smile of pure mischief, especially when saying something calculated to shock his audience. While he was certainly never malicious, as I got to know him a little I felt he was struggling hard—and not always successfully—to keep his demons under control. He did not look like a man who shared his grief very easily.

Not surprisingly, his eyes revealed something of this ambiguity. They were moist and brown, deep set, and ringed with bruised lines. They were the eyes of a lover and a mystic, a saint and a seer, yet also the eyes of a Rasputin, a master hypnotist. His voice was soft and his manner self-effacing. Since he spoke no English, he required an interpreter—and no ordinary interpreter, at that.

Pyotr Patruchev, the man chosen for this task, had fled the USSR some years earlier, making Australia his new home. Since he had been attending the conference from the start, I came to know him over the first three intense days. Pyotr had also been the interpreter for the then Australian prime minister, Bob Hawke, and he was the current writer of an enlightened science column for a major Sydney newspaper. He had one of those deeply inquiring minds that can press to the heart of the most complex issue. He also looked like a younger Marcello Mastroianni.

Sometime during the first three days of the conference,

after hearing a number of anecdotes about how dolphins can energize exhausted swimmers, Pyotr Patrushev had spontaneously recalled his own astonishing dolphin story. As a young man in his early twenties, he had escaped from the Soviet army by swimming something like thirty-five kilometers across the Black Sea to Turkey. The time that he suddenly remembered was when he was becoming utterly tired and demoralized, and it was dawning on him that he might not make the long swim. Suddenly, there beside him was a single dolphin. They journeyed together for some hours until Pyotr's mood turned positive and hopeful once more. Then his finny friend disappeared as silently and mysteriously as it had come. Of course, the dolphin had changed his life—or at the very least, greatly extended it.

Along with Pyotr's many talents, he also had wide experience in rebirthing, a technique developed to help remove some of the more unpleasant human birth traumas and imprints. He was thus a propitious choice for this most tricky of translations. The subject of underwater birthing can raise the oddest of reactions. Birth traumas run deep in our psyches and can influence our behavior during the course of our lives far more than we are likely to believe.

So it was that these two talented and unusual men took to the platform of the large conference hall at Valla Beach. The hall was a fine timber structure, with its open beams and polished wood floor—altogether excellently appointed, with the exception of that Australian penchant for structural frugality: its corrugated iron roof. While I am sure the roof worked perfectly well in its primary function—that of keeping the elements out—the hall's designer certainly had never considered the noise level of heavy rain and its impact upon people within the space. As the storm persisted in its waxings and wanings and its sudden, explosive detonations, it was like being trapped inside the snare drum of an insanely determined recruit in a military marching band. Moreover, it had not stopped raining for four days and nights.

The constant downpour had resulted in the energy being focused in the main hall and not dribbled away by the pleasures of sun and surf. This was a cetacean-oriented conference, after all, so small wonder that the humidity of the atmosphere might have approached saturation. In fact, when a small group of us made some K-powered fourth-dimensional excursions, who did we find at the helm, observing and modulating the conference, and using the very downpour as a carrier wave with which to do it, but a small family pod of orcas—the so-called killer whales.

There were something like 350 people packed into the main hall, which was dark, moist, and warm. A projector's light flickered black-and-white sixteen-millimeter films onto an overhead screen, behind and to the left of the two speakers. Our mad recruit was battering on the roof at his most determined, the roar of the rain periodically overlaying all attempts to be heard. On the platform, Igor Charkovsky and Pyotr Patrushev, happily both with microphones, were each in their own ways being stretched to their limits.

Communication was not easy for either of them. Igor was a shaman, used to talking in stories and parables, to going off on immense and endless tangents. He was also clearly unpracticed at using an interpreter, frequently speaking at great length before Pyotr was able to translate. This gave the proceedings an ebb and a flow that added even further to the hypnotic overtones created by the flickering lights and the thrumming of the rain.

Igor talked extemporaneously. Some jokes were made about Pyotr's one-line translations of Igor's five-minute diatribes, but I could see that Igor was circling in on his main concern. When it came, there was a powerful sense of female knowingness to his words as he matter-of-factly related to us some of the most difficult and unpalatable realities we have to face collectively on this planet, right now.

The Soviet Union, so he told us (this was in May 1990), was in desperately poor shape—far worse than we could understand. We were simply not being allowed to know the facts, being protected from the full horror of the situation by the shame and deceitful ways of those in power who were directly responsible for it.

Igor was in particularly close contact with the ecological nightmare through the work he was doing with babies born in Kazakhstan. This area of southern Russia, he informed us, had been the site of numerous atomic experiments and had been even more seriously irradiated than Chernobyl. As many as three and sometimes four out of every five babies born in that region were malformed, he said, and the mortality rate was frightful—almost to genocidal proportions. But such crises also bring forth great opportunities for healing, he maintained, and it was within this emergency that techniques such as underwater birthing and water treatment became crucially important.

In spite of heavy resistance from the Soviet authorities, there can be no doubt that Igor's techniques work—the results are undeniable. He is finding that women who have seriously irradiated babies can keep them living by having them spend sometimes up to a week in water. Children pronounced incurable by the Soviet medical system are surviving and are often completely healed by his processes.

"Otherwise they would have died," Pyotr was translating very precisely at this point, realizing the importance of what Igor was saying. "I can keep children living in the water for a long time, in cold water sometimes. I believe this procedure, particularly with very sick children, can bring them to a near-death situation. It will at the same time free their fears, which are locked into the cellular system, and clear out a lot of past traumas.

"The repeated immersion and diving, which appears to be excessive to some people, actually takes the baby through a period of spontaneous rebirthing. In other words, it'll have to tap into different experiences at birth—and even past-life experiences, which are revived by this repeated immersion and diving." I could see some of the women sitting in front of me fidgeting a little nervously at this.

"In the case of a stillborn child," Igor continued to our appalled fascination, "I would put the child through a period of suspended animation and reanimation—but really through an NDE—by, for example, even freezing the child. And when they come out, it appears that certain very deep traumas are released at that time and the child makes the decision to live again." Then he added, "Very often the dolphin energy can help that reanimation. Children who have gone through this later on often make contact with dolphins."

The quiet truth and power of what Igor was telling us, together with the shocking reality of the plight of the women in Kazakhstan, began to make itself felt on the audience. I saw heads drooping and bodies swaying all around me. Up to now, most of the talk at the conference from the Western practitioners of underwater birthing had emphasized the gentle and loving side of the craft. The concept of forcing a near-death experience on a newborn baby was striking at some very deep insecurities.

Igor must have picked up on this because he went on to elaborate: "Children are very solid energy systems as babies; if they don't have fear, they can endure a lot of pressure. Even when a child appears to experience fear, I believe this is the release of encoded fears. When children overcome this, they can even sleep underwater." And on the screen we could see tiny babies, face down in the water, apparently fast asleep and yet turning every minute or two to take small breaths through the corners of their mouths.

After the astonished laughter had died down, Pyotr continued translating: "A child who doesn't have a lot of psychological problems after birth can swim immediately, but because most of us have these bad imprints, we can't do this in the beginning. One particular woman I admire had a very difficult personal history: she had a curse from her grandmother, and her father was alcoholic. So when she began to work with her child, three times the baby was brought to the state of clinical death in the water. But the child refused to leave until he underwent and relived some of his traumas. Then the child was healed and has become very strong. A child who undergoes this type of treatment can end up a very powerful being with strong telepathic abilities.

"One of the conditions for the survival of the baby during this process of continual living in the water is for the parents to create a situation where they're receptive to the energy of the whales and dolphins," Igor went on. He told us of despairing women who bring their severely impaired or dying children to the sea, to use it as a departure ritual. "Not infrequently," he continued, "when the baby is in the water, a dolphin will make contact with it, and on some occasions this has resulted in a reanimation and a healing."

In fact, Igor went so far as to suggest that underwater birthing has been fostered and directed *by* the dolphins. "In some way," he said, "they make contact with the fetus, which in turn encourages the mother to make herself available for water birth." Under these conditions he recommended as little interference—or assistance—as can reasonably be extended to the woman in question, since she was already being helped by the dolphin energy. "Dolphins are the greatest psychotherapists in the world," he stated, "and they should be credited with achievements like these."

"After such a child is born," he advised, "then best leave it as much as possible floating in the water. Sometimes I suggest that a woman fast before birth so that the baby, after being born, will go for the breast and actually suckle underwater."

Meanwhile, the black-and-white images, with some rare flashes of color, continued to flicker silently behind the two speakers. Babies cavorted and paddled in a variety of baths, swimming pools, and special glass-sided tanks. Every once in a while one of the images on the screen attracted Igor's attention, and he would launch off on another wonderful, rambling story drawn from among his almost two thousand water births.

Underwater birthing, he told us, had come to him in response to the two-months-premature birth of his own daughter. Coincidently, he had been investigating animal behavior and its relationship to water when he accidently dropped a box of newborn animals. Apparently they were badly hurt because he mentioned that after their fall they looked half-dead to him. He left fifty percent of the baby animals in the box and tipped the rest gently into a basin of water. All the animals in the box died, while the ones in the water survived. Consequently, he decided to use water to treat his sickly and failing daughter, and he found that she, too, quickly rallied and caught up with her healthier peers. "The reason for this," Igor stated, "is that weightlessness in water reduces oxygen and energy requirements so that the body's resources can to a greater extent be used to repair injuries:."

What a difference this could make if applied to standard medical procedures! Igor talked of water stretchers and of transporting seriously ill people in tubs of liquid. He even suggested hydro-surgery as a future possibility. Not only would the body be evenly supported, but the wound itself would be cleared of blood and oxygenated by the flowing water. Moreover, he told us, the organ being operated on would not collapse and become deformed; it would maintain its volume in water. Igor's daughter had not merely survived against tough odds, but she had grown strong and superfit on her father's constant water treatment. Soon afterward, Igor was delivering babies underwater.

Although he is the acknowledged pioneer of underwater birthing, Igor has not been completely on his own. Among the first to challenge conventional birthing practices in Europe was the English doctor Grantly Dick Read, who advanced through the early part of this century what he called birth without fear. In Russia, in the 1920s, physicians started experimenting with hypnosis, which, though later abandoned, led Professor A.P. Nicolayev to develop psychoprophylaxis, or natural childbirth. This flowered briefly in the 1950s and '60s but has also since been discarded by the Soviet medical authorities. Fortuitously this concept reached France through Switzerland and subsequently became popularized by Dr. Fernand Lamaze. Frederick Leboyer then adapted the methodology, calling it birth without violence, and it spread rapidly through the West among those questioning the metal-surface mentality of so much of modern medicine. It took Dr. Michel Odent in France to bring natural childbirth to its next logical step. He found that it was possible to give the baby a gentle and fearless start in life by delivering it in water.

But here Igor had something of a differing viewpoint, as the film on the screen was vividly illustrating. Holes were being cut in the ice of a frozen lake and small children, babies, and adults were plunging in and out. Igor was saying, "This little girl in the film can swim up to ten minutes in icy water. I have children swim in the ice water to mobilize their immune systems and to purify infections. Incidentally, there is in Russia a long tradition of children being baptized in icy water. It appears to turn on certain motor functions in the child, who very quickly learns to crawl on all fours." (I recall thinking: Yeah, to get out of there!)

Igor went on to say that although he does not have any footage of it, women have even given birth in ice holes: "Children born in this way appear to have telepathic contact with dolphins. I will take them and their mothers out to sea at night, and dolphins will immediately appear. All children born underwater seem to have an unusual contact with ecological consciousness. They have an increased sensitivity to every kind of natural phenomenon."

By now, the tension was growing quite palpably in the hall. Igor's gentle, hypnotic manner, the surging, rhythmic battering of the rain on the roof, and the strangeness of the information were having their effect on all of us. I found my own head nodding and then jerking back convulsively as I struggled to remain fully conscious—a reaction to my own birth difficulties, I assumed.

We were all crowded together in the darkness of the increasingly warm and humid space. The psychic atmosphere was tightening up with a stomach-wrenching apprehension.

"The fear of water," Igor was saying, "that most of us seem to have appears to have a bearing on the ecocide that we are now projecting toward the water resources of our planet. Through water birth, and through the facilitation of our contact and rapport with that particular environment, we will create a new generation of people who will not engage in ecocide, particularly toward the living marine environment.

"For thousands of years we've been breeding a species of biological suicides. If you subject any animal species to the procedures we conventionally experience, they'll also suicide. The Soviet Union has gone furthest in this ecological suicide, so we've got a model we can study there.

"I've experimented with separating newborn rats from their mothers, and they don't live very long. In the Soviet Union there's been a conventional practice of separating women from their babies on economic grounds. They would take twenty women, separate nineteen of them from their children, put them in lecture halls studying Marxism or working machines somewhere in a factory, and make [the remaining] one of those women the so-called educator for the children. Gradually the women will get used to the separation and the rupture of the bond that existed between them and their babies, and through that very deleterious process they can later be subjected to any stupidity or process. I believe we have bred a generation of people who have all sorts of sociopathic and sadistic tendencies and impulses."

As the deeper impact of Igor's words sank in, a pall of fear filled the hall. The rain was now so cacophonous that it seemed to be beating into us the harsh reality of his message.

"If you take children whose bonding has been ruptured and mothers who are unbonded with their children," he explained, "you can train the children to become engineers, scientists who may be engaged in military research, and producers of mass destruction. Such people will have no qualms murdering people of their own nationality—even people who are in kinship with them."

At this point, the psychic pressure finally reached an intolerable peak of intensity. Suddenly there was an impossibly noisy commotion in the darkness—chairs being knocked over, gasps, and cries—and a young woman rushed out onto the veranda, where she screamed and screamed. An awful, primordial despair filled the space, and the space between the spaces, and a silence viscous with horrified guilt hung over us. I believe we knew, in those moments, that she wailed for all of us. The tragic errors in judgment that have been made in the name of progress—of technology and economics, of authoritarian medical procedures, of materialisms, dialectical and otherwise—would surely have to rebound on us, as they had started to do environmentally. The rain crashed. The light flickered. We sat in numbed terror. We had seen Igor's truth—and it was hideous.

Thank heavens for the power of toning. Within moments, Chris James, the Australian tone-master, stepped in. He had been acting as a sonic caretaker for the gathering, breaking up accumulated tensions by leading well-timed vocalizations and body stretches.

"Aaahhhhhhhhhh. Breathe deeply, everyone . . . aaaahhhhhhh." We drew the tension and fear into our bodies and then, with the toned outbreath, began the process of blessed release. After three or four deep exhalations and some nervous laughter, the atmosphere became noticeably lighter. The woman on the veranda, however, by this time deeply into her own primal regions, continued to wail into the rain.

While these waves of sound and emotion were coursing through us, I saw that Igor was constantly moving his hands, as if he were stroking the energy field into a more manageable form. When we had finished toning he spoke again. "I am terrified by what I am saying, too! What I'm talking about has created this tension, and people who are supersensitive would have that kind of reaction. The situation is traumatic and tragic. The radiation we have unleashed during the process of technological evolution, with Kazakhstan and the nuclear testing sites alone, has diffused through the ecosystem." He looked up at the film flickering away behind him, before slipping fluidly to his next subject.

"Many children are now being born with weak joints," he went on. "By manipulating these joints . . . [and coincidently there on the screen was a tiny, half-hour-old infant being pulled and pushed by Igor Charkovsky in what appeared to be a most forceful manner] and allowing the baby to use certain of its muscles [push, shove], within some hours the baby will begin to use these muscles. This is not quite Benjamin Spock [pull, crack], and a lot of mothers who think of themselves as very loving will reject this kind of discipline.

"Inversely, if you take a wild animal and begin to subject

it to the lack of discipline human beings have, then you have domesticated pets [wrench, twist] who are as weak as ourselves. In the wild, a small deer has no choice but to move very swiftly following its mother—otherwise it'll get eaten by a predator."

A woman shrieked from the back of the hall: "You're a barbarian, Charkovsky!"

A murmur of angry agreement swelled up, presumably from some of those same very loving mothers Igor had previously mentioned. But this was territory Igor knew well. He was a born agent provocateur.

"Some of the native hunters," he continued without missing a beat, "who are also barbarians [his sly grin here], will run ten kilometers after a deer because he knows that if he doesn't, he will miss a meal and probably starve. He will run until the deer drops from exhaustion. Then he'll cut open the belly of the deer, crawl in, and wait for his hunting mates to join him for the meal."

Referring once again to the baby being manipulated on the screen, he told us in no uncertain terms: "In special regard to the cerebral paralysis caused by low-level radiation, some people who regard themselves as very loving toward the baby will allow it to become a cripple. Whereas I will torture that baby, moving its joints to a point where the blood is attracted to that joint, and I will rehabilitate the child." With that, Igor Charkovsky excused himself and walked rapidly back through the crowd to attend to the woman outside, who was still screaming in the downpour.

The natural drama of the situation, the quiet conviction of the man, the evident truth of much of what he was saying, and the innate power of his subject matter left deeply felt ripples that continued affecting us throughout the night. Everyone was talking about Igor, comparing notes and attempting to bring into fuller focus what he had been telling us. Most of those I talked with agreed that he had activated many of our own birth traumas. A New York attendee, Michelle Margetts, volunteered that the presentation had made her confront her whole range of doubts regarding her potential motherhood and that she had found it extremely difficult to breathe throughout. A number of people made specific reference to the extensive and unusual use Igor put to his hands. In moments of high tension and also during meditations, he seemed to be carving out these odd figures in the air—mudras, perhaps—as if, in the most intimate way, he were conducting the group soul.

That he was a magician, there can have been little doubt. He left an intense effect on everyone, forcing us back on our deepest intuitions. Deep down I knew that the fearful reality he was presenting, while doubtless true within the confines of the materialist nightmare, had no real spiritual staying power and would therefore fade away in the face of higher realities. Meanwhile, the lessons to be learned from facing and moving through the pessimism inherent in soulless, authoritarian government would result in a strength of individual spirit that would shine forth radiantly in the coming worldwide renaissance.

The weather had broken by the time Igor came to give his two-day workshop immediately after the conference. The rain had washed the air particularly clear and clean, even by immaculate Australian standards, and the sunny, autumnal brilliance encouraged us to use the outdoor pool for Igor to demonstrate, hands on, some of his techniques with babies.

The fact that the water was icy cold quite naturally did not deter the shaman one little bit. In the water, Igor was another man. He was truly amazing with the children, folding and pushing and pulling them, dunking them in and out of the water. It was all done with a level of supreme confidence that communicated itself instantly to the children, though possibly a little less readily to their parents, who struggled earnestly not to display—heaven forbid they should communicate it to their child—any of the anguish they were undoubtably feeling.

Igor had emphasized a number of times just how sensitive babies and small children are to the projected fears of their parents, and in many cases he preferred to work without the parents present. It was an act of great trust on all sides. One of the mothers told me later that after seeing him handling her child with such extraordinary grace and natural authority she had total confidence in the man.

It was obvious from his treatment of the babies he was given to handle that he related to them much as a coach would—as one born to manipulate bodies (Charkovsky's training was in physical education). As Michelle Margetts observed, "He doesn't approach mothers and children with any assumption of unsolvable problems."

Igor did half a dozen quite extended healings, including one on a baby girl whose parents, I knew, were deeply concerned about her very weak and impaired chest. She had been a water baby and yet had been constantly ill since she was born. Igor spent much concentrated time dipping her in the pool, holding her out by her thighs, and keeping her underwater for increasingly extended periods of time so that she was forced to open her little chest and, while in the air, to breathe in deeply. The mother showed enormous faith and courage by standing in the pool, keeping in close eye-to-eye contact with her daughter, while a Russian shaman pushed her child to the point of death.

Yet it worked! I have kept in contact with the family, and although the child went through something of a healing crisis immediately following the workshop, she has now developed marvelously powerful lungs and chest and has had no recurrence of her previous ailment. She also loves being in the water, so her father tells me, and no longer seems to mind if it is cold.

The contrast between what were clearly two different Igors became more evident through the course of the workshop. The tenderness that came through in the films, and the caring and confidence with which he handled the children, alternated—sometimes ominously—with a very dispirited and scornful Igor who made no pretense about hiding his frustration at some of those present. He seemed particularly disdainful of those who espoused the more gentle and protective features of underwater birthing. Igor felt that his approach, with all its apparent harshness, was of vital importance at this turning point of evolution, and he adamantly refused to have it watered down.

Reflecting on all this, I conclude that both paths will have their immense value. Underwater birthing is here to stay, and Igor will have to come to terms with the fact that people in the West can adapt it—and are doing so—quite naturally to their own conditions, needs, and desires. By now many hundreds of water babies have been delivered outside of Russia and are demonstrating some of the same capabilities that Igor cites. My experience in New Zealand, meeting the group of water babies, showed me that very clearly.

Looking at it with detachment, I have to say that Igor, being a highly open and sensitive man, appears to have taken on the psychic brunt of the failure of the Soviet experiment. Possibly the assumption of this responsibility is the next step in his personal spiritual development, and how he deals with it may well be the measure of the growth of his soul. What must be hard for him to remember, from within the teeth of the crisis, is that the entire planet is in transformation: all the old ways are being dislodged as we move irrevocably into the fourth dimension. And we are certainly not the first planet to do so.

There are quite evidently enormous numbers of inhabited planets and a great many of them must be populated by technological societies. The process of atomic power, radiation, and the resultant pollution and globally distributed mutagens must be readily understood by those who created these processes in the first place. To think anything else is naive.

Nothing significant occurs that is not meant to happen. This is an intuitive truth that transcends the dilemma of free choice and determinism. We live on a world, so we are told, that has suffered an inordinate amount of pain and spiritual darkness, and yet out of this crucible something entirely new is emerging. If there is to be some discomfort along the way, there are vast numbers of experienced and willing souls prepared to undergo the trials of incarnation in order to further the greater planetary mission.

However uncomfortable are some of the short-term effects of technological evolution, the transformation of our world could not be happening right here, right now, without it. And if low-level radiation is indeed mutagenic, then who is to say whether, in time, it might not be among the key factors in the mutation of the new phylum—the coming race?

23

Life with Wild Dolphins

The Watchers take our female dolphin out of her body to Phinsouse, in the heart of the Andronover Nebula, to the great architectural sphere that has been designated the center of space activity for this area of the galaxy. There she is shown that every inhabited world has its own chamber: part meeting place, part museum, part vivarium—a constantly changing biomontage representing the state of life on their home planet. She is able to see what in many ways she is unable to appreciate from the Web: that the secondary species, the split fin, have, over the recent few hundred solar cycles, allowed appropriate stewardship of the biosphere to disintegrate into a somewhat sorry state of affairs . . .

One of the features of the dolphin journey is that I never quite know what is going to happen next or where it is all leading. The value of writing a book like this, of course, is that it encourages a bit of stocktaking every few years. Admittedly, I set out with a relatively simple goal in mind—this time it was to examine telepathy and dolphins. I had hoped, as I invariably do, that it would be a straightforward affair, but I did not then understand a fundamental factor about telepathy: it is not mere thought transference, as I might have supposed, but seems to involve a dimensional shift of consciousness, which is much more complicated.

I have found that it is not possible to approach dolphin

telepathy without gaining some idea of alternate realities or parallel dimensions. When I started the series of adventures recorded here, I was already working with the premise that multiple realities exist in a very real and tangible sense. It had been the only way I could explain to myself how some of the odder events in my life might have occurred.

Naturally, the concept of multiple levels of reality is by no means my own, as it is hinted at—and in some cases even spelled out—in a number of arcane and occult traditions, and it has even become the focus of a branch of quantum physics. The study of angels also presumes an appreciation of varied life forms existing at different vibrational frequencies. Castaneda's don Juan lays down the *nagual* and the *tonal* as two quite separate realities; Seth, the entity channeled by Jane Roberts, presents a worldview that encompasses many alternate realities; and the bicameral-mind approach of renegade Princeton philosopher Julian Jaynes rests on the distinction experienced between realities generated by the left and right hemispheres of the brain. However strange it may seem to those still struggling to make sense of *one* reality, there does seem to be a recurrent theme in life that suggests the existence of worlds other than the one we consider to be consensus.

The simplest way of knowing more about multiple realities is to reach down inside yourself and take a moment to contemplate those occasions when reality has, quite literally, shifted. These times can be very pronounced, as in cases of crisis or when a death point has been reached, or quite subtle, as in moments of high creativity or in shamanic ritual. Over the years I have found that these shifts in reality most frequently happen at points of peak consciousness, and I have come to understand them as sidestepping.

In its most extreme form, this reality-shifting phenomenon can be observed in certain life-threatening situations. Two examples from true and trusted friends should serve to illustrate what I mean by this.

My friend Alexandra Manzi Fe has told me how she was crossing one of the larger California deserts in her van with her daughter, Goldie, who was about five years old at the time.

They pulled off the road sometime after midnight and were settling down to sleep. Alex recounted that she lay there, Goldie already asleep, when suddenly, through one of the small windows in the rear of the van, she saw quite distinctly the form of a man with a shotgun. She remembers the thick, double barrel glinting in the moonlight. He walked slowly around the van until he found the side-panel window open. Lifting his shotgun, he started poking it in the window. At that moment, Alex said, she focused all her concentration and prayed for the reality to change. Change it did. The man and the gun disappeared before her eyes. All else remained the same.

The second example is more personal—except that I was asleep at the time. It also occurred on the highway. This time, my friend, the late Carolina Ely and I were driving across the United States, from New York to New Mexico. It was late at night. I was slumped snoozing in the front seat, and Carolina was driving our U-Haul moving van. She was tucked in behind a large tow truck, and both vehicles were traveling at about sixty-five miles per hour. She was jerked out of her driving reverie to see, to her horrified fascination, that a heavy tire iron had bumped loose from under the truck in front of her, had bounced once, and was hurtling directly toward our windshield. Feet away from the glass, it simply vanished in thin air.

These are not isolated examples, and most of us have a few totally strange and inexplicable encounters with the twilight zone in the course of our lives. That many of them also occur at moments when our lives are in danger should not be surprising either since, in our culture, we seem to know so little about the nature of death.

Over the years, I have heard a number of stories from people who have somehow "survived" death by sidestepping to a parallel reality in which the immediate threat no longer existed. They did not understand how they did it, but the fact that they were recounting their story was evidence enough that they had managed it. In fact, death itself can possibly be better comprehended as dying to a consensus reality that no longer serves as an adequate teaching device for the person concerned. Life in the third dimension is a university, after all.

When I started this line of thinking, it had been my observation that these alternate realities, however they are generated, appear to cluster down into three primary levels, or reality streams, to which we are all more or less intimately connected. But that, it turned out in the face of experience, was something of an oversimplification. Primarily through my encounters with the angels, I have now become convinced that there are, at the very least, seven parallel levels of reality, or dimensions, to which we all have access through our chakras, our internal subtle-energy system. It is also true to say that we are living, with different degrees of consciousness, in all of these seven dimensional realities at the same time.

Without a doubt there are other dimensions within which we coexist, but it appears that these seven are the starting points in our appreciation of our multidimensional natures. Given the vibrational structure of matter—and of the material universe—it is evident that these realities exist simultaneously and can sometimes only minimally interpenetrate one another. In other words, bizarre though it may seem, we appear to be living in seven separate but broadly interconnected realities at the same time. Sometimes we have sight of this, and on occasion a number of these realities can become aligned, allowing us a brief glimpse of our part in the Multiverse. I believe that these realities can be entered through working with our chakra systems because they are the "windows" from one state to another.

The realities span from the devic to the divine. The first, or root, chakra, located at the base of the spine, gives access to the mineral intelligence; the long, low waves of gravitational telepathy; and the links that bind all stars and planets into one cosmic family. The second chakra, in the area of the sexual organs, opens into the wisdom of the trees, flowers, and vegetables; the fecundity of the plant kingdom; and the richness of the devic life that accompanies it. The third chakra, in the solar plexus area, is the inner window to the animal kingdom, to our animal nature, and to the power and mobility inherent in the higher orders of physical life.

Our heart chakra, the fourth, the angels tell us, is our intended domain; it is the linking bridge between the outer manifestion of the created material universe and the inner nature of the top three chakras. It is by being in the heart that we can open ourselves to higher mind, whether it be insight into the eternal verities or the simple joy of living a loving life. But experience shows that we can go into these higher realms only to the extent that we have cleared and released blockages in our three lower realms—a fail-safe mechanism that prevents inappropriate discovery and misguided manipulation.

The top three chakras allow us access to the inner levels from which plans, designs, and patterns are projected onto the screen of three-dimensional matter. The fifth chakra, in the throat, accesses the angelic kingdom and can act as a seat of telepathic dialogue—of listening with the "ears of the throat." Our guardian angels guide us through this energy system. The sixth chakra, behind the center of the forehead, opens to the domain of the archangels and is, I suspect, a mental link to our vastly far-flung cosmic family. The seventh chakra, at the crown of the head, is the key to our divine nature, the indwelling Spirit.

When we become subject to dolphin telepathy, I believe we are accelerated into a fourth- and sometimes fifth-dimensional level of reality. This is the experience of time slowing down, of an entirely new lucidity of mind, of a wonderful, peaceful gnosis; all are recurrent themes of this communication and all are features of these dimensions of beingness. Glenda Lum, the Australian musician who has played such extraordinarily evocative music with cetaceans and whom I have come to know through spending time down under, has described to me what it was like to find herself in the water with more than one hundred dolphins. I caught up with her in her beautiful garden in New South Wales while she was making and painting the shamanic masks that she now uses in her performances. I asked her about the encounter.

"It was a particularly shiny morning," she remembered, "and I was in a bit of a negative state. I went down to the beach and forced myself to run because I wanted to start breathing more fully. I ran down toward the south end and passed my friend Swa on the way. He was lying down, so I just kept running. When I got down to the point, I looked out. And there, seven yards away, among this little batch of rocks, I saw a mass of fins—up to a hundred—simply floating in the water. I was totally overcome—completely ecstatic. I was talking to myself: 'Oh God! What's happening?'

"I didn't have my bathers on. There were people down at the other end of the beach, but I didn't care. I just took my clothes off and slipped into the water. And they all just stayed there, all those fins. I started to breaststroke out to them, and then I remembered to put my head underwater. They were all whistling and clicking, and it was going through my body. It was almost too much for me; it just sort of jumped a dimension.

"The water was really green, end-of-winter clear, and I put my head under and I could hear them all whistling. I kept listening to them. They didn't go away, so I started swimming even nearer. Suddenly this big dolphin swam toward me and in front of me. I got the strongest feeling that he said to me, 'Don't flap your arms around! Just lie there and float.' Then he went straight back to the pod, and they all turned their fins and started to slowly cruise off.

"I got out of the water. I couldn't bear to experience this by myself—I knew I had to have another person with me. So I ran all the way back to get Swa, who was still sleeping on the beach. We ran back together and went into the water with them. Swa could hear all their whistling; then they started moving out again. It was like I'd asked them to wait—I had to go get someone, to have an extra strength with me because it was too much.

"My heart was beating really fast. Swa suggested we get out of the water. We started to walk, and for two hours down that beach we went, a small pod of dolphins stopping for fifteen to twenty minutes at a time, doing the most incredible acrobatics. They did everything to have us screaming and dancing for joy, and then that pod would swim farther down and make way for the next lot, who would stop in front of us for another twenty minutes.

"Every time a new pod came, they'd do something like coming up out of the water—or there'd be twenty of them riding a wave right in; they'd nearly beach themselves. They'd be coming in on a wave, then suddenly they'd flip direction, then flip again and again. Then they'd leap right out of the water just in front of us. Because they spent lots of time with their heads out of the water, in bunches of four or six, I think to them it was like seeing us. They were really saying, 'It's as you think it is!' Then they'd move off, and another pod would appear and do the same thing."

I asked Glenda if she felt any particular communication was going on. "I felt something really good was happening for them," she said. "There was a huge gathering of them, and there were 'people' there—fellow dolphins—they hadn't seen in a long time. That was my feeling. Some were passing through, and they were doing this for us, since we were the only ones watching. It was so deliberate. Every time they did something, it would send this electric shock through our bodies, and we'd just jump and shriek and wave at them. It was pure joy—an utter joy."

"You mentioned something about jumping a dimension. In what way did you experience this?" I asked her.

"I felt it straight away. I can only go back to when I was a child, where I experienced so much light. The language *was* light, so it never had to do with meaning. I'd get to that extradimensional shift where I'd hear music. It's not like Earth music; it makes a shift in my ears and my eyes to my own inner space. It's the same sort of light that surrounds me and the whole event."

"Is there a shift down after it?" I wondered.

"Funny that you say that. I was blown out the whole day, of course. Next day I was really sick. I remember thinking that I'd had such a blast of energy. Maybe it was a kind of clearing, in a way."

"Dross rising to the surface?" I suggested.

"It was an elimination," she concluded. "I would have thought that I'd feel on air for days, but this was so intense. Absolute shock. That's why it was great to have someone with me. If I had had to witness it by myself, what would it be? It's the sharing, isn't it? Because the dolphins were so sharing, and deliberate."

Having spent sometime with the dolphins at the Britannia Beach Hotel in Nassau in the Bahamas, at the beginning of my own dolphin journey a decade ago, I am also including the following personal experience of Cathleen Civale, a woman I have never met but whose tale I intuitively trust. Handed onto me by my friendly walk-in, Michael Miller, her story contains something of the wild, passionate magic that is waiting to greet us all.

"I was spending two months in the Bahamas," she wrote out for Michael, soon after the encounter. "Every day or two I'd walk to the cove next to the Britannia Beach Hotel on Paradise Island and watch a diver feed some dolphins lunch. I felt a tremendous sense of affinity for those beautiful mammals and spent a great deal of time watching them and meditating on their beauty and grace. I had a deep feeling of appreciation that I am sharing a planet with a whole species that's enjoying itself as much as I am.

"Toward the end of the second month of my stay, I witnessed something unfortunate and dreadful. In another cove near the hotel, a group of French scientists had captured four dolphins, two adults and two babies. The dolphins didn't resist the men's efforts to contain them, though they could have easily broken free, and I have no idea why they didn't. I went through a whole variety of feelings—alarm, horror, anger; I almost even got in the water with them and I don't swim, having almost drowned twice as a child! As this went on, I moved closer to one of the dolphins, now motionless and strapped into a carrying bag. He was hot and uncomfortable. I took a jar of Vaseline™ out of my beach bag and gently caressed him, stroking him on the sides and back, and sending him soothing thoughts. I felt a tremendous wave of sadness, but that was all I could do.

"A few weeks later, I was back on the mainland, on Key Biscayne in Florida. I knew dolphins had been seen around there, so I went down to the beach and waded into the shallow water. Two friends were with me. When I got into the water, there were no dolphins in sight, but within moments two dolphins appeared out of nowhere and swam around my legs. I felt surrounded by their auras.

"I have no idea what got into me, but I took a leap of faith. Completely uncharacteristically, I lunged forward and jumped onto the back of the larger of the two dolphins. I held onto his fin and let my legs trail behind. Before I knew it, we were off. The other dolphin would swim around us, gently massaging my legs with its body as we all headed offshore. I was never more *here,* more *present,* in my life. I had no thoughts and no sense of time; I was simply with these beautiful beings. My friends told me afterward that we had paralleled the shore for about a hundred yards and then veered straight out to sea.

"Finally a thought burbled to the surface of my mind: what would happen when they dived down into the crystal blue sea? At the very moment I had the thought, my beloved new friend turned and made a beeline for where they had picked me up. There seemed to be no surprise at this perfectly natural communication—they simply knew.

"Throughout this journey, the oddest thing is that I don't recall feeling any physical sensations. I didn't feel wet or dry, cold or warm. My hands didn't feel tired in any way, just secure and safe. Nor did I feel surprised at this; it was almost expected and all in the greatest of fun.

"When we arrived back at the spot where we had all met, I simply stepped down onto the sandy bottom. But the dolphins weren't finished having fun. They'd only brought me back to reassure me that I was safe, but it was far too early to end the party! They swam around my legs again, and this time I knew what I was doing and climbed on carefully. We were off again, this time faster and maybe a hundred feet out from the shore. It was effortless. Ahead I could see a snorkeler cruising the reef. I felt a sense of humorous intention in my dolphin. He sped up and headed directly toward the poor man, only to turn a sharp ninety degrees at the last moment. I can still see the look on the guy's face. Again, the oddest thing: I felt no abruptness at this movement, no gravitational inertia affecting the lightest of grips I had on the dolphin's fin.

"After a few hundred yards of play, they brought me back again. A small crowd had gathered, including my two friends and also some of John Lilly's people who'd watched the whole event through binoculars."

Cathleen's account once again emphasizes the sense of being enveloped in a dolphin's aura, the biofield that Igor Charkovsky talks about.

On the eastern coast of Australia, dolphins swim freely in some of the clearest, cleanest waters in the world. The beaches are long, sandy bays, wild and remarkably free of people. I have come to know this area in the course of my visits to Australia, and it seemed a perfect place to hide away and get this book written. Mostly I just wanted the proximity of the dolphin energy, since the book was to focus so intimately on them. Naturally, I had hoped to see them, perhaps even to get to swim with them, but fortunately I have learned to surrender any expectations where dolphins are concerned.

Of course, everyone has his or her dolphin story in the tiny hamlet where I was living. It is tucked between a long, golden, deserted beach and the mouth of a broad river, and the dolphins are sometimes daily visitors to the rich fish life of the estuary

John, of the village store, was privileged to witness a dolphin birth while out on his surfboard the other day. It was a thick, misty morning—he could not see the shore from where he was catching waves—and there before him, between where he sat on his board and the beach, he saw the wriggling tail emerging, watched the midwife dolphins supporting the tiny form, felt the happy wave of release from the pod, and saw them all move off together. The coincidence with his own imminent paternity (his wife, Tracey, was very pregnant) was not entirely lost on him.

Another neighbor, Charmaine, told of walking by the river with a young man she described as "a cynical city slicker down from Brisbane." Dolphins were playing on the other side of the water, some two hundred yards away. Charmaine bet that she could get one of the dolphins to swim over to where they stood. Our young sharpie dismissed the idea with a sarcastic sneer. Immediately, one of the dolphins detached itself from the pod, swam very rapidy over to them, and executed a perfect tail stand—with a fish balanced on the end of its beak!

As usual, the dolphins were evidently following very much their own schedule. Over the six months I was there, despite their constant psychic presence I saw them a mere three times. Only on one of those occasions did anything like a meaningful exchange take place or did I feel that slight shift in consciousness that accompanies dolphin telepathy.

It happened that one day my Australian partner, Elli Bambridge, and I walked down to the wide, wild beach, watching big Pacific breakers rolling in over the sandbars. As we came over the dunes, Elli shouted out loud, "Hallo, dolphins!" Moments later, we both saw a pod of about seven swimming some fifty yards offshore. It appeared that they were feeding, since they were moving around in small circles. They were traveling slowly up the beach with the current.

Enchanted, we walked up the beach, too, keeping pace with them as they slowly circled north. Elli was soon up to her waist in the roaring surf, but she was almost immediately dumped by a huge wave and could not see the dolphins from the water anyway. So we settled for walking up the beach together, calling and happily waving our arms around.

The dolphins appeared utterly disinterested in our antics. Always the compulsive experimenter, I suggested we send a visualization together of one of the dolphins leaping out of the water. We focused the visual image, did what we could to project it at the dolphins, held it for a few moments, and then released it.

No response. We continued pacing the dolphins for about thirty seconds, and then we both stopped at the same time, turning to each other with the same thought. Elli verbalized it: "Who wants to do a somersault when you're eating your dinner?"

No sooner was that said than we turned to look at the dolphins again, and one large, black tail came high up out of the water, pointing directly toward us, and very leisurely slapped down a great sheet of spray in our direction—once . . . twice . . . three . . . four times. At no other point, before or after this, did any of them repeat this action, and I have since heard from a knowledgeable dolphin trainer that such tail flapping has been seen among captive dolphins—but seldom among those in the wild. It was a tacit lesson in telepathic etiquette.

After we had been walking with the dolphins for about ten minutes, politely keeping our thoughts to ourselves, they started coming in closer, over the second sandbar to within fifteen yards of the shore. More dolphins that we hadn't seen earlier joined them, and together they came surfing in on the waves in perfect formation, four or five beaks and smiling faces sticking out from a moving wall of water.

If this was an invitation, I was not ready for it. Perhaps with a few months' more confidence in the ocean—the unexpected rips and the wild waves—I would have plunged in more willingly. At that point, however, we just stood and watched them. When it was obvious that we were not going in to join them, and coincidentally we found that we had walked the half-mile or so to one of our favorite spots in the dunes, the dolphins chose to leave us and slipped easily and rapidly back out into deeper water and away.

As I stood on that now lonely beach, the black fins cutting the water far out beyond the breakers, I experienced a feeling such as I have never had before: a feeling filled with such poignance, such gentle wonder, such tender, sad joyfulness—all at once. A flooding. In those moments I was wholly in my heart. The dolphins had worked their dimensional magic on me, again when I least anticipated it.

They showed me a key to what we are collectively about to go through as we move more fully into the era of the great transformation. The challenge, of course, is to stay firmly in touch with the fourth-dimensional reality of the heart, surely slipping back every once in a while, but always returning to the way of love. The key is the heart. If we do this, we naturally and fluidly open to the fifth-dimensional awareness in which telepathic contact with dolphins, extraterrestrials, and angels will all seem perfectly normal.

However dark and terrifying we have allowed our fear driven realities to become, they are not the true reality to which we are transforming, and therefore they can only dissolve in the light of the fundamental optimism, the good common sense, and the fine humor of the kingdom of the heart. The dolphins are here, among other things, with the express intention of helping us through these rapids of time and to allow us to move more freely into the dimensions and realities awaiting us as we rejoin our cosmic relations.

An Exultation

With the Watchers, our female dolphin exults inwardly: seeing the sorry state of the biosphere, she is overjoyed, for she knows presciently that such challenges can easily be met and mastered with the full cooperation of the two species. Knowing this, she rejoices.

She is filled with pleasure at the shared destiny of the two species as it becomes unveiled for her. She opens to the wonder of her assignments ahead. She knows suddenly, amazingly, what lies in front of her as our beautiful, little blue-green planet, seemingly so far from the main star routes, floats wondrously, irrevocably, into its own great transformation. For it is our planet itself, our sweet Mother Gaia, who has come of age. It is she who is about to become, once again, reunited with her cosmic brothers and sisters. Our female dolphin sees all this and exults.

She knows and comprehends the destinies of all, of ALL, as the two great species once again rejoin and rejoice at having found one another, cosmic cousins in this great unfolding galactic drama.

—Notes from *A Dolphin Journey*

Appendix A
Dolphin Sonics and Telepathy

A dolphin's brain is somewhat larger than that of a human being, and it is also more richly convoluted. This increase in surface area is generally thought by scientists to be a sign of high intelligence. While the dolphins' visual apparatus is simpler than ours, their acoustic capabilities, both in the emission and reception of sounds, have been calculated by Dr. John C. Lilly to be some twenty times faster and more complex than those of humans.

Dolphins are also able to use three different ways of generating sound at the same time. Best known to us is their echo-recognition ability, called sonar. This is perhaps analogous to clapping hands in a dark room and getting a rough idea of where the walls are. However, because sound travels faster, farther, and more clearly in water than in air, dolphins are able to perceive a very precise picture of their world by interpreting the echoes they hear.

It is also becoming evident that this means of communication most likely leads to some form of telepathic contact. A dolphin's sonar is clearly able to discern between the densities of different metals, and we know that they can "see" into the body as if their sonar gave them x-ray vision. They always know, for instance, when human females are pregnant—sometimes before the women themselves are aware of it—and consistently give special attention to them. Glandular changes in the bodies of all mammals reflect variations in emotional and physical well-being. Dolphins, with their thirty-million-year history, are able to gauge their companions' welfare with an accuracy that we would find literally supernatural.

While watching a research film in the late seventies, I first saw what I felt was an obvious example of dolphin telepathy in action. It was not commented upon in the film, so I had no idea at the time whether the scientists involved could see what to me was so clearly evident.

The film, a twenty-minute, sixteen-millimeter documentary by the English cetacean researcher Horace Dobbs, featured Donald, a lone dolphin who appeared in the cold waters off the northern English coastline. Games and play were areas of much sharing and mutual learning, and to encourage this Dr. Dobbs had built a wooden surfboard that he and his staff could tow behind their motor boat.

In the scene in question, the cameraman was sitting in the bow of the small speedboat, filming over the shoulder of Dobbs's female co-worker in the direction of the sea behind her. The boat had just been pulling the scientist along on his homemade surfboard when Donald came alongside the board, easily keeping pace with the speedboat. Then, with a wicked nudge, Donald pushed the scientist off the board and threw himself onto it, managing to get himself towed along at high speed!

After a few moments of this, the female researcher evidently felt enough was enough, and she started to speak to the cameraman, "We must go back to pick up Hor—"

At that *exact* point in time, in mid-sentence, Donald slid off the surfboard and turned back toward Dr. Dobbs, who by this time was just a bobbing black head in the distance. The strangeness of the moment was underlined by the tone in the woman's voice when she turned to see that Donald was already on his way. It was a mixture of tenderness and embarrassment, as if she felt slightly raw at being caught so openhearted.

There was no way Donald the dolphin could have heard the woman's remark in any conventional sense. It was a low aside to the camerman in a noisy speedboat, and the dolphin was a good thirty to forty feet behind. Dolphins also have relatively poor hearing of airborne sounds in comparison to their brilliant underwater abilities.

A coincidence, perhaps? One of those happy sychronicities that seem to accompany the dolphin trail? Possibly. But I doubt it. I saw Horace Dobbs's film before I had the chance to swim with dolphins. In fact it was one of the things that so intensely provoked my interest in the first place. Now I have no doubt from numerous personal experiences that dolphins, orcas, and many of the whales are indeed able to detect what we are feeling and thinking.

Telepathic, yes, but not in the manner we might immediately or directly appreciate. We tend to think of telepathy as simple thought transference, but it is something far more complex than that. Joan Ocean, another dolphin researcher, has coined the word "telempathy" to attempt to describe the empathic nature of telepathy, but the nearest I have gotten to comprehending it is as holographic thought clusters. It can sometimes be like receiving a message through all five senses simultaneously—almost too much for the frailer human nervous system to handle. I have known people who have been zapped by an orca's call who say that every cell in their bodies rang like a bell for minutes afterward.

Appendix B
The Surgeons of Avalon

The Urantia Book tells us that at a certain point in the evolution of an inhabited world, the universal authorities—the angels whose job it is to nurture planets into progressively higher levels of being—permit an intervention from a small group of what we might term "extraterrestrials." Strictly speaking, they are not actually extraterrestrials, since they hail from the more subtle inner realms, but they are further along in their development than we, having already been mortal beings on their own worlds.

Because of the radically different densities of the material bodies of these beings, they have to be given physical vehicles to enable them to function in this dimension. This, we are told, was accomplished with the aid of a special group of surgeons brought in from a planet called Avalon. According to *The Urantia Book,* small samples of bioplasm were removed from one hundred human volunteers who were drawn telepathically to the earthly location chosen by the extraterrestrials as their domicile. These samples were then genetically manipulated to produce physical bodies for our visitors: fifty males and fifty females.

As might be imagined, these were no ordinary bodies, although it is likely that they looked somewhat similar to ours. They were designed to be virtually immortal, sustaining themselves over vast periods of time through the consumption of a certain plant, which was also shipped in from the higher worlds and cultivated here. Significantly enough, as our visitors would find out later much to their misfortune, the plants' efficacy was dependent on certain incoming cosmic rays with which it interlocked. This shrub has been remembered by some of our planetary cosmologies as the Tree of Life, since it was evidently of such importance to our extraterrestrial friends.

This intervention occurred some half million years ago, and our group of one hundred then set about building a city on the shores of the Persian Gulf. After this, they proceeded in the long and arduous task of educating those human beings either drawn telepathically to the city or selected and brought in from among the tribes of the world as being the finest specimens available. These humans would subsequently return to their tribes and pass along what they had learned, thus starting the long, slow upliftment of culture and the orderly development of higher evolutionary life that has occurred on this planet.

It is perhaps significant that Zecharia Sitchin, in his remarkable series of books called *The Earth Chronicles* in which he has deciphered numerous Sumerian tablets and cylinder seals, also postulates an extraterrestrial intervention at approximately the same time in the history of Earth, and in exactly the same location.

Appendix C

Grounding and Releasing Meditations

One of the most important tasks facing us on the planet today concerns the releasing of fears, guilts, and other negative thoughtforms. Therefore, I am including here both the grounding and releasing meditations that have been shown to my colleague Alma Daniel and myself in the course of a series of seminars we have been teaching on making contact with guardian angels.

We find from experience that it is vitally important to be fully grounded, to be really in contact with the Earth, our dear Mother Gaia, in order to release the thoughtforms we have literally trapped in our emotional bodies. These can often be the cause of diseases as they become progressively more entrenched, until ultimately they filter down into our physical bodies. If we are able to rid ourselves of these thoughtforms before they become crystallized into our physical vehicles, then we can save ourselves a great deal of pain—and doubtless a lot of doctor bills.

For those unaccustomed to thinking of emotions as thoughtforms, it is worth saying briefly that thoughts have a considerable power that is largely unrecognized by contemporary belief systems. The mind of a human being is much more creative than we have hitherto imagined, and thoughts themselves—especially strongly held or emotionally powered ones—have a quasi-life of their own. A powerfully felt fear, for instance, can attach itself to the auric field (the emotional body) and stay there, feeding off the suffering it causes until it is in some way removed. Occult science has long known of the existence of these thoughtforms, and I would encourage the interested reader to look at *The Astral Plane* and *Thoughtforms,* two slim volumes by C.W. Leadbeater, as they are still the best in the field.

The techniques I am presenting here, I should add, are tried and true, since we have been holding meditations for more than four years in many countries of the world. Hundreds of people have found that they have been able to apply these processes successfully to their busy lives and have opened up to realms that are, in fact, our spiritual birthright.

For the fullest benefit, I recommend that you tape-record the meditation instructions, changing the words if necessary to suit your own sensibilities. As you become more proficient at it, you will find that the whole process can be considerably speeded up so that you will be able to do it under all manner of circumstances. For a start, though, I suggest you either find a quiet spot out in nature where you will not be interrupted or use a place in your home that you generally reserve for meditation. You might wish to light a candle or incense, fill a small bowl with water, or burn some sage to cleanse the atmosphere before starting. If you are at home, for obvious reasons it is important to unplug the phone.

Recording the instructions and playing the tape back while you are meditating has the additional benefit of the security of hearing your own voice. When you record, speak slowly and clearly, and give sufficient pauses where indicated. You will probably find that you establish your own rhythms, and you might want to rerecord the instructions after doing the meditation a few times.

It is well worth continuing this process and giving it a really good chance. Although it might appear at first glance to be rather simple, it is extremely effective. In addition, negative emotions, such as unworthiness and blame, often cloak other, more deeply buried ones. By removing the superficial thoughtforms, these deeper ones will come to the surface to be released.

One brief word about denial: Our very human capacity to deny negative emotional states is one of the hardest locks to break in our journey toward enlightenment. Nobody wants to think of himself or herself in a poor light. But it is worth remembering that we all contain the full gamut of human emotions. These are neither good nor bad; they simply are. Many of us, for instance, have been trained to think of anger as bad or, for men in our culture, that crying in sadness is somehow unmanly. Consequently, we suppress and deny these quite valid emotions. Often we have done this for so long that we have lost contact with our true feelings.

If you are patient with this meditation, you will find, over time, that it is like stripping layers off an onion. You will discover that it is not worth denying any emotions that may arise. Each will teach you something about yourself. That is, after all, their function. You will also find that obsessive negative states—states that you might well have convinced yourself are the normal lot of human life—will simply drift away as you take more conscious control of your emotional body and psychic well-being.

True feelings, not superficial emotional turbulence, are the basis of telepathy. In taking charge of our emotions and releasing the fear-trapped thoughtforms that have plagued our lives, we are demonstrating to the higher realms that we are ready for the next leap in our own spiritual evolution. And that is something for which each of us receives unlimited support and invaluable guidance.

We have been shown that it is helpful to sit upright, either cross-legged in a lotus or semi-lotus position (if this comes naturally to you) or in a straight-backed chair with both feet flat on the floor. As will become clear, this allows for the alert but relaxed state of consciousness necessary for these meditations. After you become more experienced, you will find that you can do them under a wide range of different conditions.

Meditation I

Take a deep breath and close your eyes. As you breathe in, breathe in the light; and as you breathe out, let out the tensions. Relax your body, paying particular attention to your shoulders and neck. Let go of any physical discomfort by relaxing on the out-breath.

Breathe deeply and regularly. Keep your attention on your breathing, drawing in the light and letting go of the darkness. [*Pause.*]

When you feel ready, start visualizing roots, like the roots of a great tree, wriggling down from the base of your spine. If your feet are flat on the ground, see the roots also sprouting from the soles of your feet. See these roots in your imagination as they push down through the floor of your dwelling, through the apartment(s) below you if you happen to live in an apartment house, or through the foundation, down into the earth and rock upon which your house is built.

Keep breathing deeply. Breathe in the light, and on the out-breath allow the roots to sink deeper and deeper, down into the heart of our Mother, the Earth. As your roots descend, picture the tensions and toxins your body has accumulated pouring down through them, deep into the Earth. Don't worry about polluting the Earth with the debris of your life. She is ready to receive it, and it *is* biodegradable. Our Mother needs this information to reshape the chemistry of future generations, so relax in the knowledge that releasing into her is correct and benefits all.

When the roots have gone down as far as possible—to the very center of the planet, if necessary—then reverse the process, and on the in-breath draw up from the Earth the healing, nourishing energy that is waiting for you. Draw it up through your roots as you would suck liquid up through a straw, and let this healing energy accumulate at the base of your spine.

Feel the warmth growing in the lower half of your body as more and more nourishment pours up the roots. Keep breathing deeply and regularly.

As the healing energies are gathering in the base of your spine, in your root chakra, take a moment to feel your mineral nature. Your root, or base, chakra is your access to the mineral kingdom, so feel your kinship with the rocks and metals of the Earth. What kind of rock are you? Round and smooth? Large and craggy? Are you buried in the ground or on the surface? Are you in sunlight or in rain? On a beach? In a riverbed? What does it feel like to be you—to be solid and confident and utterly secure in your rockness? Allow that feeling to spread through you, emanating from your base chakra and filling you with a sense of safety and invulnerability. [*Pause.*]

When you are ready, allow the energy that has gathered in your root chakra to gently and easily move up your spine into your second chakra. This is located in the area of your sexual organs, and you will probably feel a warm, tingling feeling as the energy starts filling you up. Keep breathing deeply and regularly, drawing nourishment up from the Earth and letting it rise up through your first chakra and into your second.

Relax any tensions you might be carrying in the area of your sexuality, and, as before, breathe them down the roots on the out-breath. Simply let go. You are perfectly safe.

When you feel clear and open, take a moment to focus on what the second chakra actually is. It is your access into the vegetable kingdom, the place in which you intersect with the nature spirits who care for the plants and trees. Feel that relationship and take the time to experience your vegetable nature. What are you today? A tree? A plant? A field of wild flowers? Are you grasslands? Seaweed gently swaying in the current? What color are you? What shape and form?

Feel the sun on you. Now the rain. Now the passing of the seasons. Feel how fruitful you are, how luxuriant and fertile. Experience the rivers of creativity that quite naturally run through you. Breathe deeply. Breathe down your roots any obstacles or resistances you encounter in your second chakra. Just let them go. They have served you well.

They have brought you to this point in time and to this degree of consciousness. [*Pause.*]

When you are ready, allow the energy that has gathered in your second chakra to rise easily and naturally up your spine to your third chakra. This is located in the area of your solar plexus and is the seat of your power and your animal vitality.

Once again, breathe the nourishing earth energy up your roots, through the first and second chakras, and feel it flowing up and into your solar plexus and the whole area of your lower belly. Allow any tensions or obstacles to rise gently to the surface of your consciousness, and then simply breathe them down your roots, back into the arms of your Mother.

As the first and second chakras are your access to the mineral and plant devic kingdoms, so also is your third chakra a portal to the domain of the animals. As the good, healing earth energy is flowing up and into your third chakra, look inside and see what kind of animal you are right now. What is your power animal? Let it emerge naturally. Is it friendly or fierce? Large or small? Hairy or smooth skinned? What is your relationship with it? Does it have a message for you?

Whatever it is and however it emerges, make your peace with it. Your power animal is part of you, and it has served and will serve you well. If you experience any nervousness or hostility, breathe it down the roots and once again make a joyful peace with the animal that you are. [*Pause.*]

As the healing energies fill up the bottom three chakras, allow the flow to move slowly and steadily up into your heart. Open your heart to receive it. Breathe it in, and feel your whole chest expanding with warmth and joy. If you feel any resistance or any hard-heartedness, visualize the problem being detached from your heart chakra and flowing back down the root system into the ground.

Your heart is the bridge. It is the link between higher and lower, between the created world of the devas and the yet-to-be-manifested world of the angels. The heart is the special province of humanity, and it links us with all living beings. Everything ultimately joins in the heart. It is the heart of the matter, the heart of the universe.

Feel your connection with all living beings. Feel for a moment the presence of those you love and of those you will love in the future. Love joins us all in the heart. Feel the love of the universe and the love of the Creator welling up in your heart.

Breathe deeply and evenly. As you breathe in the love of God, remember who you are and what you are doing here. As you breathe out, release the lies and distortions you have come to believe about yourself. Take a few minutes to totally relax into the safety and security of an open-hearted state of being. [*Pause.*]

When you feel ready, visualize the earth energy moving up from your heart to your throat chakra. You might find it natural to sound a tone, any tone that comes easily to you. As you tone, visualize the healing energy massaging your throat muscles and delicately opening up this center of communication. Breathe deeply, and, as before, visualize any blockages you experience flowing down your root system.

Your throat chakra is your immediate point of access to the angelic realms. When your angel speaks to you, you will most likely hear it in your throat. So make a triangle in your imagination with a line joining your two ears and the lower point resting in your throat.

Silently open yourself to your angel and extend a loving greeting to it. You may well feel its presence, but do not be concerned if you do not. Your subtle-energy systems are still being cleared, and there is a releasing yet to come. If any sense of impossibility or a feeling of unworthiness surfaces, be sure to acknowledge it and breathe it back down into the earth. Now take a little time to be in the loving space of the angels before moving the energy on up into the sixth chakra. [*Pause.*]

The sixth chakra is located in the center of your forehead and is also called the third eye, or *ajna,* center. Allow the energy to rise up into it. Feel it gently circulating around, stroking and opening this most delicate of subtle organs. If you experience any difficulty or obstacles, use your breath to dislodge them and visualize them flowing back into the Earth.

The third-eye center is your access point to the seraphic or archangelic realms, so take a moment to feel what that means to you. Open to receive whatever it is the archangels have for you to learn right now. [*Pause.*]

When you feel complete with the ajna center, visualize the energy, which is now streaming in a constant flow up from the Earth. See it moving naturally and easily into your seventh chakra, the crown, at the very top of your head.

The crown chakra can be understood as the seat of the divine within you, so as the energy surges up into this chakra, feel the closeness of your relationship with God. Remember once again who you are and why you are here. [*Pause.*]

Breathe deeply and regularly. Then, as the energy builds in intensity, visualize it pouring out from the top of your head in a great geyser of light. As it surges up, visualize the energy curling over at the highest point like a fountain, and then bring it down all around you, clearing and cleaning your aura. Feel the tingling freshness as the healing, clarifying energy falls all around you. Then bring it up into your base chakra and direct it back up your spine, through all your chakras, and out of the top of your head again.

Keep this energy movement flowing for a short time until you feel cleared and rejuvenated. Then, when you are ready, bring yourself to rest in your heart. [*End of the grounding and clearing phase.*]

You are now ready to start the releasing process. We have been shown by the angels that the body stores memories, especially traumatic memories, on a cellular level as well as in the more subtle energy systems of the emotional body. This is particularly true of repressed fear, guilt, and pain.

The angels offer us a simple and straightforward way of releasing these cellular memories and fear-trapped thoughtforms and of healing wounds that have troubled us for years—possibly even lifetimes. They emphasize, however, that a person needs to be willing to release these trapped cellular memories. Free will is, as always, the key. You may well find, every so often, that particular memories or traumas are needed for awhile longer. The angels urge you to honor your deepest intentions, and if you come across something you are unwilling to release, leave it be. Its purpose will reveal itself to you in good time.

It helps this process immensely if you can suspend any judgment you might have about your own negative imprints, which we all have. In fact, one of the ways we have locked these cellular memories into place is by finding them so frightful or unacceptable that we want no part of them. However, the problem is a circular one: we cannot release or give something away unless we have first owned it. Therefore, courage is needed to perform this process fully and effectively—the courage and willingness to look at these negative emotional thoughtforms, hopefully one last time, before sending them back to where they belong.

When doing this meditation, it may help you to visualize the thoughtforms literally being drawn out of where they have been trapped all this time. Open your heart to accept and acknowledge them, and know that your heart can contain them safely and securely until you have looked at them and the effect they have had on your life. Feel all the associated emotions, however painful they might be. When you have looked squarely at the worst aspects, take a moment to inwardly make contact with your angel, or Higher Self, or the Holy Spirit, or whoever you believe dwells within you whom you acknowledge as more powerful and knowing than your everyday self. Ask that one for aid in the releasing of the particular fear-trapped thoughtform. We have found that naming the thoughtform—guilt, envy, fear, anger, unworthiness, and so on—and being as specific as we can in our description of it helps. Although sometimes rather tempting, general releases are not nearly as effective as more specific and focused requests.

As you release each thoughtform, you will become aware of how each of these emotional blocks has impacted your life and how all of them together constitute the interlocking parts of the persona you have developed. Then, when you feel ready to release the thoughtform in question and you feel the immediate presence of your inner helper, take a deep, full breath and literally breathe the thoughtform down your spine and down your roots into the Earth. Go as deep and as far into the Earth as you can before taking another deep breath and repeating the process. Doing this three times, while visualizing the thoughtform being propelled down the roots, effectively dislodges and releases it.

You may also find it helpful to tone on the out-breath, as this adds a kinesthetic dimension to the process and helps your body remember that it need no longer be host to the evacuated negative thoughtform. Toning at this point also helps to realign the physical and subtle bodies, bringing you into more congruence. As you do this process, you will discover for yourself some very important information regarding the nature of thought: that thoughts actually do have quasi-lives of their own. They certainly have had a great influence on all our lives, and as such, they need to be respected—not feared or deferred to, but acknowledged and treated as we would hope to treat any life form. In fact, we have found that an attitude of gratitude is the most positive and effective way to approach these thoughtforms. They did, after all, get you to this point in time; and thus, in a way, they have earned the journey back to their home, too.

Meditation 2

To be most effective, the rhythms of this exercise should be entirely yours. By all means, create a tape guide if you wish, or simply memorize the sequence of releasing. It will become progressively easier and more natural as you practice it. It is advisable to do this immediately after the grounding meditation.

Sit quietly with your consciousness centered in your heart. Allow whatever emotions you are experiencing to rise to the surface. Are they painful? Disturbing? Fearful? Do you want to run and escape into your head?

Allow them to be. Invite them into your heart, and open courageously to receive them. The more specific you can be, the better. So ask the emotions questions: What are you? Where do you come from? Why are you here?

Listen and watch for the answers. They will come naturally and give you all the information you need. Take one at a time and focus on it. Allow the emotion just to be for a moment. Then open to when you first might have started feeling it. Find out how it got to be there or who might have done or said something that made you originally feel it. See how it has affected you. How has it crippled your well-being or stopped you doing what you really wanted with your life? [*Pause.*]

When you have explored this emotion and felt all its aspects—where it stemmed from and where it has gotten you—make sure you are ready to release it. Now ask the Holy Spirit—or your Higher Self—for its help in moving the thoughtform out of your body. Breathe it down your roots and back into the Earth. Breathe it down three times, and then thank your inner helper for its cooperation.

Bring your attention back to your heart, and invite the next negative thoughtform to step forward. Repeat the process. Do this as many times as is necessary. You will find that it will get faster and more efficient as you do it more, and each time there will be less to release.

Because this process appears so simple, it can be easy to dismiss. How can negative thoughtforms that have plagued us for years or decades be released in a matter of minutes? But do not forget the power of the creative imagination or that you are working with the highest force available to you: your indwelling Spirit.

In my experience, through some years of working with people and using this technique, I have observed that it is not unusual for particularly bothersome or ingrained, habituated thoughtforms to make a brief return appearance. These are not by nature subtle, and you will probably recognize them fairly quickly since they have lived inside you for so long. Merely take a moment to release them once again. The art of releasing is in remembering to do it when you first encounter the problem. I have found it rare that the same thoughtform will return more than two or three times at the most; and if it does, then it merely means there is some as-yet-unacknowledged piece of information that is still being presented to you. Pay attention. It will be as though the thoughtform is testing you to see if you really want to be rid of it. But without its solid hold in the undercurrents of your psyche and the cells of your body, it is a puny thing and can be dealt with easily.

More techniques for releasing and for taking the next step of making contact with your guardian angels are available in a manual, *Ask Your Angels,* which I have coauthored with Alma Daniel and Andrew Ramer. It is available from Ballantine Books, and the interested reader is encouraged to peruse it.

Appendix D
The Lucifer Rebellion

The Urantia Book tells us that approximately 203,000 years ago, on the capital planet of our system of one thousand worlds—607 of which were inhabited at the time—there was a rebellion among those angels whose function it was to administer the planets in their domain. The beings known to us as Lucifer and Satan, far from being imaginary or mythical devil figures, were in fact the high angels in charge of this sizable operation. Although their realm was by no means large, by the vast standards of an inhabited universe of trillions of worlds, they doubtless had a responsible and important posting. (The book mentions in passing that it was apparently not the first rebellion in our sector of the universe, there having been two previous ones not of immediate concern to the well-being of life on this planet.)

The motives of the angels concerned, which eventually involved a large number of what we might think of as junior bureaucrats, are complex and hard to fathom. It is recommended that the interested reader examine *The Urantia Book* while remembering that, as a document, it represents the opinions of the very universal authorities against whom the angels were rebelling and is therefore bound to have a somewhat conservative bias. For a fuller understanding of this upheaval and its contemporary relevance, the first volume of this series, *Dolphins, ETs & Angels,* contains a more detailed analysis of both the rebellion and its impact on our planet and the thirty-six others who sided with the rebellious angels.

What is relevant here is the reaction of the authorities to the incident. They simply isolated the dissenting planets from the incident. They simply isolated the dissenting planets from what would be their normal evolutionary birthrights and allowed the rebellion to wind down in its own time. It was this action—and presumably the incapacity of the rebellious angels to minister responsibly to their wards—that has made this such a dark, difficult, and dangerous planet upon which to incarnate.

There are compensations, of course. We have been bred very spiritually sturdy and exceptionally self-reliant and are eminently capable of believing without seeing—a status very much of value to us, by all accounts, as we progress in our universal careers.

For yet a broader appreciation of this rather horrifying phase in our world's history, the reader might be interested once again to compare Zecharia Sitchin's fascinating series, *The Earth Chronicles.* From his analysis of Sumerian tablets, he, too, has established that a mutiny occurred among the extraterrestrials on this planet—and again, within much the same time frame.

Any planetary cosmology, however detailed or accurate it purports to be, cannot be relied on to communicate the entire truth of any of these tumultuous events that happened so long ago. And quite right that they should not—it would then all be too easy! It is often only by cross-referencing many relevant sources that we are able to arrive at an overall comprehension of how matters have come to be the way they are.

Appendix E
Universe Overlays

The following is a synthesis of *The Urantia Book* cosmology with transmissions I received from the Trinity Teacher Son who came to me on that warm Florida evening at Peter Anderson's house. Like all the information I have been given, much of which I have included in this book, I do not present it as established fact but would rather urge you to check it carefully with your own intuition. I trust it will serve to spur further dialogue.

The Urantia Book speaks of creation being divided into two vast categories. Its authors tell us that there is a Central Universe, outside of time and space entirely, from which energy is down-stepped and modulated to be made available to co-creators of the many universes of the time/space continuum. This original creation sets the pattern for the development of the slower-moving energies that we perceive as the electronic building blocks of the material worlds.

Our Creator, so say the Urantia angelic communicants, presides over this primary Central Universe in the form of a Trinity of great beings. This is the One-in-Three and the Three-in-One spoken of in various earthly cosmologies. And, since the inhabited cosmos is so intimately a family affair, the direct offspring of this Trinity, a divine pair known as the Creator Son and the Divine Mother Spirit, are the modulators of the dual polarities of our material energy systems.

Therefore, these two are effectively the designers and creators—from the original patterns, of course—of all natural phenomena, including our physical bodies. These are carefully developed and experimentally perfected over the aeons, as we might make an extraordinarily elaborate robot, ready to receive the indwelling Spirit of our mutual Creator, the Father/Mother of us all. Yet the building blocks themselves, which the Urantia cosmic scientists call ultimatons—each an infinitesimal quantum of energy, one hundred of which cluster within the confines of the basic electron—carry at their center, in a manner almost impossible for us to grasp with our limited brains, the patterns of the Central Universe. Thus it is from the very core of matter that the universe as we know it is created.

According to *The Urantia Book,* the universes of time and space, though truly massive affairs, are gathered into seven quite distinct groupings called superuniverses. Each of

---

Master Universe Structure (based on The Urantia Book, p. 129)

- **a.** Central Universe (pattern creation) includes Paradise and Havona
- **b.** Seven superuniverses
- **c.** First outer space level
- **d.** Second outer space level
- **e.** Third outer space level
- **f.** Fourth and outermost space level

- Distance between b and c: approx. 400,000 light years.
- Width of c: at least 25 million light years.
- Our local universe (10 million inhabited planets) is one of the 100,000 local universes that compose the seventh superuniverse.
- Each superuniverse sustains approximately one trillion inhabited planets.
- The "layers" of the Master Universe rotate in opposite directions: time comes by virtue of motion and because mind is inherently aware of sequentiality.

these units contains within it something of the order of one hundred thousand local universes, and each one of these local creations supports about ten million inhabited or to-be-inhabited worlds. These local universes are each presided over by their own divine pair and consequently have a quality and tone all their own that depends on the individual natures of that particular creator pair. It should come as no surprise that the underlying tone of our local universe is *mercy and forgiveness.* This might go a long way toward suggesting why we witness so much apparent evil in our corner of creation. After all, if the emphasis is to be on mercy and forgiveness, there has to be something to be merciful and forgiving about!

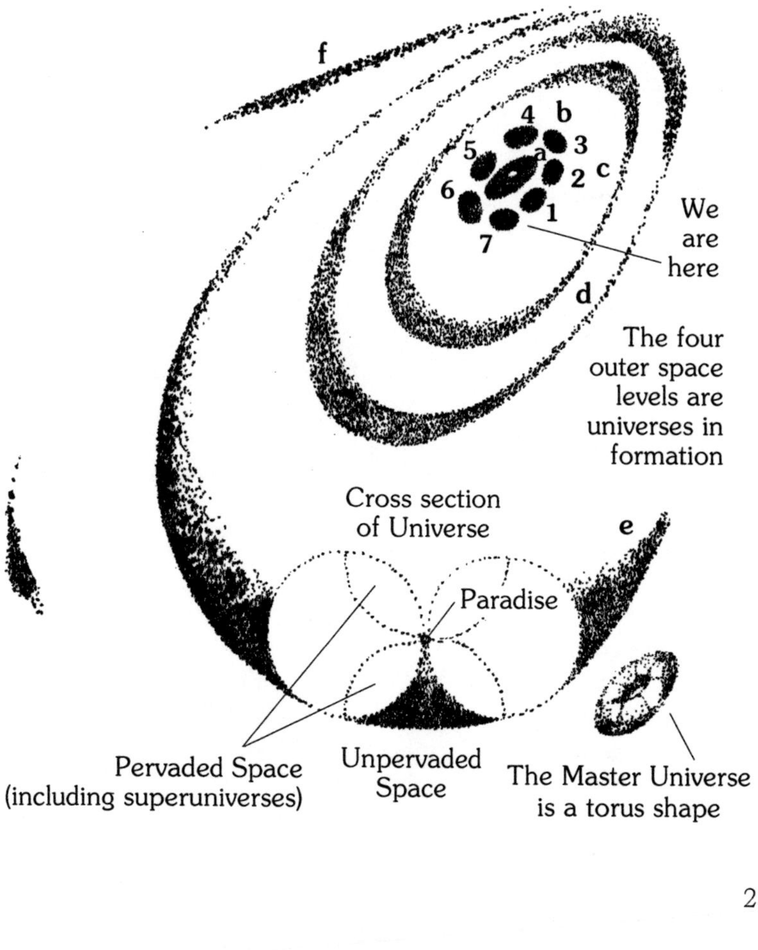

As I was writing the above in my journal, I was joined by a Trinity Teacher Son, one of the high angels sent from the Central Universe to oversee the events that are transpiring on our planet at this exciting point in time. I then received in automatic writing the following:

> The actual building blocks are already created by the Trinity, the ultimate instigators of the universes of space and time. The binary nature of your level of creation is a pattern overlay by which the Creator Son and the Divine Mother order these pre-existent building blocks, down-step them, and in a sense create your local universe.
>
> Each local creation is therefore modeled, inasmuch as it can be, on the nature and experiences of the particular pair who finally create that which you experience within the aegis of matter. Before they down-step and remodel these primary energy sources into dualistic interplays, this divine pair are bathed only in the energies of the Creator of all, the First Source and enter.
>
> It is therefore no surprise when, at these closing moments of the great drama, there are those who enter as if from a central point of reference. They are finding the way well laid into all the systems you are likely to explore.

After I had received this message, I felt the angel withdraw. Then I went on writing in my journal, simply recording my own thoughts on the relationship of the overlighting I had just experienced to the principle of overlays in the natural world.

The holographic nature of reality strongly suggests that the way in which different elements affect each other is repeated at different levels on the universe scale of life forms. This holographic integrity can be seen wherever we look, from the highest to the lowest frequencies. Thus, the most basic physical elements of the created universe, the ultimatons, have the overall pattern at their core. Overlaying these are the subatomic domains and the rhythms and permutations of electrons—the quarks and the charmed particles of modern physics. Overlaying those are the molecular and biological levels of organization, and over those are the DNA codings, which direct the morphology of increasingly complex life forms.

This could all be said to be in the province of the Divine Mother Spirit, since it is her "body"—matter or, more literally, *mater*—that is the substance of the physical universe. On the more complex levels of organic physical organization—the higher mineral, vegetable, and animal dimensions—these are also the domains of the nature spirits, the angelic groups directly responsible for sustaining biological life. It is undoubtably these levels of organization that British biologist Rupert Sheldrake is exploring in the light of his examination of morphogenetic patterns. Simultaneously, this upward movement of progressively more complex life forms is infused—or overlit—with spiritual circuitry being down stepped from the higher frequencies of the spiritual dimensions.

Contrary to popular skepticism, there is always an immense amount of angelic activity involved in the preparation and sustenance of a planet and its living animal and human populations. The development of a piece of biomachinery as sophisticated as a human body is not something that is left to chance. (Those interested in a more detailed description of the various orders of angels and spiritual beings whose function it is to nurture the physical universe are advised to consult *The Urantia Book*.)

It is in this manner, with material creatures of increasing complexity reaching up and out of the ground of being and at the same time the spiritual energies being projected downward from the higher frequencies of the spiritual dimensions, that the divine marriage of spirit and matter is accomplished. And we human beings, on whatever planet and at whatever level of development we find ourselves, are the sentient vehicles at the heart of this cosmic liaison. This is what all the great sages and saints knew, for this is the "Kingdom of Heaven on Earth" and the "pearl of very great value."

Appendix F
Violet Blood and Cosmic Gene Splicing

According to *The Urantia Book,* once a planet has reached a certain level of maturity, a second extraterrestrial mission is sent down with the express intention of refining and upgrading the genetic mix of the human races. On Earth this occurred about thirty-eight thousand years ago, an event that has been recorded in some planetary cosmologies as the advent of Adam and Eve. However, by this account, Adam and Eve were not the father and mother of the human race created by some local deity out of clay and ribs; they were two sophisticated and highly trained extraterrestrial biologists of what must have been almost unlimited sexual and reproductive potency. Their instructions, if we are to believe *The Urantia Book,* were to have somewhere in the region of one million children who would then mate with selected members of the human population, thus injecting the planetary bloodlines with this vital, off-planet gene.

But this world seems to have had an almost unanimously turbulent effect on all our extraterrestrial visitors, and this mission, like the one before it, came to abject failure. The plan of our two biologists—to take their task into their own hands and accelerate the process against the counsel of their superiors—proved hopelessly ill considered. Very few children were born to them before they and the majority of their offspring were hurriedly and unceremoniously shipped out.

Thus, humans continued to languish in darkness and isolation as the millennia passed. The planet was being prepared for something, but few could hazard a guess as to what that might be.

Appendix G
Ketamine: Potentials and Risks

Ketamine hydrochloride, the pharmaceutical mentioned in chapter 8, holds considerable therapeutic promise. Please note, however, that it is not suitable for casual experimentation.

Researchers in the 1960s' seeking an anesthetic that did not depress the heart rate, discovered that their first candidate, phencyclidine, was too psychedelic and disorienting for human patients as they regained consciousness. Ketamine, of similar derivation, had a milder "emergence reaction" and so became the anesthetic of choice for certain operations, especially in children.

Ketamine, which causes short-acting peripheral anesthesia, is also commonly used in veterinary medicine. Like most psychedelics, it has low toxicity. The typical anesthetic dosage for a 150-pound person is 750 milligrams, administered intramuscularly, whereas the typical dosage for a psychedelic "trip" is from 75 to 100 milligrams. *The Physician's Desk Reference* reports that surgical patients overdosed by mistake have survived doses of the drug as high as 3,000 milligrams.

Ketamine has immense therapeutic qualities still waiting in the wings. Research has shown that it is among three substances that can prevent brain damage if administered within an hour after a stroke. Ketamine, dextromethorphan (used in cough remedies), and a Merck & Company compound called MK-801 all block the glutamate that normally floods the cells after a stroke, opening the channels to calcium ions, which appear to sustain brain function.

In addition to the use of ketamine as an anesthetic, physicians are permitted to use the drug for nonanesthetic purposes. When a psychiatrist in the Southwest applied to the Drug Enforcement Administration for federal permission to use ketamine in psychotherapy, he was told that as a physician he was already so authorized.

In 1992, Russian psychologist Igor Kungurtsev and psychiatrist Olga Luchakova lectured in the United States about their experimental use of ketamine in treating alcoholism. They administered ketamine within the range of 2 to 3 milligrams per killogram of weight taken intramuscularly—an average of 175 milligrams per person—to a group of male alcoholics. One year after this single session, 69.8 percent of them had not resumed drinking. Although Kungurtsev and Luchakova's original intention was aversion therapy, interestingly the effect of the drug seemed to be transpersonal, and the patients emerged with a radically altered perspective.

Unfortunately, even though ketamine is already approved for human use, the mills of medical research grind slowly. Protocols for its diverse application in physical and psychological therapy for human beings have not yet been spelled out, and few physicians know of much of this research.

Supervision is recommended for a first experience with ketamine. The psychological effects can vary wildly among individuals—and from time to time in the same individual. Typically, people are mute and immobilized by a psychedelic dosage of ketamine, but some talk or thrash about. There are also gender differences in potency at different times of day.

Although no psychotherapeutic guidelines have been spelled out for the relatively low dosages used by "trippers," those with a history of head injury, epilepsy, hysteria, or violent outbursts should avoid ketamine until more is known about its effects. The same can be said for individuals taking antidepressants, tranquilizers, and other prescribed drugs with psychoactive effects.

Ketamine does not meet the criteria for physical addiction, but it is important to be aware that the desire for the state it produces can become disconcertingly habitual. As described in chapter 9, ketamine can also produce occasional episodes of paranoia, and there is some evidence that it can suppress the immune system as well.

People have described the effects of taking ketamine in psychedelic doses as similiar to those of a near-death experience; because the drug lowers respiration, the state it produces indeed simulates the appearance of death—something like a yogic suspension. Somewhat paradoxically, subpsychedelic doses of ketamine (say, ten to twenty-five milligrams), by anesthetizing the periphery of the physical senses, tend to make the user keenly aware of her or his inner state. With the outer shell silenced, the body can signal its needs: for example, more water or the intake of needed nutrition, including specific vitamins and minerals.

So, while there can be risks in taking ketamine, there are many positive aspects to the drug as well. Perhaps its healing potential, as well as its other therapeutic and visionary potentials, will be explored as our society becomes more open to mind expansion in general.

Appendix H
Stories of Dolphin Telepathic Abilities

ICERC's second International Dolphin and Whale Conference provided an ideal arena for meeting a variety of people who have had relationships with cetaceans. For me, most affirming was the general acceptance of dolphins and whales as telepathic, as well as being highly intelligent. With the sole exception of a young scientist who affected not to know what telepathy meant, everybody I talked to had a story or an incident that had convinced them that dolphins can communicate telepathically. They did not necessarily understand it, and many were reserved and peculiarly tender when they spoke of such encounters. Even ten years ago, I doubt if it would have been possible to talk with such mutual agreement, which surely indicates the start of a fundamental change of attitude in the way we hold our cousins of the sea.

Whether we will ever be able to prove conclusively that dolphins possess a telepathic intelligence is unlikely. Contact with wild dolphins, of necessity, is almost entirely on their terms, and it has to be the natural prerogative of a telepathic species as to whether it wishes to reveal itself. Rumors abound, of course. One was leaked recently by marine biologists at a secret navy establishment and tells of their discovery of a telepathic matrix that links all cetacea. Experiments with dolphins in one location yielded evidence that another dolphin, a quarter of a mile away, was showing the appropriate responses. The scientists involved, according to the report, regarded the discovery as too important to entrust solely to the U.S. Navy.

Governments, and more especially the military mind, of course, cannot be relied on to be particularly sensitive to the possibility that dolphins might have a telepathic intelligence, even if the dolphins were prepared to reveal it to them. The U.S. Navy, for instance, has stated that they regard dolphins as "unreliable," because when limpet mines are harnessed to their beaks they have a tendency to double back and plant the mine on the hull of an American ship. Now that sounds intelligent to me, if not downright telepathic!

Most of those to whom I spoke at the conference talked unguardedly of their encounters, and their memories seemed to open their hearts and fill their spirits. The following is a list of those people and their unique experiences:

Dr. Horace Dobbs, one of the foremost English dolphin researchers and filmmakers, who has seen for himself the positive healing impact wild dolphins can have on people suffering from acute depression. He has formed Operation Sunflower to facilitate this form of interspecies psychotherapy.

Jean-Luc Bozolli, the French artist, who was taught by the dolphins how to create breathtakingly beautiful paintings while living on a houseboat. He had never painted before.

Neville Rowe, the American psychic channel, who feels he has been in telepathic contact with a collective dolphin intelligence since 1985.

Paul Horn, the musician, whose cetaceous revelation came when he was playing his flute for a male orca—the so-called killer whale—who was mourning the loss of his mate.

Joan Ocean, writer of the book *The Dolphin Connection,* who is being befriended by a pod of spinner dolphins in Hawaii and who receives lucid telepathic messages.

Dr. John C. Lilly, the American scientist, who has probably forgotten more about dolphins than anyone else knows and who twinkles with delight at the implications of telepathy in cetaceans.

Glenda Lum, the Australian musician, who swims almost daily with a coastal pod of bottlenose dolphins in New South Wales and who, in her audiotapes *Legendaria* and *Not Talking* has created some of the most haunting and evocative human/cetacean music ever heard.

Kamala Hope-Campbell, the Australian organizer of ICERC, who drew us all together acting largely on telepathic messages she received from whales and dolphins.

Estelle Myers, the Australian filmmaker, whose fine documentary "Oceana" has been seen on networks all over the world and which presents much of this advanced material in a more readily accessible form.

Andi Cox, an English investigator of cetacea, whose adventures with the wild dolphin off Dingle on the Irish coast (already immortalized by Heathcote Williams in his luminous poem "Falling for a Dolphin") have left him in no doubt as to how telepathic dolphins might be.

Yantra De Vilder, the Australian musician, whose score for the enchanting music to *Oceana* tunes into the very heart of cetacea.

The late Carolina B. Ely, the American seer, who was witness to the true drama of the release of the Human/Dolphin Foundation's two dolphins Joe and Rosie, and who can tell a story or two about cetacean dream telepathy.

Dr. Betsy Smith, the American psychologist, who through her work with autistic children in the water with dolphins has seen something of the mystery of the dolphins' healing biofield in action.

Dean Bernal, the American dolphin trainer, who has developed a close and loving relationship with a semiwild dolphin in the Turks and Caicos islands and who needs no convincing.

Richard O'Barry, former trainer of the famous dolphin Flipper and a courageous campaigner against the U.S. Navy's exploitative abuse of dolphins, who has been around dolphins long enough to know that there is a lot more going on than meets the eye.

The late Dexter Cate, environmental activist extraordinaire, who in the course of releasing hundreds of dolphins from the nets of Japanese fishermen has demonstrated the immense power of compassionate, individual action.

There must have been many more stories from among the hundreds of people there, drawn from all over the world by a feeling, as yet largely undefinable, that the dolphins and whales have information that is going to be extremely important for the future of all life on this planet. Perhaps it is the same feeling that prompted you to read this book and to continue on your own adventures among spiritual intelligences.

There is no doubt that when the telepathic nature of cetaceans becomes sufficiently well known, and then generally accepted, our attitudes will go through a profound change. The fact that we are sharing this planet with another species of intelligent beings—indeed, spiritual cousins of ours—who use a communication skill of such impending importance for us and who are friendly and loving, is an extraordinarily powerful reality. It could be a magnificent contribution to the reenchantment of the planet. It will also be an early introduction to the vast, friendly, populated universe and all our cosmic relations—our galactic elders and cousins—who wait even now to greet us as we come of age.

About the Author

Timothy Wyllie was born in England during World War II and trained as an architect. He practiced in the United Kingdom as well as the Bahamas before joining a religious community and traveling throughout Europe and the United States. In 1977, he left the community and started a business in New York City marketing a photographic storage system that he had had a hand in devising some years earlier. By 1980 he was able to devote himself full time to his lifelong interest in spiritual intelligences. His first book, *Dolphins, ETs & Angels* (Bear & Company:1984), remains in print and is widely regarded as a classic in its field. He is also the co-author, with Alma Daniel and Andrew Ramer, of *Ask Your Angels,* the first and still the most effective of the manuals for contacting guardian angels. Published by Ballantine Books in 1992, it quickly became an international bestseller, and has to date been translated into eleven languages.

In 1995, he co-authored, with Elli Bambridge, *Contacting Your Angels: Through Movement, Meditation and Music* for an Australian publisher.

The book you hold in your hands was first published in 1992 as *Dolphins, Telepathy, & Underwater Birthing* by Bear & Company, and was possibly a little ahead of its time. Wisdom Editions has redesigned it, renamed it, and produced what is essentially a new edition.

As a storyteller, Timothy is collaborating with other musicians to create evocative and transformative sonic experiences. *A Dolphin Journey,* taken from the story that weaves its way through the pages of this book, with superb music by Glenda Lum, is presently available, as are other tapes. For further information, please write to Timothy in care of Wisdom Editions.

He is currently writing and drawing, and enjoying his new home in the high desert of New Mexico.